GEORGE THE THIRD AND CHARLES FOX

GEORGE THE THIRD AND CHARLES FOX

THE CONCLUDING PART OF

THE

AMERICAN REVOLUTION

BY THE RIGHT HON.

SIR GEORGE OTTO TREVELYAN, BART., O.M.

AUTHOR OF "THE LIFE AND LETTERS OF LORD MACAULAY"
AND "THE EARLY HISTORY OF CHARLES JAMES FOX"

IN TWO VOLUMES

VOL. I

NEW EDITION

LONGMANS, GREEN, AND CO.
FOURTH AVENUE & 30TH STREET, NEW YORK
LONDON, BOMBAY, CALCUTTA, AND MADRAS
1915

Norwood Press
J. S. Cushing Co. — Berwick & Smith Co.
Norwood, Mass., U.S.A.

PREFACE

"THE Early History of Charles James Fox" was published thirty-one years ago, in October 1880. In the following December I accepted office as Secretary of the Admiralty, and perforce abandoned literature for an indefinite period to come. At the beginning of the next Session, in the lobby of the House of Commons, Mr. Justin M'Carthy did me the honour to express a wish that there existed a Statutory power for obtaining an Order of Court to compel me "to finish Fox"; and I am very glad to think that my old friend is alive to read this book. Its two volumes, — of which the first is here, and the second has been already in part written, — will carry Fox up to the moment which, so far as personal success was concerned, proved to be the culminating point of his whole career. They will likewise continue, and conclude, the History of the American Revolution, — my tranquil and pleasant occupation during the later years of a life much of which was passed in stormier waters.

A general map of the revolted colonies at the outbreak of the American rebellion is herewith given for the convenience of readers.

WALLINGTON : *November* 1911.

v

CONTENTS

CHAPTER I

CHAPTER II

CHAPTER III

CHAPTER IV

CHAPTER V

CHAPTER VI

CHAPTER VII

CHAPTER VIII

CHAPTER IX

GEORGE THE THIRD AND CHARLES FOX

THE CONCLUDING PART OF

THE AMERICAN REVOLUTION

———◦◦◦———

CHAPTER I

THE KING'S POLICY. PERSONAL GOVERNMENT. LORD CHATHAM. THE SEVENTH OF APRIL

THE capture of Burgoyne, the evacuation of Philadel-phia by the British army, and the outburst of war be-tween France and England in the spring of 1778, were decisive events in the history of the American Revo-lution. For ten years past the resources of the mother-country had been applied, lavishly and continuously, to the object of preventing, and, (when prevention failed,) of crushing the rebellion in her Western colonies. The King and his Ministers had devoted themselves with single-minded energy to the work of coercion and re-conquest, and Parliament had refused them none of the means which, in their judgment, the prosecution of that work demanded. Strongly worded Addresses of sympathy with the Ministerial policy; penal laws of novel character and terrible severity ; armies larger than ever yet had been transported across any ocean ; multitudes of foreign mercenaries; powerful fleets; ordnance and com-missariat stores in unexampled profusion ; — whatever the responsible government demanded, or even suggested, had been at once forthcoming. The forces of the rebel-lion had been pitted against the forces of the Crown during four hot and fierce campaigns, in which Great Britain, undistracted by European enemies, exerted much of her naval, and almost all her military strength

against the power of the Revolution.   And now, in July
1778, as the result of these sustained and strenuous endeavours, there was not a single province, or even a single township, where the civil administration was in
Loyalist hands ; and, outside the fortifications which
protected the city of New York, the British army held
not one square mile of soil on the mainland of the Northern and Central colonies.

Historians have in many cases overlooked, or under-
valued, the dominant circumstance which governed the
military situation during all the closing years of the War
of Independence.   Ever since that week in March 1776
when General Howe abandoned the city of Boston to
Washington's besieging army, and took himself and his
forces away by sea to Halifax, New England was never
again assailed by a determined and formidable invader.
That vast tract of country, as large as Scotland and Ireland together, contained a population of men ardent for
the Revolution, who had established a very effective
political unanimity by the expulsion of all such as dis-
agreed with them in political opinion.   Farmers and
sailors for the most part, — hardy, shrewd, and frugal,
and as brave as need be on those occasions when there
was nothing for it but to fight, — they yielded implicit
and intelligent obedience to rulers chosen by themselves
from among tried and respected members of their own
community ; and they always were ready to rally in force
to the rescue whenever, and wherever, the Republic was
in perilous straits.   Connecticut, and Massachusetts, and
New Hampshire formed a spacious, a plentifully stored,
a powerfully garrisoned, and an altogether impregnable
citadel of rebellion.   It was the story over again of the
Associated Eastern Counties of England during our
Seventeenth Century struggle between the Parliament
and the Crown.   Once, and only once, the safety of the
old Puritan provinces was seriously menaced throughout
the seven years which followed the evacuation of Boston.
When Burgoyne, with his column of British and German
infantry, and his horde of Indian warriors, came trailing

down towards Albany in close proximity to the frontier of New England, thirteen thousand New England yeomen marched, at their own charges, to repel the aggressor ; and, if the career of the English general had not been stopped short at Saratoga, he would have had twice that number upon him in front, flank, and rear, before ever he had penetrated into the heart of Massachusetts.

So it had long been with New England ; and now the same immunity from hostile invasion had been secured for the rich and populous Central provinces as a consequence of the protracted campaign which began at Brandywine, and terminated at Monmouth Court-house. A large, an admirably appointed, and a valiant British army, conveyed and assisted by a noble fleet, had gone south from New York City in the July of 1777 ; had done its duty in conspicuous fashion ; and twelve months afterwards had returned, not indeed defeated, but foiled, disappointed, and with very small expectation of ever repeating an experiment from which no military man, who understood the business of his profession, anticipated even the possibility of success. Two great battles had been fought and won, and the capital city of the Revolution had been triumphantly entered by the royal troops ; but, as the final result of the whole matter, the disputed territory was left, then and thereafter, in possession of the Revolutionary government. That government was destined to have its own troubles and difficulties as long as the war lasted ; but they were troubles and difficulties of a nature to which the most firmly settled and long established monarchies have always been liable during a period of national emergency. There were wrangles and intrigues in Congress, just as there was quarrelling between Whigs and Tories at Westminster. There were outbreaks of turbulence in Washington's army, just as there was a mutiny at the Nore at a time when England was engaged, heart and soul, in her death struggle with the French Republic. The American Treasury flooded the country with issues of worthless paper, just as Frederic the Great had debased the silver coinage of Prussia in the agony of the Seven Years' War. But those are internal maladies of which a nation does not die; and the United States were now, to all intents and purposes, a self-contained and independent nation. The concluding phase of the great conflict was no longer a mere colonial rebellion, but an international war between Great Britain and America, in which the Americans were assisted by France, Spain, and Holland, and by the unconcealed and very efficacious sympathy of almost every other European power. The British Cabinet indeed, at a large expense of money, but with an utterly inadequate force of troops, made some ill-combined attempts to detach Virginia and the Carolinas from the Republican cause; but the British generals had as little intention of marching into New England, or of besieging Albany and Philadelphia, as George Washington had of invading Cheshire or Lancashire. The case was truly put by Nathanael Greene in his own quiet manner. " We," (he wrote,) " cannot conquer the British at once; but they cannot conquer us at all. The limits of the British government in America are their out-sentinels." And, in the month of August 1778, those out-sentinels had been withdrawn from almost every post which they had hitherto occupied on the American continent.

The King himself had renounced all hope of subduing America by campaigns and battles. " It was a joke," (such was his own expression,) " to think of keeping Pennsylvania," [1] and it was far beyond a joke even to contemplate the forcible recovery of New England; but his determination never to acknowledge the independence of the Americans, and to punish their contumacy by the indefinite prolongation of a war which promised to be eternal, was as fixed and resolute as ever. His intention henceforward was to retain his garrisons at New York and on Rhode Island, in Canada, and in Florida; to withdraw all the rest of his troops from America;

[1] George the Third to Lord North; March 13th, 1778.

and to employ them in attacking the French and Spanish possessions in the West Indies. Meanwhile aggressive hostilities against the Americans would be confined to the destruction of their coasting-trade, and the bombardment of their commercial ports; to sacking and burning their villages within a day's march of the sea-coast, and turning loose the Indians, from time to time, upon the more exposed and defenceless of the settlements which lay along their Western border. These operations, according to the royal view, would inspire courage in the partisans of the Crown throughout every colony; would promote faction in Congress; and would keep the rebels harassed, anxious, and poor, until the day when, by a natural and inevitable process, discontent and disappointment were converted into penitence and remorse. That was an infallible, and for the English taxpayer a very cheap method, which sooner or later would bring the Revolutionary diplomatists to their knees, and, (to use the King's own words,) "would make them come into what Great Britain might decently consent to." [1]

Such was the plan of action, and inaction, which George the Third had thought out for himself, and which, in a long succession of letters, he lovingly and minutely expounded to his Prime Minister. It was a foolish, and a most cruel policy; — cruel to the Loyalists who, after having been invited and induced to declare themselves for the Crown, were abandoned, unprotected by the presence of a British army, to the vengeance of their political opponents; cruel by the infliction of useless and objectless suffering, for an indefinite period of time, upon the civil population of the United States; and cruel, above all, to the people of Great Britain. The hour had come when our country, already weary of war, was to fight for her life against a combination of new and old European enemies who aimed at nothing short of her utter ruin, and her permanent humiliation. She would have to face the crisis alone,

[1] George the Third to Lord North; Jan. 13th, 1778.

and shorn of no small portion of that native strength on which she had formerly been accustomed to rely.   The military resources of America, from which Lord Chatham extracted such memorable advantage in the glorious past, were now employed not for, but against, the mother-country.   The people of Massachusetts who, when Chatham asked them for money, had taxed themselves to the amount of two pounds in every three of their year's income for the defence of the British empire, now spent their substance in keeping the flame of revolution ablaze in less wealthy States of the American Union.   The successors of those provincial militiamen, who had marched in their thousands under Wolfe and Amherst, were now embattled beneath the Stars and Stripes in the ranks of the Continental army.   The successors of those New England mariners, who had been proud to serve in the fleets of Hawke and Boscawen, were now scattered, on board of their innumerable cruisers, over the wide and narrow seas of both hemispheres, making prey on British commerce.   Of all the infatuated ideas that have crossed the brain of a ruler none was ever more illusory than this notion that the Americans would sit with folded hands, and sheathed weapons, while England and France fought their quarrel out.   The Revolution had bred and trained a multitude of restless and irrepressible warriors both on land and sea.   Paul Jones, and Anthony Wayne, and Harry Lee, and Morgan's sharpshooters, and Marion's fiery guerillas, were not the men to desert the war-path because King George had ordained that active hostilities between England and America should slacken, and cease, up to the precise moment when he himself found it convenient to begin again.   Unless he could bring himself to make peace with the United States the King was in the plight of a hunter who had hold of a wolf, or rather a grizzly bear, by the ears at a time when the most formidable wild beasts of the forest came ravening upon him.

The prospect was alarming to all far-sighted men; and the future, when it began to unfold itself, did not belie their most gloomy anticipations. As those black years rolled on, the dangers which beset our country were continually on the increase, and her hope of deliverance lessened. A conviction gradually crept over the public mind that England could never emerge, safe and erect, from the conflict with her European foes unless she consented to treat with Congress upon terms which Congress would accept. That view of the only possible solution became evident at last to the great majority of Englishmen, but not to the King. He, for his part, refused to make an acknowledgment which was the condemnation of his own colonial policy, and his own favourite system of parliamentary management. He had brought upon himself, and on his subjects, calamities and distresses almost as bad as the plagues of Egypt; but his heart was hardened against America, and he would not let her people go. He was unable to give any tenable reason for his persistence; he persuaded no man's judgment; and the time eventually arrived when he looked around him in vain for any sincere and disinterested adherent to his policy. That policy was clamorously defended by bribed senators, and pensioned courtiers, and the whole swarm of army-jobbers, and loanmongers, and fraudulent contractors who

> "leech-like to their fainting country cling
> Till they drop blind in blood."

It was supported in the Cabinet mainly by the Bedfords,— a knot of reckless statesmen, overloaded with debt, and intent only on keeping the Government in place for another, and yet another, quarter-day. The Prime Minister, and his more respectable colleagues, conscience-striken and miserable, begged piteously to be allowed to resign their offices and permit the nation to be saved by less discredited and more independent men than themselves; but they served an inexorable master, who combated their prayers and expostulations sometimes with angry reproaches, and sometimes with earnest and pathetic appeals to their personal affection for himself. King

George has met his deserts from the hands of posterity.
Mr. Lecky, writing with unwonted passion, has pronounced that his course of action, during the later part
of the American War, was " as criminal as any of the
acts which led Charles the First to the scaffold." More
than one famous writer has exerted all the powers of
his pen in drawing a parallel between George the Third
and George Washington, to the immense disadvantage
of the English monarch ; but it is unfair to try an hereditary ruler by the standard which is applied to men who
have risen, by pre-eminent merit, from a private station to
the height of power. Kings should be compared with
kings ; and, if that course is adopted, it is impossible to
doubt that the American difficulty would have been more
prudently and rationally handled, from first to last, if the
throne of Britain had been occupied, not by George the
Third, but by a monarch endowed with the solid judgment, the calm temper, and the watchful and enlightened
public spirit of his grandfather, or his great-grandson.

A most striking contrast between the position of
England in 1763 and in 1777, and between the methods
of government pursued respectively by George the
Second and by his successor, was drawn by a pamphlet-
eer of an ability unusual even in days when the ablest
men devoted their best thought and labour to the political pamphlet. Burke himself has not left behind him a
more searching analysis, or a more unanswerable condemnation, of George the Third's favourite System of
Personal Government, than this anonymous author.
"So material a change," (he wrote,) " as a little space
of time, yet short of a quarter of a century, hath wrought
in our empire, cannot be ascribed to accident. Probably
the history of mankind, and of human society, doth not
furnish such another. Let us pause for a moment, and
look up to that pinnacle of national glory from which
we have fallen. Compared with this power, — the extent to which it might have been pushed, the advantages

which might have been derived from it, — everything that
hath gone before it is trifling and insignificant. I speak
with the pride, the partiality, the enthusiasm of an Englishman. Alas! How are all our well-founded expectations destroyed! Where are we now to seek our
glorious dependencies? . . . The reign of George the
Second afforded the ministers of his successors a large
body of experience which a real statesman would have
been fortunate in the possession of. The maxims pursued in that reign were wise, not because they were to
be accounted for upon this or that theory, but because
their consequences were salutary. Strange as it will
tell to posterity, this body of experience was not sapped
by degrees, but at once, totally, and in all its parts,
overthrown by those who were called to the Administration after his present Majesty's accession. As if the
public happiness were a subject of envy to the courtiers,
that happiness was to be reversed. Men, who have
never given a proof of capacity, were placed in the
front offices; and the doctrine of the Court was that
the King's choice was not to be questioned, and that
the Royal favour was to stand in the place of all qualifications for public employment." [1]

That was most indubitably the doctrine of the Court;
and for eighteen years, with one brief interval, George
the Third's ministers had been men of his own choice,
and to his own mind. The nation, by the end of that
time, was satiated with experience as to the true worth,
in peace or in war, of a Government selected by such a
process. The internal administration of the Earl of
Bute, the Duke of Grafton, and Lord North had been
marked by abuses which loom very large in our political history, and in our national literature. Their repeated assaults on the freedom of the Press, and the
freedom of Election, kept Parliament in a chronic state
of factious and barren agitation, and plunged the City

---

[1] *Address to the public by an Unconnected Whig;* 1777. From the collection of pamphlets at the Athenæum Club.

of London into a fever of excitement varied by not un-
frequent ebullitions of popular fury. Great, indeed,
were the issues involved in those long and angry con-
troversies; and yet, however flagrant were the scandals
of our domestic history, the world was only half acquainted with the personal character, and the qualifications for exalted office, of King George's favourite
statesmen, until, in a disastrous hour for the British
empire, they began to exhibit their improvidence and
incapacity to a far larger circle of spectators, and on a
more conspicuous stage.

Unwarned by the recent lesson of the Stamp Act,
which had been written in such glaring characters
across so many pages of our history, these fatal rulers
insisted on making a grave and far-reaching innovation
in the fiscal arrangements of America without the smallest particle of consideration for American opinion; and
then, having irritated all the thirteen colonies, and
driven Massachusetts to disaffection and despair, they
entered upon a headlong course of vindictive repression.
Parliament which, under their leadership, could seldom
or never find time for the long arrears of useful legislation so urgently needed by the people of Great Britain,
was called upon to pass a whole series of Coercion Acts
devised against the people of America. The military
occupation of their townships; the ruin of their cities;
the annihilation of their commerce; the extinction of
their chartered rights, — those were some of the spells
by which these clumsy magicians undertook to exorcise
that spirit of rebellion which they themselves had raised.
But it is a work of superfluity, at this distance of time,
to pile up an indictment against men who already stood
self-condemned before the tribunal of their own contemporaries. In February 1778 Lord North informed a
dumb-foundered, and almost incredulous, House of Commons that his Cabinet had resolved to abandon the
Tea Duty; to renounce the power of taxing America
without her own consent; to repeal the Boston Port
Act, the Massachusetts Government Act, and the Act

for Restraining the Trade and Commerce of the New England Colonies; and to surrender every claim and demand, whether trivial or essential, for the sake of enforcing which England had fought a dozen battles, had spent seventy million pounds, and was now embarked upon what threatened to be the most perilous European war in which she had ever yet been implicated.

The men whom the King delighted to honour had blundered egregiously as Home Ministers and as Colonial Ministers; and by this time they had given a more than sufficient sample of their value as War Ministers. During the opening years of the American rebellion our soldiers never came short of their duty, and our regimental officers performed their part to admiration. It could not indeed be denied that British generals in the field had not always made the most of their opportunities; but the prime cause of their failure, — as every competent critic, from Frederic the Great downwards, perceived then, and as every student of our military history recognises now, — had been the senseless scheme of strategy which was dictated to them from Downing Street. It was the unhappy fate of Great Britain to enter upon an internecine war with France, and in all probability with half Europe, under the guidance of statesmen who had wasted four campaigns over an unsuccessful attempt to put down an insurrection in our own colonies. All opponents of the ministers, and many more of their supporters than chose to admit it, contemplated the future with distrust and dismay; and their worst fears were justified by the event. After four more years of squandered resources, and mismanaged hostilities, and baffled diplomatic efforts, Lord North and his partners had been judged and condemned by every Englishman who was not paid to praise them. What their best friends thought about them in the spring of 1782 was bluntly expressed by the most staunch of Tories. "Such a bundle of imbecility," (said Doctor Samuel Johnson,) "never disgraced a country. If they sent a messenger into the City to

take up a printer, the messenger was taken up instead
of the printer, and committed by the sitting Alderman.
If they sent one army to the relief of another, the first
army was defeated and taken before the second arrived.
I will not say that what they did was always wrong;
but it was always done at a wrong time." It was idle
to hope that England would ever be extricated by such
feeble and awkward hands from the net of danger in
which she was so deeply entangled. No more urgent
and vital question has ever been submitted to Parliament than the expulsion from power of those deplorable ministers, and the abolition of that system of Court
favouritism which had planted and rooted them in office.
And so it came about that, during the later period of
the American War, the Senate was even more important than the camp; and the centre of interest was
transferred from the banks of the Delaware and the
Hudson rivers to the polling-booths of Great Britain,
and the floor of the House of Commons.

Amidst the turmoil of these anxious and troubled
years Lord Chatham presented as noble, and in some
respects as pathetic, a figure as any which stands in the
gallery of history. Whether or not he was the greatest
of Englishmen, he had, beyond all question whatever,
done the greatest work for England; and he lived to
see the best part of that work undone by the hands of
others. Goethe has complained, somewhat sadly, that,
if a man accomplishes something for the sake of the
world, the world will take good care that he shall never
do it a second service; and there is no more striking
exemplification of Goethe's remark than the story of
Lord Chatham and the British empire. When Chatham,
after his long and mysterious illness, once more appeared
in public he had regained something of his ancient vigour, and all his unequalled judgment of State affairs on
a large and comprehensive scale. But those rare powers
of insight and prevision did not make for his happiness;

for he returned to find the goodly fabric of political liberty and national pre-eminence, which his own hands had raised, sapped to the foundation by the perversity of his successors. The great ex-minister knew America with a knowledge founded on long experience, and intense interest and affection ; he could read the motives and ambitions of foreign Courts as in an open book ; he was minutely acquainted with the naval and military resources of Great Britain, as compared with those of her European ill-wishers and rivals ; and he discerned, at a very early moment, the inevitable issue of Lord North's colonial policy. Before ever the Boston Port Bill had left the House of Commons Chatham foresaw and foretold the long series of calamities which was sure to follow. "A fatal desire," he wrote, "to take advantage of this guilty tumult of the Bostonians, in order to crush the spirit of liberty among the Americans in general, has taken possession of the heart of the Government. If that mad and cruel measure should be pushed, one need not be a prophet to say that England has seen her best days."[1]

During several generations after Chatham's death his legitimate fame suffered, in no small degree, from the undiscriminating admiration and gratitude of his fellow-countrymen. Some of his most characteristic attributes were lost and forgotten in the popular tradition of the overpowering orator who conquered France by animating our nation at home, and our soldiers and sailors abroad, with his own patriotic audacity and self-devotion. But his contemporaries knew him likewise as a painstaking and all but omniscient administrator, for whom no precautions were too humble, and no particulars too dull; as a master of strategy, and a consummate judge of military merit in the generals and admirals who fought our country's battles on land and sea. The diligence of recent historians has disclosed to us the full secret of

[1] The Earl of Chatham to the Earl of Shelburne; Burton Pynsent, March 20, 1774.

those methods by which Chatham repaired defeat and
organised victory. His power of speech, it is true, was
among the wonders of the world ; and it was the gift of
nature. Members of his family, before and after him,
had at their command an inexhaustible store of passionate and picturesque language which some of them applied to trivial and unworthy uses ; and his second son
inherited the Pitt eloquence, perfected to the very highest standard of culture and precision.[1] The spontaneous
rush of Chatham's rhetoric, apart from the mastery
which it gave him over the emotions of his audience,
was of practical advantage to the quality of his statesmanship ; for he was spared all the preliminary trouble
of picking words, and framing sentences, and could de-
vote his whole attention to dealing with events and
realities. When he had resolved upon the substance of
his policy, the explanation and the defence of it might
safely be left to the unstudied inspiration of the moment. "Bitter satire," (wrote Horace Walpole,) "was
Pitt's forte. When he attempted ridicule, which was
very seldom, he succeeded happily. But where he
chiefly shone was in exposing his own conduct ; " and
his conduct, during the Seven Years' War, was of a nature to bear the closest and most searching exposition.

[1] Chatham's grandfather, the Governor of Madras, (as Lord Rosebery's
readers know,) was a man of exceptionally masterful and emotional nature, whose correspondence was conducted on a high level of emphasis
and passion. His denunciations of all who ventured to criticise his very
high-handed methods of Indian administration, or to question the genuineness of his Pitt diamond, display a wealth of invective which leaves no
doubt of the source from which the Great Commoner derived his eloquence.
The family characteristics were not less deeply marked in a succeeding
generation. The biographer of Lady Hester Stanhope, Chatham's grand-
daughter, was lost in perpetual admiration of her forcible and impetuous
volubility. "She was," we are told, "unceasingly employed in laying bare
the weakness of our common nature," or, in plainer language, in haranguing
about the shortcomings of other people. On that topic she could hold
an audience, or more usually a single auditor, for many hours at a time.
The performance was, beyond all doubt, an extraordinary exhibition of
rhetorical powers ; and the voice was the voice of Chatham. "Good
God!" said her uncle, the Prime Minister: "If I were to shut my eyes I
should think it was my father."

Walpole, a loyal son, was fond of contrasting Chatham's oratory with his own father's shrewd and homely mode of addressing the House of Commons, and he was always fair to both his heroes. Sir Robert's strength, (wrote Horace,) was "understanding his own country"; and his foible may be said to have been inattention to other countries, which made it impossible that he should thoroughly, and for all purposes, understand his own. But Chatham understood every Government in Europe, every Native State on the sea board of Hindostan, and every British and foreign colony in the Western Hemisphere. One of his contemporaries, who was a well-known and much respected man of business, pronounced that, "while Lord Chatham's abilities were transcendent, his knowledge was almost boundless:" [1] — his knowledge, that is to say, of what was worth knowing, for his want of acquaintance with unimportant things was a standing marvel to that large portion of London society which concerned itself about little else.

The world-wide magnitude of Chatham's successful operations is unparalleled in modern history. Napoleon's comprehensive glance swept as wide an horizon of land and sea, and his armies were vastly greater than those that contended in the Seven Years' War; but Napoleon's schemes ended in a huge ruin, while the English minister made his country the queen of nations. The elder Pitt's arrangements for a campaign in Germany, or an expedition across the ocean, remain on record as a model which only too few of his successors have been at the pains to imitate. He ascertained beforehand the force required for each successive undertaking; and he provided that force, and something over. He selected his commanders with care, and trusted them absolutely, — depicting to them, in broad but intelligible outlines, the nature of their allotted task; leaving them a generous latitude; and perplexing them with no contradictory or ambiguous

[1] Letter of January 1770 from Thomas Bentley, the partner of Josiah Wedgwood.

suggestions.[1] But he never spared ink and paper when
dealing with a point of practical detail. His letters on
business were no formal departmental despatches, drawn
up by subordinates, with the great man's signature
scrawled at the foot of a half-read document. He took
infinite personal trouble to secure that the naval and
military authorities should be aware of each other's
needs, and should play into each other's hands. On the
eve of the final struggle with the French in Canada his
admiral on the American station was duly informed
that the Government at home had taken up twenty
thousand tons of transport, with six months' food for all
on board, and equipped in every respect for the reception
of ten thousand troops on the scale of a ton and a half
per man. On the same day General Amherst was told
how many of the ten thousand men, and the six thousand
field-tents, were consigned to him for the furtherance of
his own objects, and how many had been shipped direct
to General Wolfe at Louisburg; and Mr. Secretary Pitt,
— a very different war-minister from the nobleman who
devised the campaign of Saratoga, — did not forget to
supply General Amherst with a copy of the Secret Instructions which had been sent to General Wolfe. Special attention, according to the medical lights of the day,
was bestowed on the physical comfort and welfare of
the troops; although it was clearly laid down that, in the
last resort, no subsidiary considerations should be allowed
to interfere with the exigencies and opportunities of active warfare. Brigadier General Wolfe having represented that it would be of the greatest utility to the
health of the army to have a quantity of molasses to
make spruce beer as a preservative from scurvy, meas-

---

[1] " I am to signify to you the King's pleasure that you do attempt, with
the utmost vigor, the reduction of Canada. At the same time His Majesty, placing great confidence in your Judgment and Capacity, is pleased to
leave entirely to your discretion by what Avenues you will penetrate into
the same ; and whether you shall judge it most expedient to operate in
one Body, or by detaching, in the Manner you mention, a Corps to the
right, and another to the left." Mr. Secretary Pitt to General Amherst;
Whitehall, March 10, 1759.

ures had been adopted for enabling the privates to purchase that liquor at a halfpenny a quart. "But it is the King's express pleasure," wrote Pitt, "that you do not, on account of the Molasses above-mentioned, delay for one moment the Embarkation and Sailing of the Troops."

The elder Pitt, as became a great Englishman, was a maritime strategist of the highest order. His instructions to Admiral Boscawen, preparatory to the siege of Louisburg, have been justly admired as a shining example in their own class. Pitt there laid down the doctrine that a naval administrator, — with the view of securing the passage across the sea of his own reinforcements, and intercepting the reinforcements of the enemy, — should concentrate his ships of war in overpowering force at the point of departure and the point of arrival, and allow his transports to find a way for themselves over the comparatively secure expanse of the mid-ocean.[1] If Lord North's Board of Admiralty, in the autumn of 1781, had acted in accordance with that sound principle of warfare, the irreparable disaster of Yorktown would in all likelihood have been averted. Pitt knew geography to some purpose. He had the strength, the destination, and the probable latitude and longitude, of every French and English squadron on the high seas always present to his mind. When planning a naval campaign he never forgot, (so he himself tells us,) that the progress of a fleet is regulated "by the pace of the lag-ship"; and he took care to find out how slowly, or how quickly, that lag-ship sailed. The minute events of war were his delight and recreation, as his generals in the front were well aware. Lord Amherst's journal-letters, — obviously concealing nothing, obviously exaggerating nothing, and narrating a string of homely and petty occurrences, lighted up from time to time by the announcement of splendid

---

[1] Julian Stafford Corbett's *England in the Seven Years' War;* volume I, chapter 13.

successes,—kept the Secretary of State loyally and
frankly informed of all that happened while the British
army was hewing its path towards Canada through the
primeval forest. In fewer sentences, (for Wolfe and
Boscawen had just then less time to write,) Mr. Pitt was
told how matters had gone at Louisburg;—how the surf
ran so high that it seemed almost impossible to land even
if the French artillery had not been firing across it; how
many boats were swamped, and how many dashed to
pieces by the cannon-balls; how long it took to drive
the enemy from the beach, leaving behind them "thirty-
five guns, great and small"; and how it rained so hard
all through the siege that no British soldier had a dry
thread upon him until the place surrendered with
twenty-four companies of marines, and four battalions
of white-coated infantry. The pride and satisfaction
of an officer, selected to carry home the tidings of
victory, were enhanced by the prospect of being cross-
examined by Mr. Pitt with the well-informed and
sympathetic curiosity which is the most valued compliment that a civilian can pay to a soldier. "I send
Major Barré with this," (so Amherst wrote after the
capture of Montreal,) "that you may receive all the
intelligence of the apparent state of everything in this
country." When the Major appeared in Downing
Street, with a French bullet in his face which he carried
to his grave, the fine qualities displayed by him during
his interviews with the Minister laid the foundation of
a warm personal and political friendship between Pitt
and Barré; and that friendship, in after years, was
nobly and generously recognised by Pitt's son.

Pitt's lofty and sterling nature was conspicuously
visible in his relations with the colonial authorities of
America, and, through them, with the American people.
In a contest for British honour and British interests
which was waged on many shores, and on every sea, it
was no small advantage that a statesman, who for the
time being was supreme ruler of the empire, should
treat men of British descent, all the world over, as

self-respecting and self-governing citizens. When he had a point of importance to carry, he began his despatch by setting forth, in one or two of his rolling sentences, the reasons why he called upon the American colonists for exertions and sacrifices; and he scrupulously and exactly defined the nature, and the limit, of the demands which he made upon their patriotism. His Majesty, (so the letter would commence, for in his public communications he always spoke of George the King rather than of William Pitt the Minister,) not doubting that all his faithful and brave subjects would continue most cheerfully to co-operate with, and second to the utmost, the large expense and extraordinary succours supplied by the mother-country for their preservation and future security by completing the reduction of all Canada, urged them to raise a stated number of regiments proportioned to the resources of every province. "The King," (Pitt went on to say,) "is pleased to furnish the Men, so raised as above, with Arms, Ammunition, and Tents, as well as to order provisions in the same manner as is done to the rest of the King's Forces. The whole that His Majesty expects and requires from the several Provinces is the Levying, Clothing, and Pay of the Men." [1] That was how Pitt's requisitions were worded; and they met with prompt and eager obedience. Massachusetts, — so close-fisted against any attempt to take her money without asking her own consent, — gave Pitt a hundred and forty thousand pounds in twenty months, and loaded herself with debt when the yield from

---

[1] Mr. Secretary Pitt to the Governors of Massachusetts, New Hampshire, Connecticut, Rhode Island, New York, and New Jersey; Whitehall, January 7th 1760.

This circular is quoted from *The Correspondence of William Pitt, when Secretary of State, with Colonial Governors, and Military and Naval Commissioners in America;* edited by Gertrude Selwyn Kimball. It is a work to be studied along with Mr. Corbett's *England in the Seven Years' War.* In the year that these excellent books were published there appeared an English translation of Albert von Ruville's *William Pitt, Earl of Chatham;* but, — whatever valuable qualities this writer's work may possess, — his analysis of Chatham's character, and his theory with regard to Chatham's motives, may be laid aside in amazed silence.

current taxation shewed symptoms of dwindling. The less populous and wealthy colonies strained their credit, and ransacked their villages for recruits, at the call of a leader who accompanied his appeals for assistance with explanations which they believed, and exhortations which fired their public spirit. The Governor of South Carolina, writing in the name of his province, expressed an earnest hope that, under the blessing of Almighty God, the next campaign would expel the French from the Continent of America ; that the inhabitants of that Continent would for the future be safe from an insatiable and cruel hereditary enemy ; and that Mr. Secretary Pitt himself might live to enjoy the effects of the vigorous measures which he had so wisely promoted. Under that glorious administration every member of our race, in whatever corner of the universe he had been born, deemed it, like William Cowper,

> " praise enough
> To fill the ambition of a private man
> That Chatham's language was his mother tongue,
> And Wolfe's great name compatriot with his own." [1]

Those were the arts by which Chatham secured for England the affection of her colonists, and those were the methods by which he brought her enemies to rout and ruin. But power and responsibility had been transferred to other hands than his ; and the statesman, who had extended and consolidated our empire, was thenceforward a sad and anxious, though not a silent, spectator of a policy which had brought about its disruption, and which threatened to result in its downfall. He had combated at each successive stage, with weighty arguments and glowing words, the action of the King's government in relation to America. That action produced the consequences which from the first he had predicted. America renounced her allegiance to the British Crown ; and it was too late for even Chatham's

---

[1] *The Task;* ii, 235.

oratory to undo the mischief. He did not, however, deem himself absolved from the duty of counselling Parliament; and, when the occasion presented itself, he gave utterance to warnings and prophecies every one of which was scouted by men in office, and every one of which was fulfilled by the event. He had told the Ministers, at a very early moment, that it was idle to dream of reducing the whole of British America to obedience with three or four slender brigades of infantry. In the late war, (so he reminded them,) the expulsion of the French from a comparatively small part of that region had required the exertions, "during five full years, of forty thousand men, under the command of one of the ablest generals in Europe, Sir Jeffery Amherst." His advice was neglected. Only ten thousand troops were sent; and, so far from overrunning the thirteen colonies, they were not enough to defend even the single town of Boston, where they would have been captured to a man if they had not been withdrawn by sea.

France was Chatham's ancient adversary, whose projects he divined as a swordsman divines, and anticipates, the intention of his opponent to plant a thrust. In January 1775 the Ministers, with a light heart, and no eye for future European complications, exhorted the House of Lords to approve by an overwhelming majority the forcible subjugation of the revolted colonies. Chatham reminded his brother Peers that America did not stand alone in the world of nations. "France," he said, "has her full attention upon you. War is at your door; and carrying the question here by your votes to-night will not save your country from the extremity of peril." And now in December 1777, a few days after the reception of the news from Saratoga, the Cabinet thought it well to adjourn Parliament over the space of six entire weeks, as if it were a matter of paramount importance that the Peers and Commoners should not miss their Christmas hunting. Lord North, in the Lower House, had encountered the objections which

were offered to the proposal by an easy and offhand
assurance that France and Spain had no mind to molest
us, and that, in any case, England was prepared at
all points to meet either of them, or both of them together. Such was not the view of Lord Chatham.
" At so tremendous a season," he said, " it does not
become your Lordships, the great hereditary council
of the nation, to retire to your country-seats in quest of
joy and merriment, while the real state of public affairs
calls for the fullest exertions of your wisdom. It is
your duty, my Lords, to advise your sovereign, to be
the protectors of your country, to be conscious of your
own weight and your own authority." Lord Chatham
wished to keep Parliament sitting, not for the purpose of
making fine speeches, but in order to lose no opportunity
of enforcing practical suggestions of immense importance,
and bringing to the public knowledge significant and
momentous facts. He was almost the first, and quite
the most earnest, to recommend an immediate em-
bodiment of the Militia. Using the modesty of true
greatness, — as if he had been rather the witness,
than the author, of those judicious measures which
in former days had saved and aggrandised England, —
he told his audience how, during the late war,
he had enjoyed the satisfaction of visiting no less
than three extensive and admirably situated camps,
swarming with a well-trained and well-armed Militia.
" I remember," he said, " when appearances were
not nearly so melancholy and alarming as at present,
that there were more troops in Kent alone, for
the defence of that county, than there are now in the
whole island."

Chatham's speeches made all the deeper impression
upon the country at large because, for the most part,
they remained without an answer in the assembly to
which they were addressed. We are told that " it
became fashionable, if not a rule of conduct, with the
Court Lords " to treat his censures and proposals with
an affected indifference, and to talk contemptuously

about his waning powers.[1] But that sort of conversation was reserved for the dinner-table and the supper-table; and the Treasury Bench in the House of Peers, when Chatham was concerned, seemed seldom or never in a fighting mood. Lord Sandwich and Lord Weymouth, on whom the main burden of the debate lay, were voluble enough when there was a meek or discredited opponent in face of them; but they both had the strongest personal reasons for not venturing to engage at close quarters with an antagonist, himself of unimpeachable character, who wielded with such terrible effectiveness the lash of moral reprobation. The Ministry, unable to refute so powerful an adversary in open debate, endeavoured to disparage his authority by the agency of mercenary pens. In pamphlets written by State pensioners, and in newspaper paragraphs paid for out of the Secret Service money, Lord Chatham's past history was held up to reproach, and his good fame bespattered by calumnies. Those were not, and never had been, Chatham's own weapons. " Mr. Pitt," (it has been said,) "to his immortal honour, employed no writer to justify his administration. He nobly declared in the House of Commons that he wished for no approbation of his measures but that which was constitutional. The moment those who were the best judges of his conduct disapproved it, he would withdraw into retirement." [2] As a senator he always answered argument with argument; and as a war-minister, (so Horace Walpole finely said,) he replied to abuse by victories.

Lord North's government reverted to Sir Robert Walpole's practice of subsidising the press, and carried it to a height which it had never attained before. It was matter of common knowledge that many thousand pounds of public money were distributed annually among people who, in the language of the Opposition,

[1] *History of Europe in the Annual Register of 1778;* chapter 3.
[2] *London Evening Post;* Saturday August 7, to Tuesday August 10, 1779.

were "a set of dishonest scribes"; but, whatever epithets these gentry may have deserved, they had the merit of keeping faith with their employers whenever they were told off to attack the Earl of Chatham. "The Duke of Newcastle," according to the *Morning Post*, "used to say that Mr. Pitt's talents would not have got him forty pounds a year in any country but this. His lips dropped venom. When he had obtained enormous legacies, pensions, and sinecures, the mask fell off. His treachery to the cause of the people still loads his memory with curses." Lord Chatham had insisted, with extraordinary force, upon the distinction which should be drawn between German rulers who hired out soldiers to put down the rebellion in America, and German rulers who, in the Seven Years' War, had sent their troops to serve with British allies, and in British pay, for the purpose of repelling a French invader from the soil of the German Fatherland. The ministerial journalists professed themselves unable to see any difference between the two cases. "That vain old dotard with the short memory," (such was the description of Chatham given by one of the ablest among them,) "seems to have forgot the meaning and use of auxiliary troops. I am astonished that this new-made Lord should, in the House of Peers, take the liberty to abuse his betters, the German Princes, who are much older gentlemen than himself, with all the black-guardism of modern patriotism, when so many Noble-men sit there who can claim their pedigrees from a descent of above a hundred years. If this goes on much longer he, and his gang, shall hear some private anecdotes not very pleasing to them."[1]   To us it seems strange that an Englishman should ever have lived who thought a Landgrave of Hesse, and a Margrave of Anspach, the betters of Chatham.

The stream of Treasury gold which poured through the subterranean channels of literature was wasted

---

[1] Letter from Vindex in the *Morning Post;* Dec. 11, 1777.

money for any effect which it produced upon the serious
judgment of the country. The times were such that
Englishmen did not care to take their politics from
Grub Street. When the tidings from Saratoga were
followed closely by an announcement that France and
America had joined hands, — when a conviction flashed
upon the public mind that we had no army at home, and
only an outward show of a war-fleet in the channel; —
the world, as if by a single and simultaneous impulse,
bethought itself of the statesman who, just twenty years
back, had rescued England from almost as poor a plight,
and within the space of thirty months had mounted her
on a pinnacle of triumph. The hour had come round
once again, and the man was still there. Everyone
who had anything to lose, everyone who cared for the
interests and honour of the nation, joined in a cry for
the return to office of the Earl of Chatham. The journalists in Government pay began to change their note.
One newspaper, which had repeatedly assured its
readers that, if ministers had taken Lord Chatham's
advice, they would have rendered themselves the laugh-
ing-stock of Europe, suddenly inquired why the great
Earl, whose health was now completely re-established,
held aloof from attendance in Parliament. It was no
answer, (said another Tory journalist,) to repeat that
Lord Chatham was past his prime. Mr. Pitt had
always been thought older than he really was, " for the
same reason that the same error prevailed with regard
to the celebrated Voltaire," because he came into
public life earlier than most of his contemporaries, and
was already a distinguished ornament of the House of
Commons at the age of six-and-twenty. It soon became
evident that those gentlemen were writing under orders.
Lord Barrington, who then was still Secretary at War,
took upon himself to inform the King that a general
dismay existed in all ranks and all conditions, arising
from an opinion that the Government was unequal
to the crisis ; — an opinion, (he confessed,) so universal
that it prevailed among those who were dependent

on, and attached to, the ministers, and even among those ministers themselves. "Lord North," (in the works of Mr. Lecky,) "implored the King to accept his resignation, and to send for Lord Chatham. Bute, the old Tory favourite, breaking his long silence, spoke of Chatham as indispensable. Lord Mansfield, the bitterest and ablest rival of Chatham, said with tears in his eyes that, unless the King sent for Chatham, the ship would go down." [1]

Men of all parties, save and except the Bedfords, were united in calling for Lord Chatham. But the King's repugnance was inexorable. In these days we are told that History has no right to concern itself with Ethics. Whether such be the case or not, a prudent historian will gladly leave to the moralist the unpleasant task of explaining the motives of George the Third's hatred for a statesman who had made him the greatest monarch in the world; who was old enough to be his father; and whose reverence for the kingly office, and the kingly person, was blamed as excessive even by indulgent critics. The royal vocabulary, often bald and barren, teemed with depreciatory epithets whenever the subject under discussion was the greatest of living Englishmen. Lord Chatham's political conduct was so abandoned, — it was so absurd to expect from him gratitude, "when the whole tenour of his life had shown him incapable of that honourable sentiment," — that he, and his family, must hope for no mark of favour from the Crown "until death, or decrepitude, had put an end to him as the trumpet of sedition." [2] That was the strain in which King George had habitually written about the Earl of Chatham; and, when the leading men in politics, with Lord North at their head, urged him to accept the object of his dislike as Prime Minister, his anger was hot and his resolution stubborn. He acceded to the pretence of a negotiation; but the conditions

[1] *History of England in the Eighteenth Century;* chapter 14.
[2] George the Third to Lord North ; Kew, August 9, 1775.

which he exacted were such as to render an agreement impossible ;[1] and, lest there should be any mistake about the royal intentions, Lord North was informed specifically that, if Lord Chatham should ask for an interview with the King before giving his final reply, the King would certainly refuse to see him. No one could expect, — no one, then or now, could wish, — that Chatham should have stooped to accept such an offer. The attempt at an arrangement fell through, to the undisguised relief and satisfaction of the monarch ; while Lord North sadly and reluctantly abandoned the hope of transferring his responsibilities to the group of statesmen for whom his Sovereign could find no more respectful appellation than " Lord Chatham and his crew."

George the Third might safely have dispensed with that ungracious outburst of self-revelation. The famous statesman, whom he misunderstood and misprized, had no desire whatever to impose his services upon an unwilling master. Ambition was extinct in Chatham's breast ; and, though patriotism sat enthroned there as supreme as ever, he felt that he was no longer able to fulfil the expectations of his countrymen. His health was shattered beyond repair; and his strength would not support the ceaseless vigilance, and relentless labour, which devolve upon a Minister who is directing,

[1] The King laid down the limits of concession, for Lord North's guidance, in a sentence of which the grammar was confused, but the meaning plain, and the spirit imperious and inexorable. " If," he said, " Lord Chatham agrees to support your Administration, or, (if you like the expression better,) the fundamentals of the present Administration, and Lord North at the head of the Treasury, Lords Suffolk, Gower, and Weymouth in great offices of their own inclination, Lord Sandwich in the Admiralty, Thurloe Chancellor, and Wedderburne a Chief Justice, I will not object to see that great man when Lord Shelburne and Dunning, with Barré, are placed already in offices ; but I solemnly declare nothing shall bring me to treat personally with Lord Chatham." *King George the Third to Lord North : Queen's House, March* 16*th,* 1778. 28 *minutes past* 8 *a.m.*

In the course of this letter the King speaks of his unwillingness to accept the services of " that perfidious man "; and Lord Russell, in his memorials of Fox, quotes the expression as meaning Chatham. Macaulay notes in the margin of the book: " No. Lord Shelburne certainly."

instead of leaving to the hazard of fortune, the operations of a great war.   An ever-present sense of fatigue,
both of mind and body, warned him that the day was
already spent, and the night very close at hand.   It was
a calm and mellow sunset.   Nowhere might be found a
more united family or a more peaceful home.   Lady
Chatham, a true helpmate in joy or sorrow, was one
with her husband in affection, in opinion, and in her
views of duty.   They had around them their three sons,
whom they were launching into life, which in the case
of Chatham meant that he was giving them to his
country.   The eldest son, as soon as the French war
became imminent, had returned to the military profession ; and he now was on the eve of sailing to join
the garrison at Gibraltar, which henceforward was
the scene of danger.   The third son, a lad of great
promise, and amiable disposition, — "the young tar,"
said Chatham, "who may, by the favour of heaven, live
to do some good," — had just passed as lieutenant, and
was looking forward to his first independent command.[1]
The second son, William, marked out by nature for a
great career, was waiting for one-and-twenty, and
meanwhile served his political apprenticeship as the
confidential assistant, and inseparable companion, of
his father.   "My dear Secretary," the old man called
him : — and he added, with a humorous side-glance at the
King and his Secretaries of State, "I wish *Somebody* had
as good and as honest an one."   The new year of 1778
found Chatham fairly well, and exempt from pain and
discomfort.   "Perhaps," (so he told his physician,)
"I may last as long as Great Britain."   Early in February he had an attack of gout which aroused hope,
rather than apprehension, in those of his friends and

---

[1] James Charles Pitt served on the West India station under Rodney,
who appointed him to the *Hornet* sloop, where he died of fever at the age
of twenty.   When Lord Chatham sank down unconscious in the House of
Lords it was observed by the reporters that the youth, though apparently
not more than seventeen or eighteen years old, displayed a sailor's handi-
ness and presence of mind "in assisting his venerable father."

well-wishers who, according to the accepted theory of
their generation, regarded that disease as a remedy.
Lord Granby wrote in much the same language as his
brave father might have addressed to Mr. Secretary
Pitt twenty years before. "I hope," said the young
Peer, "that your Lordship's gout continues favourable,
and will be productive of such a stock of health as may
enable your Lordship to save us from the cloud of
misfortune which impends over our heads." But
Chatham did not mistake his own symptoms and sensa-
tions, and was aware that the end could not be far distant.

Lord Chatham, while the nation clamoured to be
governed by him, stood almost isolated in his attitude
towards the question of the moment. He made no
secret of the policy which he would adopt if he was
raised to power. He would cease to contend in arms
with the American rebellion. He would withdraw
every British and German soldier; abrogate every
obnoxious statute; renounce every disputed claim; and
trust, for the future reunion of the colonies with the
mother-country, to the healing influence of time and
the bonds of a common race and a common religion.
In the debate on the Address of November 1777 he had
given the House of Lords his opinion about the conflict
with America. "In a just and necessary war," he then
said, " to maintain the rights and honour of my country,
I would strip the shirt off my back to support it. But
in such a war as this, unjust in its principle, impracticable in its means, and ruinous in its consequences, I
would not contribute a single effort, or a single shilling."
On that point he agreed with Lord Rockingham and the
Duke of Richmond in the Peers, and with Sir George
Savile and General Conway in the Commons; but they,
one and all, recognised, — as a stern fact, and an established certainty, — that the war with America would
never cease until the Independence of America was
acknowledged by the government of Great Britain. In
such an acknowledgment Lord Chatham refused to
concur. He could not bring himself to speak the

irrevocable word which would divide the English people. His position was criticised by Horace Walpole with shrewd and unsparing logic. " He would recall the troops," (said Walpole,) " and deny the Independence of the Americans. He is right to recall an army that cannot conquer ; but a country that will not be conquered, and that cannot be, is in an odd sort of state of dependence." [1] It was an inconsistency very natural, and very noble, in an old statesman who was dealing with colonies which he had saved by his genius, where he was still passionately beloved, and where, (as he beautifully expressed it,) his heart was garnered.

On the seventh of April, 1778, the American question was brought forward in the House of Peers by the Duke of Richmond. Chatham insisted on being present at the debate, and, when the Duke ceased speaking, he rose from his seat amidst the anxious sympathy of an awe-stricken assembly. "His Lordship," so the report runs, "began by lamenting that his bodily infirmities had so long, and especially at so important a crisis, prevented his attendance on the duties of Parliament. He declared that he had made an effort, almost beyond the powers of his constitution, to come down to the House on this day, (perhaps the last time he should ever be able to enter its walls,) to express the indignation he felt at an idea, which he understood was gone forth, of yielding up the sovereignty of America." But to narrate once more the story of what then occurred would be like telling over again how Nelson was struck down on the quarter-deck of the *Victory*. Lord Chatham was carried, from the scene of the catastrophe, by easy stages to his home in Kent. There he lay, between life and death, with all his family about him, except the eldest son, whom he affectionately, but firmly, dismissed from attendance at the bedside to his post of duty on the battlements of Gibraltar.[2] On the eleventh of May

[1] Walpole to the Countess of Ossory; Dec. 5, 1777.
[2] A full year elapsed before the new Peer made a hurried visit to England. " The young Earl of Chatham took the oaths and his seat in Parlia-

Chatham breathed his last. He was saved, by the good fortune of a timely death, from the distress of seeing a war with France conducted in accordance with the methods of Lord George Germaine and the Earl of Sandwich. Nor is he to be compassionated because he was forbidden by fate to embark on the hopeless task of resuscitating the loyalty of America towards the British Crown. " Heaven," (it has been truly, and not unfeelingly, said,) " spared him the anxiety of the attempt, and, we believe, the mortification of a failure." [1]

Edmund Burke, in the finest passage of an admirable speech, had reckoned the name of Chatham as among the solid and valuable possessions of the nation. " A great and celebrated name," (so he called it,) which had kept the name of England respected in every other country of the globe.[2] The citizens of London, in Common Council assembled, expressed an earnest desire that their favourite statesman should be buried " in their Cathedral Church of St. Paul." Rigby translated the known sentiments of the King into his own rude and blustering language, and scoffed at the idea of bestowing a compliment upon the Aldermen of London, whom he vehemently attacked for their degenerated respectability, and their detestable politics. The King himself told his Lord Chamberlain that they might do what they pleased with the corpse, but that he would not let his Guards march in procession into the City. Whatever may have been the motives of the refusal, the decision itself cannot be regretted. The Commons voted Lord Chatham a public funeral, and a monument in Westminster Abbey which, in conception and execu-

ment on Thursday last. His Lordship was dressed in his regimentals, which were scarlet turned up with green, and he presented a very elegant, manly, and graceful figure. He is as tall as his late father, has the appearance of much mildness in his countenance, and is said to be a most exemplary young gentleman in his morals and general character." *London Evening Post* of Thursday July 17, to Saturday July 19, 1779.

[1] The *Quarterly Review* of June 1840. The article was from the pen of Mr. Croker.

[2] Mr. Burke's speech on American Taxation of April 19, 1774.

tion, proved worthy of the man whom it commemorated;[1] and ample, though not excessive, provision was made for the bereaved family. Lord North's personal behaviour, throughout the proceedings, was marked by delicacy, and by genuine good feeling; and the House of Commons honoured itself by the tribute of respect and gratitude which it paid to one who in earlier days had been its own greatest glory.

It was otherwise in the House of Lords. A whole string of insignificant peers, among whom not the least insignificant was Lord Chancellor Bathurst, delivered themselves as if they were so many members of a third-rate debating club assembled to discuss a motion condemning the political conduct of the late Earl of Chatham. They inveighed against him as an arbitrary ruler; as a spendthrift of the public resources; as a plausible and misleading orator; and as a war-minister who owed his reputation to better men than himself. One speaker after another, with suspicious unanimity, reminded their audience that our successes in the Seven Years' War were due, not to Mr. Secretary Pitt, but to Lord Hawke and Prince Ferdinand of Brunswick; and Parliament, (they added,) had not thought fit to treat those distinguished warriors with the liberality which it was now invited to exercise towards the Pitt family. Lord Camden replied, on behalf of his old friend and chief, with intense, but studiously guarded, indignation. He acknowledged that the professional qualifications of Lord Hawke, and of Prince Ferdinand, were beyond question; but the one, (he maintained,) was Lord Chatham's admiral, and the other, his general; "and so far from their individual merits lessening those of the deceased Earl, or diminishing the value of his services,

---

[1] A Whig member, who wished to gratify the City, complained that the proposed statue in the Abbey "would be too near the ceiling"; a feature which is the most striking and characteristic merit of the whole design. The tombs of Chatham and of his august coæval Lord Mansfield, — noble monuments, and nobly placed, — go far to redeem the North Transept of the Abbey from presenting the appearance of a statuary's shop.

they went directly to enhance both." Lord Chatham
was warmly defended by several other Whig noblemen;
but the honours of the day rested with a member of His
Majesty's Government; for Lord Lyttelton, who with
all his faults was a gentleman, argued forcibly and
eloquently on the same lines as Lord Camden. There
had been many commanders, (he said,) who in past days
had led our soldiers and sailors to triumph on land and
sea; but England, in the course of her history, had
never seen the like of Chatham. At a dark hour in her
fortunes he had thrust his way to the front by the mere
force of his abilities. He had silenced faction; had
restored energy to the administration; and had reduced
those national enemies, who at the outbreak of hostilities were assured of success, "to sue with the most
abject and mortifying humility for peace." As was most
appropriate when dealing with a question involving
the expenditure of public money, he gave examples
of Chatham's disinterestedness, and of his high-souled
scorn for what then were the customary perquisites of
office.[1] Lyttelton's fervour thrilled the assembly, and
persuaded most of the ministerialists who had not
already committed themselves in debate. After he
had resumed his seat cavil was hushed; and the financial proposals, which had been sent up from the Lower
House, were carried by a large majority. The Lord
Chancellor, and the Archbishop of York, whose own
services to the world were remunerated by colossal
incomes, put on record a Protest against "an unwar-
rantable lavishing away of public money during an
expensive war." But only two other peers could be
induced to sign the document.

---

[1] "The noble Earl," said Lyttelton, "had gone through offices, which
generally seemed to enrich his predecessors, without deriving a shilling of
advantage from his situation. When he was Paymaster General, a subsidy
to the King of Sardinia passed through his hands. The usual perquisite
amounted to more than twenty thousand pounds. The noble Earl declined
to touch it, and the whole sum was found in the bank years afterwards.
It was then offered to the Earl of Chatham as his right. He refused it;
and the money was applied to the public service."

The funeral took place on the ninth of June. The great officers of the Court were absent from the ceremony; and Cabinet Ministers remained at home, as if, (said Horace Walpole,) their modesty shrank from a comparison with Lord Chatham. Gibbon, as a supporter of the Ministry, was anything but pleased with his leaders. "The Government," he wrote, "ingeniously contrived to secure the double odium of suffering the thing to be done, and of doing it with an ill grace." Before ever the grave in the Abbey was closed, the work of detraction and calumny recommenced. Thurlow, who succeeded Bathurst as Lord Chancellor within a week of the funeral, had set the tone in Government circles by a sarcasm which was exceptionally brutal, even for him; and aspirants to official preferment launched their gibes against Lord Chatham in epistles written to be shown in high, and in the highest, quarters.[1] The hirelings of the newspaper press continued, all summer through, to slander and ridicule the dead statesman with a pertinacity which, even at this distance of time, provokes contemptuous disgust. Their efforts to belittle him went for less than nothing. Four years back Edmund Burke had analysed the elements of that atmosphere of national respect and regard by which Lord Chatham was surrounded, — "his venerable age, his merited rank, his superior eloquence, his splendid qualities, the vast space which he filled in the eye of mankind; and, more than all the rest, his fall from power, which, like death, canonises and sanctifies a great character." And now death itself had come; and the feeling of England

---

[1] Some curious letters in this class have been preserved in the collection of *Steevens's Facsimiles* at the British Museum. Sir Beaumont Hotham, for example, wrote thus to the Right Honourable William Eden. "The 'Chathamania' is very strong upon us. What a wonderful people we are! If Lord Chatham had happened to have lived till Parliament had risen, in all probability this wonderful furor would have subsided long before it met again; and in that case his family would have remained in the same condition as other families descended from expensive and thoughtless ancestors."

about Lord Chatham, from that moment onwards, was a sentiment altogether above and outside party. The strength of that feeling was curiously tested when, after no long interval of time, young William Pitt stepped over the threshold of manhood into the confidence and affection of his fellow-countrymen as naturally and easily as an heir-at-law succeeds to the estate of his predecessor in title. That was the noblest inheritance which ever descended to son from father.

CHAPTER II

CHATHAM had passed away, old and very weary; and the times, as he himself confessed, required the services of younger men. His life's work had been ruined by a monarch and a minister who belonged to a later generation than his own; and the deadly peril, which the policy of George the Third and Lord North had brought upon the nation, could only be averted by a political leader in the vigour of life, who possessed the spirit and enterprise of his years. When the news of Saratoga arrived in London, Charles Fox was still but eight-and-twenty. He had begun early. At fourteen he attended the theatre, dressed and powdered in the latest French style. He soon fell romantically in love with the reigning toast of the day; and his sweet and pretty aunt, Lady Sarah Lennox, could discern nothing but what was graceful and becoming in the manifestation of his boyish passion.[1] At sixteen his good sayings, — and very good they were, — were duly reported to George Selwyn, even when they were uttered at Selwyn's own expense; and men of fashion were already glad to win his money, and to take his advice about the cut and colour of their finery, and about the matching of their horses at Newmarket. By the age of five-and-twenty he had despoiled himself of a younger son's landed estate, and a magnificent fortune in money; and he still was a jovial, an ill-ordered, and a very far

---

[1] " Charles is in town, and violently in love with the Duchess of Hamilton. Think of his riding out to see her! You know how he hates it. He is all humbleness and respect, and never leaves her. He is now quite manly, and is very much liked in the world. He is a sweet boy, and I hope will continue as he is." Letter of Dec. 16, 1764, in the *Correspondence of Lady Sarah Lennox.*

from irreproachable member of society. But his mind was tending towards nobler interests; and the time gradually approached when, in his own peculiar way, he became a reformed character. He ceased to gamble. He lived contented within his slender means. His home-life with the woman whom he loved, — both before and after he married her, — was admired by his uncensorious contemporaries as a model of domestic affection, and mutual sympathy in the insatiable enjoyment of good literature and quiet rural pleasures. Nothing at last remained of the old Charles Fox except the frankness and friendliness, the inexhaustible good-nature, the indescribable charm of manner, and the utter absence of self-importance and self-consciousness, which combined to make him, at every period of his existence, the best fellow in the world.

It is worth while to place side by side, but not in contrast, three separate accounts of Charles Fox at three different and distant epochs of his life. " I have passed," (so George Selwyn wrote in 1774,) "two evenings with him at Almack's ; and never was anybody so agreeable, and the more so from his having no pretensions to it." Many years later, when he was near forty, he paid a visit to Gibbon in his pleasant hermitage at Lausanne ; and the historian,— who had conversed with most English, and not a few European, celebrities, and who knew all that could be told in books about the best and greatest men of many ages and countries, — declared that no human being was ever more perfectly exempt than Mr. Fox from the taint of malevolence, vanity, and falsehood. Such, in his early youth, and in middle life, Charles Fox showed himself to his elders and his political opponents. How, after the lapse of twenty more years, he was beloved by the younger members of his own family circle, is recorded in Lord Holland's narrative of the great statesman's last illness. "On my approaching my uncle's bedside," (Lord Holland writes,) " he said, with a melancholy smile which I can never forget : ' So you would not leave me, young

one, to go to Paris, but liked staying with me better!'"
The hour had arrived when on his own account Fox
was not unwilling to have done with life; but he could
not speak without deep emotion of his wife, or of the
public causes which he had nearest at heart. " Do not
think me selfish, young one," he said. " The Slave
Trade and Peace are such glorious things. I cannot
give them up even to you." His last intelligible sentence was, "I die happy." In that placid mood, which
was so habitual to him, he left a world the pleasures of
which he had keenly relished, and where he had endured, good-humouredly and gallantly, very much more
than his fair share of abuse and injustice, of disappointed
hopes and baffled labour.

By the time that the American War had run half its
course the parliamentary position of Charles Fox was
unique in the history of national assemblies. The Lower
House was an aristocratic body, including almost every
commoner who was prominent in fashionable society,
and pervaded by a spirit of easy and unceremonious
equality. Fox was familiarly known to all his brother-
members, and quite as much at home among them as a
clever and popular undergraduate among the students
of a great Oxford or Cambridge College. The politicians
at Westminster had always heard a great deal about
him while he was still at Eton, and had met him in
London and at Ascot far more frequently than his
schoolmasters ought to have permitted. He was elected
for Midhurst at the age of nineteen; he was on his legs
before many months had passed; and, when once he
knew the sound of his own voice in Parliament, he seldom or never was a silent member for four-and-twenty
consecutive hours. In the course of two sessions, according to his own story, he spoke every day but one, and
was sorry he had not spoken on that day likewise; and,
strange to say, the rest of the House was sorry also.
The extraordinary effect which, from the very first, was
produced by his masterful rhetoric, is established by the
unanimous testimony of impartial, and even hostile, wit-

nesses; but it must be taken on trust, for it is impossible to define, and difficult even to conjecture, the nature of the spell which the wayward and audacious young patrician cast upon his audience. His politics, anti-democratic to excess, were for some years the politics of a boy, and not the best or wisest of boys; but the greatest orators of a great generation envied the skill and force with which he expounded and defended the perverse and absurd opinions which it pleased him to adopt. His speeches were admired by his adversaries of the Opposition more than they were liked by the Government which he supported. The Cabinet was deeply committed to a warfare against the liberty of the Press, and the rights of the Middlesex electors; and Charles Fox was perpetually exhorting Ministers to intensify the rigour of their harsh and unconstitutional policy. However far and fast Lord North and his colleagues travelled along the path of repression, they could not save themselves from being upbraided as lukewarm guardians of authority and order by the young Draco who sat behind them, and sometimes amongst them. Always an object of terror to the leaders of his own party, Charles Fox was never so formidable to them as during those intermittent periods when he condescended to adorn the Treasury Bench as a subordinate member of the Ministry.

The change came, just in time for his own reputation, and for his usefulness as a servant of the public. In the spring of 1774 Charles Fox broke, finally and irreconcilably, with Lord North's government; and, (what was more to the purpose,) he broke with his old self likewise. The deaths of both his parents, and of his elder brother, within the space of half a year, — together with the knowledge of that distress which his unspeakable folly, and unbridled extravagance, had brought upon those whom he loved, — set him thinking soberly and remembering sadly, and produced in him a penitence which was sincere and lasting. He was governed from within by more honourable impulses than had actuated him in the past; and the political

associates with whom he now consorted were men whose
advice and example he could safely follow. Edmund
Burke, and Sir George Savile, were very different men-
tors from the Right Honourable Richard Rigby, and
the Earl of Sandwich. In another respect, moreover,
Charles Fox enjoyed a rare advantage, which, (as it is
not uncharitable to believe,) was due to his good luck
rather than to his foresight and discretion. In his salad
days, when he was green in judgment, he had never
uttered a word about America, — good, bad, or indifferent, — which remained on record. And therefore
when Lord North, throwing open the casket of Pandora,
invited Parliament to wreck the prosperity of Boston
and extinguish the freedom of Massachusetts, Fox, to
the astonishment and amusement of the House of Commons, presented himself in the very unusual attitude of
a cold and cautious neutrality. "Without heat," (so
Walpole tells us,) "he left himself at liberty to take
what part he should please." The world was not long
left in suspense as to what that part would be. During
the remainder of the session, the last session of a bad
Parliament, Charles Fox was an unflinching opponent
of those penal laws which provoked the armed resistance of New England. He spoke seldom, — for him,
— but always with effect ; he was fertile in embarrassing
objections, and in practical amendments which the
Government had no choice but to accept ; and, above
all, he established his claim to be heard amidst the
noisiest tumult of an excited house, and at the closing
hour of a prolonged discussion. There was that about
him which repelled insult. It frequently happened,
while those fate-laden measures were being rushed
through Parliament, that the protests of Conway and
Barré, and even of Burke himself, were interrupted by
jeers and drowned in clamour. But, when Fox rose
to his feet, he never failed to command universal and
willing attention by his impressive vehemence, his persuasive logic, and his unerring tact. Nor would he consent to resume his seat until the whole row of Ministers

had listened to every syllable of that impassioned rush of closely-reasoned sentences in which he conveyed his disapproval of their policy.

The new parliament met in November 1774; and within three years from that date Charles Fox, — with no suspicion of intrigue, or even of conscious intention, on his own part, and without jealousy on the part of others, — had advanced naturally, and by gradual stages, into the undisputed leadership of the Opposition in the Commons. He spoke on every important occasion with increased acceptance, and immense authority. His prophecies had all come true, and the Ministers themselves could not conceal their regret that his warnings had been allowed to pass unheeded. He had reached the summit of his intellectual and physical powers. Henry Grattan, drawing on his long experience of the Irish and English parliaments, pronounced that Fox, during the American War, was the best speaker whom he had ever heard. His method in controversy, then and afterwards, was singularly chivalrous and straightforward. "He never," said a careful observer, " misrepresented what his opponent had said, or attacked his accidental oversights, but fairly met and routed him where he thought himself strongest." [1] He wasted no time in preliminary skirmishes, but flung himself upon the key of his adversary's position, pouring in his arguments as a fighting general hurries up his successive waves of reinforcements in the crisis of a battle. Intent on convincing, he reiterated the substance of his case in fresh forms, and with new illustrations, until the stupidest of his hearers had caught his full meaning; while the cleverest, and the most fastidious, never complained that Charles Fox spoke too long, or repeated himself too often. Always the pre-eminent debater, at this period of his career he was a superb orator. Joseph Galloway, the Pennsylvanian loyalist, who was a frequent attendant in the House of Commons, observed him with the eyes

---

[1] *The character of Charles Fox*, by William Godwin.

of a bitter and implacable enemy. The person of Fox,
(according to Galloway,) was short and squalid; his
appearance was mean and disagreeable; his voice in-
harmonious, and his countenance strongly Judaic. And
yet, when it came to the speech itself, this jaundiced
critic was all praise and admiration. " Fox is not supposed," (so Galloway continued,) " to possess a great
fund of information; but his mind supplies the deficiency
from its own inexhaustible treasure. His delivery is
rapid in proportion to the quickness of his conception.
The torrent of argument comes rolling from him with
irresistible force. He does not leave his hearers to follow.
He drives them before him. The strongest sense is not
proof against his power. He sways the whole assembly ;
and every man communicates the shock to his neighbour." [1]

Eloquence, if it is to rule the world, must be inspired
by strength of conviction, and by continuity of purpose.
Charles Fox converted to his own way of thinking two
successive parliaments, and extricated his country from
the whirlpool of danger in which it was engulfed, not
only because he could make wonderful speeches, but
because he had a policy, while his opponents had none.
The Ministers of the Crown had well-nigh exhausted
the national resources in a contest with our own colonies,
for the pursuit of ends every one of which, after four
years of civil war, they had publicly renounced and
abandoned as impossible of attainment. That was the
case as concerned the past. A more serious crisis had
now arisen; and statesmen in office, to whom the country
had a right to look for guidance, stood once again at the
parting of the ways, on a lower and more precipitous
stage of the descent along the road to ruin. A French
war, for which France had long been silently preparing,
was already on foot; and a Spanish war was surely
coming. There was hardly a government in Europe
which did not wish us ill, and intend, if the opportunity
offered itself, to do us a mischief. Our Treasury had

[1] *Considerations on the American Enquiry of the year 1779, by Joseph
Galloway, the Speaker of the House of Assembly of Pennsylvania.*

run dry; the best of our battle-ships, and almost all our regiments, were on the other side of the Atlantic; and America was still unconquered. It was a moment, above all others, when it behoved the rulers of England to look facts honestly in the face. But Lord North and his colleagues, instead of applying themselves with vigilance and resolution to the altered circumstances of their task, went on trifling and dawdling, as they had trifled and dawdled in the past; — irritating America by threats and taunts; cajoling Parliament; manipulating the Press; and attempting to conceal from public knowledge the solitude of their barrack-yards, and the nakedness of their arsenals. Their management of the war was in flat contradiction to the dictates of good sense and sound strategy. They had reduced our Home-fleet to such miserable proportions that, in the summer of 1779, a combined French and Spanish armada paraded unopposed in and about the British Channel for fifteen livelong weeks. They angered the Baltic powers, and the Mediterranean powers, by their arbitrary and high-handed treatment of neutral shipping, during a war in which they themselves failed to provide their own national commerce with that reasonable amount of protection which British merchants had a right to expect from a British Admiralty. At a time when every available soldier was required for the defence of Kent and Sussex, and for service in the East and West Indies, they kept one army idle, or worse than idle, within and around the City of New York, and consumed another army in the series of desultory marches, and bloody engagements, which led up to the catastrophe of Yorktown. They did not even themselves believe in the ultimate success of their own hand-to-mouth policy, and the efficacy of their own half-measures. The Prime Minister, when he spoke the truth in private, confessed that the prolongation of hostilities in America was morally unjustifiable, and foolish to the verge of madness. But, in the words of a precise historian, "his loyalty and personal attachment to the King were stronger than his patriotism. He was cut to the heart by the distress of his sovereign, and he was too good-natured to arrest the war." [1]

Charles Fox was quite as good-natured as Lord North; but that was not the shape which his good-nature took. He did not, in November 1778, conceive it expedient to recognise, openly and immediately, the independence of the United States. His present idea, (so he told Richard Fitzpatrick,) was in favour of withdrawing the whole Royal army from America, abstaining from all aggressive operations against the revolted colonies, and going straight at the throat of France, and of Spain also, if Spain thought fit to thrust herself into the dispute. "Whatever," (he said,) "may be the conditions of alliance between the United States and France, I cannot help thinking that the States will act very lukewarmly against England when they find themselves wholly uninterested in the war, and engaged merely by a point of honour." His industry and his ability were thenceforward directed to a triple purpose. He laboured strenuously to deter the Ministry from wasting the resources of England on ill-advised and fruitless efforts for the subjugation of America; he urged them, by every means in their power, to hurry forward the equipment of our fleets and armies; and he did all that could be done by a private member of Parliament to see that the forces of the Kingdom were employed, with unflagging vigour, and at the right points, against the rapidly increasing multitude of our European foes. His comprehensive glance embraced the entire military and political situation; and he had a marvellous faculty for presenting that situation to the minds of others. In his more important speeches he reviewed the American question, and the French question, at great length, and in all their bearings. Singular as it may appear to men who know the distaste for being lectured which is a permanent

[1] Mr. Lecky's *History of England in the Eighteenth Century;* chapter 14.

characteristic of the House of Commons, those
speeches were as attentively heard, and as rapturously
applauded, as any orations that have ever been delivered at Westminster. A sense of personal responsibility for the adequate defence of the country was
now the governing motive which urged Charles Fox
to activity; and his efforts were not confined within
the walls of Parliament. He was often at the militia-
camps, an intelligent and deeply interested spectator
of the manœuvres; and he passed weeks at Portsmouth
and at Plymouth, watching the progress of the work
in the fitting-basins and the building-yards, and living
on ship-board with the admirals and captains, among
whom he had some intimate friends, and many acquaintances emulous for the privilege and pleasure of his
company. He did very much to further the national
preparations for giving the French a warm reception
on land and sea; and he threw into the business more
heart and spirit than all the Cabinet Ministers together.
Never, since the days of Demosthenes and his Olynthiac
and Philippic orations, did any public speaker, not
endued with the power and authority of office, exert
so commanding an influence over the conduct of a war.

Charles Fox, like other great men who are the
natural product of their age, was provided with a
theatre expressly suited to the display of his gifts, and
the exercise of his capacities. The long period of years
during which Pitt, and Murray, and Henry Fox contended for supremacy in Parliament had fixed the
standard of debate, and had created a distaste for any
speaking that was not unstudied, forcible, perspicuous,
and always to the point. Set orations, (said Horace
Walpole,) ceased to be in vogue, " which added to the reputation of those great masters." Similes, quotations,
and metaphors had fallen into disrepute; allusions to
ancient Rome, and ancient Athens, were less liked than
formerly; and the style which, by the end of George
the Second's reign, had become the fashion, was " plain,
manly, and argumentative," and based upon a thorough

knowledge of essential facts.[1] It was a fashion which
suited Englishmen, who nowhere seemed so completely
English as within the walls of their own representative
assembly.   The aspect of our parliamentary proceedings was surprising to a foreigner.   A travelling
German clergyman has recorded his impressions of
the House of Commons, in the days of Fox and North,
with the convincing fidelity of a witness who finds the
reality of a famous scene something very different
from what he has pictured to himself beforehand.   The
interior of the building, (this gentleman said,) was mean-
looking, and reminded him of nothing so much as
of the choir of a Lutheran church in Prussia.   The
members kept on their hats, and wore greatcoats,
and even boots and spurs.   There was no end to their
going in and out, pausing in front of the Speaker, and
making him a bow like boys who ask their master's
permission to leave the schoolroom.   "Those who
speak," (he continued,) "deliver themselves with but
little gravity.   If a member rises who is a bad speaker,
or if what he says is deemed not sufficiently interesting,
so much noise is made, and such bursts of laughter are
raised, that he can scarcely distinguish his own words.
On the contrary, when one, who speaks well and to the
purpose, rises, the most perfect silence reigns; and his
friends and admirers, one after another, make their
approbation known by calling out ' Hear him ! ' " [2]

An authentic description of the inside of the House
of Commons, during the height of the American War,
may be read in the speech of a Somersetshire member.
He was known from others of his family as Mr. Temple
Luttrell; for in those upper-class parliaments a round
half-dozen of Luttrells sat for one or another West
Country village ; and, between them all, they had
something under four hundred constituents.   Highway

[1] *Memoires of George the Second*, by Horace Walpole.   The spelling of
the title is Walpole's own.
    [2] *Travels, chiefly on foot, through several parts of England in 1782, by
Charles P. Moritz.   Translated from the German by a Lady.*

Bills, and Enclosure Bills, (according to Mr. Temple Luttrell's account,) generally consumed the time until four o'clock of the afternoon; and the number of members present when public business commenced seldom, or never, amounted to three hundred. On a very great night, — if a Congratulatory Address to the Crown, or an augmentation to the Civil List Revenue, was under discussion, — a hundred more would drop in before the division; "and indeed," (said Mr. Luttrell,) "some scores of the majority members thought it sufficient if they repaired from their outposts towards the close of the debate, and made a forced march to the standard of the Minister. Hence it was that, when the Ayes and Noes were finally cast up at eight or nine at night, there was a respectable attendance of near four-fifths of the whole body." [1] As soon as the question was put from the Chair the door was instantly and inexorably shut, and the vote taken. The three minutes' grace for the benefit of truants and laggards had not then been conceded; and everyone, who desired to place his opinion on record, was obliged to be actually within the walls of the Chamber at the precise moment when the debate ceased. While a division was in prospect every bench was uncomfortably crowded with sitters; and a dense mass of members stood below the bar, and behind the Speaker's Chair, packed like Wilkites in front of the Middlesex hustings. The late-comers were full of wine; and those who had remained on duty through the dinner-hour were impatient for their suppers. It was a terrible audience for an ambitious orator who had not accurately judged his own value; and any gentleman of slow invention and short memory, who rose with a paper of notes in his hand, might count upon being shouted down into his seat before he had come to the end of his first sentence. But even then the House could enjoy a true debate,

---

[1] *Debate on Mr. Temple Luttrell's Motion for the admission of Strangers into the Gallery of the House;* April 30, 1777.

where argument answered argument, and trenchant hits were capped by telling repartees; especially when Charles Fox wound up the evening with a flood of common-sense, red hot, and fresh from the furnace, which sent his followers forth into the lobby boiling with excitement, and carrying with them not a few of their Parliamentary colleagues upon whose votes the Government whips had hopefully counted.[1]

The influence of Charles Fox inside Parliament owed much to his extreme popularity in that limited and well-defined circle of fashionable society which was almost identical with the sphere of politics. His kingdom was of this world; and a jolly, easy-mannered, world it was. The rural life of the governing class was on a generous scale. Landed proprietors, relatively to the rest of the community, were far richer than at present; and Whig statesmen were not the least affluent among them. We are told that the list of peers who, in the winter of 1778, protested against the prolongation of the American War, was "one of the most respectable that had appeared for

[1] Mr. Speaker Brand used to maintain that the institution of the three minutes' law before divisions, between the first and second bells, had worked a greater change in the style of House of Commons speaking than any other circumstance whatsoever. Up to that moment, when a matter had been enough discussed, the debate was summarily stopped by the throng of members who were waiting for the question to be put; and a debate it was, and not a succession of speeches, some of which are meant to waste time, while others savour of the study.

The author, during thirty years of Parliament, listened to many fine orations; but there is only one scene which stands out in his memory as a sample of what an encounter between Fox, and Burke, and Wedderburn very probably may have been during the heats of the Middlesex Election. That was the tornado of passion which swept the House of Commons on the seventh of May 1868, when, in consequence of an unexpected incident at a time of intense political excitement, Mr. Bright, Mr. Gladstone, and Mr. Disraeli met in sudden and furious combat. Mr. Disraeli, in particular, spoke as perhaps he had never spoken before, and as most certainly he never spoke afterwards, — with no sparkling epigrams, or fanciful turns, or picked phrases; but with unwonted emphasis and abundance of natural gesture, and amazing vehemence of emotion. The whole affair was over in forty minutes; but it left an indelible impression upon all who witnessed it.

some years; as, independent of their great characters in private and public life, there were ten of them whose fortunes made up above two hundred thousand pounds a year." [1] They lived on their paternal estates in homes which they took infinite trouble to enlarge and beautify. All through the middle of the eighteenth century companies of Italian workmen travelled from one end of England to the other, decorating the ceilings and cornices of the great country-houses with those plaster-mouldings which, in the history of domestic ornament, bridge the interval between the work of Grinling Gibbons and the work of the brothers Adam. But the taste for artistic improvement displayed itself most conspicuously in what was around, and not within, the mansion. The strength and prevalence of that taste may be measured by the celebrity of Lancelot Brown, who raised himself from very small beginnings to be the monarch, or rather the despot, of landscape gardening. It was he who, with a very questionable claim upon the gratitude of posterity, extirpated those antique and formal pleasure-grounds which Pope had satirised in his lines on Timon's villa; and it was he who surrounded the most famous country-houses in England with immense masses of forest-trees, with deer-parks and cattle-parks brought within sight of the windows, and with artificial lakes thrown in wherever, in his judgment, nature would have done well to place a sheet of water. His services were so much in request that he refused to exert his talents upon any landed estate of which, (to use his favourite catchword, the origin of his nickname,) he did not recognise " the capabilities"; and he had very decided views of his own upon politics. He disapproved of Lord North's American policy; he regarded the Earl of Chatham as the first of living statesmen; and, if Lancelot Brown's employers thought otherwise, they were careful, in his presence, to keep their opinion to themselves. " This," (so he wrote from Burleigh House,) " is a great place, where I have had twenty-five years' pleasure in restoring

[1] *Morning Post* of December 1778.

the monument of a great minister of a great queen. I wish we had looked at the history of her time before we had begun so unfortunate and disgraceful a war as we have been engaged in." [1]

Our rural magnates of the eighteenth century made their homes splendid, not as show-places for the admiration of the general public, but for their own personal enjoyment, and the gratification of their intimate friends and social equals. To all who came within that favoured class their hospitality knew no limit in profusion or duration. The select few had the run of all the country-seats which were best worth visiting; they arrived on the day that suited their own convenience; and they stayed as long as they were amused, or until a touch of gout took them. There exists a specimen letter from the Earl of March to George Selwyn, written, on the last day of the year, from a house the name of which is not given. " I have fixed," he said, "no time for my return. I want to make a visit to the Duke of Grafton, but I like everything here so much that I have no inclination to leave the place. There is an excellent library, a good parson, the best English and French cookery you ever tasted, strong coffee, and half-crown whist. The more I see of the mistress of the house, the more I like her; and our landlord improves on acquaintance. We are now all going to the ice, which is quite like a fair. There is a tent, with strong beer and cold meat, where Lady Spencer, and our other ladies, go an airing. Lord Villiers left us this morning." That was the sort

---

[1] *Harcourt Papers* for the year 1778. " Capability " Brown, when requested by George the Third to introduce some alterations into the French gardens at Hampton Court, " declined the hopeless task out of respect for himself and his profession." But he performed wonders at Kew ; and Londoners owe to him that Rhododendron Walk which is perhaps the most attractive of all their possessions. The servant made use of his opportunities to speak a word in season to the master, and plainly told His Majesty that he listened too readily to the Earl of Chatham's enemies. No man, (he said,) was a more loyal subject than his Lordship, or loved England better; and the King, in reply, paid Lord Chatham's patriotism the somewhat stingy compliment of acknowledging that he had too much good sense to wish harm to his country.

of company which men like Lord March came all the
way from St. James's Street to consort with; but they
looked with infinite disdain upon "the country squires,
(God help them!) with their triple-banded and triple-
buckled hats; and the clod-pated yeoman's son in his
Sunday clothes, his drab coat, and red waistcoat, tight
leather breeches, and light worsted stockings, — calling
for porter in preference to ale, because it has the air of
a London blade; and depriving of all grace a well-fancied
oath from the mint of the metropolis by his vile provincial pronunciation." [1] The fine ladies, and their admirers, who posted across half England to spend the inside
of a month at Euston or Chatsworth, came to meet each
other, and not to meet the local gentle-folk. Those who
have studied the comedies of Goldsmith and Foote, and
the novels of Fanny Burney, do not need to be told how
people inside the fashion then regarded people outside
of it, and with what careless insolence they permitted
their sentiments to colour their behaviour. There were
occasions, however, even in the most stately and well-
kept mansions, when a fastidious London guest came in
for more of rustic company, and rustic politics, than at
all pleased him. Once in the month, — or even once a
week, when an election was pending, — a wealthy nobleman would keep open house for neighbours of every
rank and every calling; because in that generation a
vote was a vote, and a peer with twenty thousand acres
would have fallen many points in his self-esteem if a
couple of politicians of the opposite interest to his own
had been returned for the county in which he resided.[2]

The best of the great English land-owners were
neither triflers nor dandies. Aristocrats of the right
sort, they were fiery, if not very laborious, politicians;
well-read gentlemen, for the most part; and sportsmen

[1] The Reverend Doctor Warner to George Selwyn.
[2] "The house," wrote one of Selwyn's correspondents from beneath
Lord Coventry's roof, "is full of tobacco ; the yard is full of tenants ; and
the peer, with an important face, is telling us how much he pays to the
Land-tax."

every inch of them.   Those of them who lived within a
day's journey from London made a point of entertaining
a houseful of political allies and adherents from the first
day, to the last, of that parliamentary recess which then
covered the whole of January.   An honest fox-hunter,
who had come all the way from Devonshire or Yorkshire to vote sturdily against Lord North throughout
the November session, was amply repaid for his trouble
by an invitation to pass the Christmas holidays at
Goodwood, accompanied by an assurance that room
might be found in the stables for his horses.   The Duke
of Richmond treated his guests with the heartiness of
a soldier, and the courtesy of a perfect host; but he
yielded no man precedence in the hunting field, — at all
events when Lord John Cavendish was not there to
outride him.   There were other famous houses where
the gamekeeper was a more important personage than
the huntsman.   Shooting was still a science, which
demanded thorough acquaintance with the habits of
wild animals, sympathetic knowledge of dogs, and
minute familiarity with the features of a countryside.
A lord of the manor, were he Earl or Marquis, had to
rise early in order to intercept the pheasants on their
feeding-grounds before they betook themselves to cover;
unless he was prepared to spend the rest of the day
among the brambles and the underwood, with a brace
or two of well-broke spaniels hunting close around him.[1]
The practice of lazy and wholesale massacre was still
in the far future; and it would have been well worth
a man's while to hear the language in which Coke of
Norfolk would have replied if he had been invited to
take part in killing three or four hundred hand-reared
ducks and drakes on a single morning.   When that
typical patrician, after serving fifty-five years in the
House of Commons, at last condescended to become the

[1] The passage on pheasant-shooting in Colonel Hawker's *Instructions
to Young Sportsmen* shows that the conditions of the sport did not alter
during the next half-century; for Colonel Hawker had been wounded at
Talavera long before he wrote his admirable and authoritative book.

Earl of Leicester, he still went out with his gun on every week-day during the season. At the age of seventy-eight, in the year of the great Reform Bill, he killed twenty-four head of game in twenty-five shots; and that amount of firing was reckoned sufficient for his day's amusement by a nobleman who ranked among the finest sportsmen in the country.[1]

These wealthy and high-born Englishmen had been subjected to a system of instruction not ill adapted to prepare them for a public career. A classical education, whatever may be said against it in theory, is a discipline by which very great men have been successfully trained for the conduct of great affairs. There have been eminent statesmen who brought nothing to their life's work except an intense and glowing mind, a clear insight into the circumstances of the contemporary world amidst which they moved, and a passionate admiration for the masterpieces of ancient literature. That, and little else, constituted the intellectual outfit of Lord Chatham, and of his famous son, when they first entered upon the scene of their labours. A youth of promise, with a turn for elocution, learned from old Greek and Roman examples how to express his ideas in an elevated, a lucid, and a manly style; and he might learn from the same source more important lessons still. Lord Camden, (as his biographer remarks,) owed an inestimable debt to Eton. Not only was his taste refined by the exquisite, if not very profound, scholarship which was a special feature of the place, "but from his Livy, and from a stealthy perusal of Claudian, he imbibed that abhorrence of arbitrary power which animated him through life."[2] It was the same at Harrow, under

---

[1] Ten years later on, the Earl of Leicester was too old to range the stubbles, and his sons maintained the credit of the establishment. "At Holkham," (so Lord Melbourne told Queen Victoria,) "they shoot from morning to night; and, if you do not shoot, you are like a fish upon dry land." Lord Melbourne was then not long past sixty; but the heroic age of the great Whig sportsmen was already on the wane.

[2] *Lord Campbell's Lives of the Chancellors;* chapter 142.

the influence of Samuel Parr, the most efficient, and, (it must be admitted,) the most pompous and self-opinionated of all assistant-masters.   One of his pupils, himself a man of some distinction, relates how the eloquent tutor inculcated and enforced " the love of freedom, and the hatred of tyranny, which breathed in the orators, poets, and historians of Greece and Rome." [1] The lively young Whigs, who swarmed on that classic hill, had soon an opportunity of testifying their attachment to those generous doctrines in a practical form. The Head-master died ; and the Governing body chose his successor from Eton.   Parr, who applied for the post, was passed over, — according to his own account, because he had voted for Wilkes at Brentford ; — and the Harrow boys, among whom both Parr and Wilkes were favourites, manifested their indignation by mobbing the Governors, and wrecking the carriage which had brought them down from London.   Parr resigned his mastership, and set up a rival educational establishment in the neighbouring village of Stanmore.   He attracted away with him from Harrow a large number of his former pupils, who are described, in stately diction, as " the flower of the school in the zenith of its glory."

There were few men of rank and opulence who did not entertain, — or, at the very least, affect, — a keen interest in the literature and art of their own generation. They were intelligent critics, and munificent patrons after a fashion which encouraged merit, without breeding servility.   They kept their book-shelves, all our island over, as well supplied as their cellars and their ice-houses ; and they never hesitated about paying down their two guineas, or three guineas, for a bulky quarto fresh from the printing-presses of Millar, or Strahan, or Dodsley.   They freely purchased the *Fermier Général* editions of the French classics ; and those Italian engravers who dedicated their ponderous and superb volumes, in terms of fulsome panegyric, to Roman

---

[1] *Memoirs of Thomas Maurice*, the Oriental scholar and historian.

Princes and Cardinals, found their most numerous, and certainly their most solvent, customers among British Peers and squires.[1] For a student, whose estimate of beauty and charm in books is not regulated by the conventional values of the auction-room, there is no inheritance more desirable than a library collected by ancestors who read and travelled during the middle portion of the eighteenth century. The culture that permeated society was faithfully reflected in its conversation, which was brilliant perhaps as never before or since, and singularly exempt both from pedantry and triviality. Gibbon, writing at ten o'clock on a Saturday night, relates how he had just seen off from his door Burke, Garrick, Sheridan, Charles Fox, Lord Camden, Lord Ossory, and Topham Beauclerk. That was a London supper-party of the year 1778. Beauclerk, of all who sat round the table, was in his own days the least known to fame; and yet Beauclerk left behind him a library of thirty thousand volumes, and possessed talents which Doctor Johnson confessed himself disposed to envy.

Our progenitors lacked the mechanical appliances, and many of the imported luxuries, which are now regarded as indispensable; but what they had was good, and they never pretended to be above enjoying it. Their habits were different from ours, and very different from those which prevailed among people of their own class on the Continent of Europe. A French gentleman, — who, after spending six weeks in our

---

[1] In 1764 Robert Adam, the King's architect, brought out his great book on Diocletian's palace at Spalatro in Dalmatia. The London subscription-list, for six hundred copies of that costly work, included almost every territorial potentate, and every man in a public position whose name is now remembered. Lord Shelburne applied for five sets; Sir Thomas Robinson, the ex-Secretary of State, for six; and Lord Bute, — a Scotchman opening his purse-strings to a brother Scotchman, — for no less than ten. The whole continent of Europe together took six-and-twenty copies. When, a few years later, Volpato gave to the world his reproductions of Raphael's Arabesques in the Loggia of the Vatican in a magnificent tome forty-two inches high, most of the copies, before very long, had made their way from Rome into British country-houses.

island, without understanding our language, published an exhaustive work on our character and manners, — regarded Londoners as the most incomprehensible ascetics. Till late in the day, (he said,) they took nothing but tea, and two or three slices of bread and butter, so thin as to do honour to the dexterity of the person who cut them. Such was the mode of life in an English household a hundred and forty years ago, and it continued to be the same in mercantile and professional families throughout the first quarter of the nineteenth century. Breakfast was of the lightest; and those who required luncheon were mostly content with bread and butter again. A certain country-house in the East of England still sends out to the shooting-field the historical noon-tide meal of bread and cheese, and a bag of onions, which satisfied the vigorous appetites of Coke of Norfolk, and Charles James Fox. But the period of abstinence ended when the day's work finished; and it finished early. There were hearty dinners at four o'clock in the country, and pleasant dinners lasting from five till eight in town, with a good supper to follow. Elderly people, in the year 1778, — as had been the case in almost every successive generation since the Norman conquest, — grumbled about the growing lateness of the dinner-hour. Horace Walpole complained bitterly that his afternoon callers would not go home to dress for the evening until four o'clock had struck ; and, when he was in a particularly bad humour over the American policy of the Government, he asserted dolefully that the glory of Britain had departed, that everything in public and private life was altered for the worse, and that he could not even get his dinner before nearly six at night.[1]

The culinary art, as then practised in England,

[1] Gibbon to Holroyd ; March 5, 1777. Walpole to Mann ; Arlington Street, December 18, 1778 ; and February 6, 1777.

According to Bishop Watson of Llandaff the dinner-time at Cambridge was three o'clock. When the bishop was a Trinity sizar in 1754 every college dined at twelve, and he never grew reconciled to the change of hour.

owed little to exotic teaching and example. Here and there might be found a nobleman who paid his French *chef* a salary of ninety guineas a year; but the made-dishes of native origin were very few in number; and, in this country of ancient and continuous tradition, it is still possible to ascertain how detestably they must have tasted.[1] The merit of a London or provincial dinner depended not so much upon the cunning of the cook as upon the intrinsic excellence of the viands; and there is little doubt that the immense and undisputed reputation of turtle and venison has been handed down from the days when epicures looked to substance rather than to style. Our ancestors had plenty of turbot and john-dories, when they lived near the coast, and, (if they chose to break the law,) they could buy game anywhere; but they counted among their luxuries some articles of food which are very seldom placed on a modern table.[2] George Selwyn's favourite parson, when located many miles away from Billings-gate market, was contented with perch " plain boiled, or in a water-zoochey," and a fine jack with a pudding inside of it. Another of Selwyn's correspondents announced the return to town of a gentleman who had repaired from St. James's Street to the purer air of Brighthelmstone in quest of an appetite. " Fanshawe,"

---

[1] In cookery-books of that date the usual side-dishes are collared eels and mutton-pies, repeated twice, — or, at a great banquet, even four times, — at opposite angles of the same table. Collared eels may still be eaten at Sunday breakfasts in Trinity College, Cambridge ; and mutton-pies, made after the receipt of 1764, were, within the author's memory, served as an entrée at Johnson's Club on an evening when a new member was initiated. Two of them would have made a dinner even for Doctor Johnson himself.

[2] One of Edmund Burke's visitors wrote down the bill of fare on a day when there was a houseful at Beaconsfield.

"First Course: a boiled turkey, roast beef, soup, calves-head, cow-heel.

Second Course: Woodcock, Hare, tarts, asparagus."

It could be wished that a guest at the Tusculan villa had left as precise an account of the dinner which Marcus Tullius Cicero gave his friends in the country.

he wrote, "set out this morning. He will arrive in London the very quintessence of wheat-ears; for he has eat nothing else for this week past, and it is feared that he has destroyed the species." Pike, and perch, and wheat-ears would now be archaic items on a bill of fare; but there is still a cheerful ring about the form of words which in the eighteenth century was proverbial of intimate rural hospitality, when one old friend invited another to come down to his manor-house or rectory to help him "eat a trout." Whether the food was good, or less good, the board was crowned with the very best of liquor. The young and the imprudent drank Burgundy, while more cautious diners were at great pains to procure the choicest vintages from Bordeaux. People who were at a distance from their wine-merchant would trust no one short of George Selwyn, if they had a claim upon his good offices. "Get me the best Chambertin you can," wrote the Earl of March; "and you may give any price for it." And Mr. Anthony Storer, — a not less important, and far more respectable, member of fashionable society than Lord March, — told Selwyn that, as long as he could pay his way, he would have his Vin de Grave, such as Madame de Sévigné used to drink, although it cost him four shillings a bottle.

That was the social atmosphere in which Charles Fox moved, with an energy of motion that kept everything alive around him. He carried to excess all the tastes which were in vogue among his contemporaries, and he had mastered all the attainments and accomplishments upon which they prided themselves. Fox was a scholar in that sense of the word which gives scholarship its true value. His Eton compositions, in Latin verse and prose, were something better than an ingenious, but lifeless, mosaic of antique phrases. Slight, graceful, and spontaneous, — and of an amatory cast whenever the subject admitted of it, — they might have been written in the days of Augustus by a young Roman of quality, who had spent his time over Propertius and Tibullus when he ought to have been reading his Stoic philosophers. As the years went on, Fox became more and more imbued with a passion for the classics, not of Greece and Rome only. No famous Englishman ever lived who had a more ardent and disinterested love of books. Fox acquired some command over every language which then could boast a literature. Spanish he knew well, and Portuguese imperfectly. He read Italian as easily as French; and he could talk French, and write it, as rapidly and as intelligibly, although not so elegantly, as English. At a later period of his life the poetry and history of the past occupied and absorbed his mind almost to the extinction of personal ambition ; and, even during the bustle of the American controversy, he contrived to get through an enormous amount of reading in that bed which he sought unwillingly towards daybreak, and left with all but insuperable reluctance at two in the afternoon. He already had a good selection of books, of which some were scarce and valuable ; and George Selwyn wondered why "he did not keep them at Brooks's, where they would have been unmolested." But such a precaution was altogether foreign to the nature of Charles Fox. He had gone security for one of those friends who had often gone security for him ; and the contents of his house were seized in execution by a creditor. The removal of his goods was the sight of the day in St. James's Street ; and their sale was an event of the London season. General amusement was excited by the shabby condition of his furniture ; and the pages of his books were examined with curiosity for the sake of the notes which were pencilled on the margin. Such, (said Horace Walpole,) was the avidity of the world "for the smallest production of so wonderful a genius." Charles Fox came off on this occasion better than he merited. Half Brooks's was there to watch over his interests ; and the Earl of March, (who otherwise in all probability would have been worse employed,) spent the whole of the day in the auction-room buying in the best of the books with the object of restoring them to their owner. Fox meanwhile, by a strange whim of fortune, for the first time in his life had a continuous run of luck at cards, and kept the money. He re-furnished his house within a fortnight; and, to the unutterable surprise of all who knew him, he had it cleaned and painted. He relieved the anxiety of Lord Carlisle by paying off the obligations which that devoted friend had incurred on his behalf; and he could thenceforward annotate his favourite volumes in full confidence that they never again would come to the hammer.

Charles Fox paid a heavy penalty for his early greatness. He is habitually cited as the instance of a statesman who was a confirmed gamester ; and yet he ceased to be a gamester at an age when very few indeed, besides himself, have taken rank as statesmen. While still a stripling he was diced and wagered, — and, as his elders believed, was glaringly and transparently cheated, — out of an immense fortune. For some years afterwards he continued to play high; but in the spring of 1782, at the period of life when an aspiring member of Parliament begins to hope for an appointment as a Junior Lord of the Treasury, Fox became the leading Minister of the Crown in power and influence, although not in title. Thenceforward he gambled less and less frequently, until, after no very long while, he dropped the practice altogether. Prudence and self-respect made him mend his ways; and he had counter-attractions, congenial to his better nature, which gradually inspired him with a distaste for the most sordid and irrational of all pastimes. The drawing-room at White's or Almack's, after the hazard-table had been lighted up, was no paradise for men of sense and intellect. "Alas! alas!" said Lord Carlisle. "We do nothing but drink gin-negus, and two or three other febrifuges, all the time. And, then, looking at the candle for nine hours together is so good for the eyes!" Fox no longer cared to fritter away his evenings on such dreary and debasing pursuits

when Dante and Boccaccio were awaiting him at home, or
when Johnson and Burke were talking across the empty
chair reserved for him at the dinner-table of the Literary
Club.   His familiar associates, moreover, were great
peers and commoners who had long ago grown ashamed
of trying to win money, which they did not want, from
people less wealthy than themselves.   Richmond, and
Savile, and Rockingham played whist for small sums of
silver, when they played at all; and Coke of Norfolk
had sworn off from gambling before he came to full
manhood, and kept his oath ever afterwards.   Other
converts, who had weaker wills than Thomas Coke,
fortified their good intentions by a device singularly
characteristic of the world in which they lived.   When
a member of Brooks's judged that the time had come
for him to set up as a serious-minded politician, he not
unfrequently called in the aid of a bet to assist him in
keeping his virtuous resolutions.   " Lord Northington,"
(so it stands recorded,) " has given Lord George Cavendish ten guineas, to receive twelve hundred if Lord
George Cavendish loses on one night one thousand
guineas, from Dinner to Dinner, at Hazard before the
tenth of May next." [1]

Fox took part in all bodily exercises, which then were
popular, with an enthusiasm very flattering to those
who made proficiency in such exercises the principal
study of their lives.   He played well at cricket, and
very well at tennis ; and he was devoted to the gun, although he possessed no manor of his own to sport over.
His share of the paternal acres had long ere this gone

---

[1] George Selwyn was under a running engagement to pay Lord Carlisle
twenty guineas, for every ten guineas, above fifty, which he himself lost,
on any one day, at any game of chance.   The forfeits were all to go for the
benefit of the little Howards.   " I reserved fifty," said Selwyn, " for an
unexpected necessity of playing, in the country or elsewhere, with women ; "
for the ladies were too often insistent gamblers, inexorable creditors, and
evasive losers.   This peculiar form of moral insurance was applied to other
temptations than those of the gaming-board.   One man of high position
received five guineas from a friend, in return for a promise to pay a
thousand if ever he went to a certain house, in a certain street, known to
both parties.

the same road as all else which he inherited.[1] But the
owners of shooting were always ready to place it at the
disposal of Fox. When inclination prompted, and the
weather served, he did not wait to be invited ; and, asked
or unasked, he was welcomed everywhere. How he
got about the country, with so notoriously deficient a
store of ready money, was a source of wonder to George
Selwyn, who was forever minding the business of other
people, and more especially the business of Charles
Fox. But Fox had a way with innkeepers, as with all
his fellow-creatures, and he never failed to command
post-horses from the commencement, to the close, of
the shooting season. He travelled into Derbyshire, to
kill grouse at Chatsworth, — a brace or two in the day,
where they are now killed by scores, — and where he
carefully recorded the exact weight of the finest bird
which his bag contained. He made rapid excursions
from London into one or another of the home-counties
whenever a hard frost gave hope of woodcock ; and he
spent his Septembers among the partridges in Norfolk,
which, — in the days of Walpoles, and Townshends, and
Cokes, and Keppels, — was more thickly studded with
Whig houses than any other district in England. Fox
shot better as he grew older and cooler ; but, before he
had turned five-and-thirty, he was often too excited to
do himself justice when game was afoot. He took an
unselfish pride in the marvellous performances of his
brother-sportsman, Thomas Coke ; and Coke repaid him
by the trouble that he expended in providing horses
sufficiently powerful to carry his illustrious friend about
the country. Fox had overcome his boyish dislike of
the saddle ; although riding was to him almost as great
an exertion as walking, or even running, to a man of
ordinary bulk. He might be seen on the course at
Newmarket, waiting opposite the spot where his jockey
had been ordered to make the final effort ; and from

[1] On an occasion when Charles Fox encountered in debate his fiery
young kinsman from Somersetshire a nobleman, who knew them both,
observed that it was a drawn battle between Acland and Lackland.

that point onward he galloped in with the horses,
" whipping, spurring, and blowing, as if he would have
infused his whole soul into his favourite racer." He
worked at the abstruse problems of weights, and dis-
tances, and public running, and private trials, as hard
as he worked at everything except the conscious preparation of his speeches; and he was very generally regarded as the most expert and trustworthy handicapper
in the South of the island. Fox enjoyed existence
thoroughly; and he was willing that all other people
should enjoy it likewise, according to their opportunities,
and their own notions of what constituted pleasure. He refused to discountenance bull-baiting. The outcry against
the inhumanity of the common people was, (he said,) unjust,
as long as their betters fished and hunted; and he was "de-
cidedly in favour of boxing." In the course of his life
he must have seen more than enough of it as he looked
down upon the crowd from the Westminster hustings.[1]

---

[1] The Fox papers include several confidential letters on racing topics.
The following document is a workmanlike production; and, (so far as a
non-racing man can judge,) it contains nothing incompatible with the
spirit of a genuine sportsman. It is docketed as of the year 1779. Fox
very seldom dated his earlier letters to Fitzpatrick, and generally omitted
to append his signature.

" Newmarket, Wednesday night.
" Dear Dick,
    The horses came in in the following order. The race was on the Flat.

	stone		lb.
Rosemary	8	—	2
Diadem	8	—	2
Rodney	8	—	12
Trotter	7	—	2
Fumus (?)	8	—	2

It was a very near race among the four first; and your horse was beat a
great way, and very easily. I am rather inclined to think the race a very
true one; and, if it is, your horse must be what I always believed him, —
a very bad one. If you should happen to meet the Duke of Queensberry
in a matching humour, and you should find him willing to run Drowsy
against Rosemary, provided it is not less than a mile, I think you cannot
make a bad match; though, if it could be across the Flat, I should like it
better. I do not think there is much chance of making a match; but, if
you can, pray do. Diadem and Rosemary are both disengaged the latter
end of the First Meeting; and, as to Rodney, I know he is afraid of him.
                                       Yours affly.
Both Rodney and Trotter seemed to run faster than the mare, though

When Fox was in London he established his head-
quarters at Brooks's, which was within a few doors of
his house. There he was much more comfortable than
under his own roof ; and there he was in the bosom of
his family. For the club was his castle, garrisoned by
a staunch body-guard of friends, in the midst of whom
he was safe from duns, and bores, and Ministerial supporters, — except those of them who, like Gibbon and
George Selwyn, were so fond of his company that they
could tolerate, without a protest, the unreserved out-
pouring of his political opinions. No party test as yet
barred the portals of Brooks's against a professed Tory ;
but admission to the club was guarded by a rigorous
standard of social exclusiveness ; and it so happened
that those candidates, who were most acceptable for social reasons, very generally belonged to the Opposition.
The mark of a fashionable Whig, (in the words of
Horace Walpole,) was to live at Brooks's, "where politics were sown, and in the House of Commons, where
the crop came up ; " and at Brooks's Fox might usually
be found, — when he was not at St. Stephen's, or between
the blankets, — marching to and fro, like other famous
talkers in the flower of their youth, and expounding to a
sympathetic audience his estimate of Lord North and
Lord George Germaine, and his anticipations about the
next stand-and-fall division in the House of Commons.
The club owns an admirable water-colour by Rowland-
son, showing the great drawing-room, adorned by a ceiling
and chimney-piece in the Adam's style, with pairs of
veterans intent on their games of ècartè in each corner,
and the vast circular table surrounded by a multitude of
players, with a tank full of gold in the centre. In the
foreground of the picture Charles Fox, — two or three
years older, and somewhat fatter, and even less aesthet-
ically dressed, than during the American War, — is holding forth to the unconcealed delight of his hearers.

she won at last. Foley thinks Trotter as likely a horse to match to advantage as either of the others. You must set him down in your mind to be a
stone worse than Rosemary for a mile, and 18 lbs. worse across the Flat."

The drawing-room is still the same as ever; and the round table remains, innocent of dice and cards. The club-house has been doubled in area, and brought up to a modern level of sanitation; but those who remember the Brooks's of five-and-forty years ago can form for themselves a very lifelike notion of the eighteenth century. Solid and unpretentious luxury, of an antique type, ruled within its walls. A dinner, the absolute perfection of English cookery, was served by a numerous band of attendants, respectful and confidential after the manner of the good old school, in that full evening costume, with knee-breeches and black silk stockings, which is now worn only in kings' palaces. There was no recourse to scientific methods of illumination, but each little table was lighted with two portly wax candles. Before the disruption of the party in the summer of 1886 there were nights when a member, who came up from the House of Commons or the House of Lords, bringing the latest news with him, might see none but friends, or intimate acquaintances, around him. The talk went across the room, from table to table, as freely as in the days of Fox; and the place was full of his associations. Three or four times every year a party of sound politicians, a club within a club, honouring him in a fashion which would have met his hearty approbation, dined together very sumptuously, and drank "The memory of Mr. Fox, in solemn silence." It was currently, but perhaps not very authoritatively, believed in Brooks's that the annual subscription had been increased from ten to eleven guineas in order to pay off some of his debts; and any proposal to build bath-rooms and dressing-rooms died away in presence of the tacit, but instinctive, sentiment that those facilities for washing which had satisfied the unexacting requirements of Mr. Fox were good enough for the best of his successors.

Frederic the Great once expressed his surprise when he was informed by a tourist, who was on a visit to Potsdam, that Englishmen might sit in Parliament at one-and-twenty. The King remarked that Peers and

Commoners in Great Britain evidently acquired the talent for legislation much sooner than a Patrician of ancient Rome, who might not enter the Senate before forty;[1] and, no doubt, if these young gentlemen had been his own subjects, he would have set them to employments which, in his view, were much better suited to their years. The House of Commons in the eighteenth century swarmed with eldest sons; with cousins and nephews of great noblemen who were patrons of family boroughs; and with wealthy squires, who scorned a peerage, but made it a point of honour to stand for their own county at the first general election after they came of age. Charles Fox, at nine-and-twenty, was already a Parliamentarian of ten years' service; and he exercised unbounded authority over the gilded youth who supplied so large a contingent to the ranks of the Opposition. His immediate contemporaries had always believed in his future at a time when the rest of the world, with much excuse, thought him a trifler and a ne'er-do-well. As early as 1774 George Selwyn complained that there were people at Almack's who cherished a fanatical belief in the necessity of Charles Fox being the first man in the country, both for his own sake, and for the well-being of the nation. And now, in 1778, if Fox was not the first man in England, at all events there was no one, from King George downwards, who did not either fear him, or follow him.

The host of young Whig members at last found a leader, and, (which they had not counted upon,) a drill-master. They had enjoyed easy times in the past. Rockingham, and Savile, and Lord John Cavendish, excellent and immaculate as they were, loved their own leisure too well to feel themselves justified in reproving the laziness of others; and Edmund Burke who, with solitary and undaunted perseverance, had spared no exertions to indoctrinate the Whig party with a sense of

[1] The age at which a Roman citizen could enter the Senate was more probably about thirty. But King Frederic was sadly to seek in his knowledge of the classics.

their public obligations, had little influence on the daily
conduct of his younger parliamentary colleagues. He
was above them, but not of them. They looked upon
him as a superior kind of schoolmaster, whose notions
of duty were too severe, and whose lectures were a great
deal too long ; and they kept out of his way as sedu-
lously and respectfully as, not many years before, they
had kept out of the way of their Eton tutor. But there
was no escaping the eye of Charles Fox. The most
ubiquitous of mortals, he was with them in their goings
out and comings in, — in the card-room of the club, in
the gun-room of the country-house, at Ranelagh and
Vauxhall, at Epsom, at Ascot, at Newmarket, and even
so far north as Doncaster. He talked politics as irre-
pressibly, as persuasively, and in as curious and inappropriate places, as Socrates talked ethics. His comments
on the Cabinet Ministers were infinitely diverting, his
forecast of the course of State affairs was cheerful and
sanguine, and he was always ready to back his prophecies by a wager. But, despite his joviality, and his
sympathy with every form of human enjoyment, he had
within him the essential qualities of a disciplinarian.
His adherents and supporters might amuse themselves
wherever they pleased between-whiles, as long as they
answered his call whenever the summons to action came;
and they, on their part, yielded him the implicit and unquestioning obedience which youth pays to youth, in a
case where a right to command has been recognised
and conceded. He could not be eluded, or hoodwinked;
for he had been one of themselves. He was acquainted
with all their haunts and hiding-places; he fathomed
the hollowness of their excuses when a critical division
was impending ; and he let them know his mind, in
language which went home to theirs, if on any such
occasion he missed their faces in the Lobby. His familiar correspondence, — and the familiarity of Charles
Fox embraced a wide circle of people, — was largely
made up of rebukes to the delinquent, and reminders
to the forgetful. A fair example may be found in a

letter written during the closing months of the American controversy. "I never," (so Fox told a friend in February 1782,) "was more sorry to hear you were out of town. Monday is likely to be of as much consequence, towards deciding the fate of these people, as any day this year. If you can possibly come, pray do ; for it is really childish, when attendance is of such real importance, to give it up for mere idleness."

Charles Fox might admonish others with a clear conscience because he himself took public life very seriously. He had been educated in the tenets of a loose and vicious creed, the creed of old Holland House, by a father who was at once the most fascinating and corrupting of preceptors. But his superb mental constitution at length threw off that deadly poison ; and he thought out for himself a just, a lofty, and, (for his generation,) a most original conception of the statesman's duty. Fox was drenched with calumny when alive; and it has been the fashion ever since, among writers of a certain school, to ignore the priceless services which he rendered to liberty and humanity, and to judge him solely by their own interpretation of his attitude with regard to the foreign policy of Great Britain. But his detractors, then or now, have never been able to call in question his highest title to honour. No man has denied, and no man ever can deny, that, during all the best years of his life, Charles Fox sacrificed opportunities of power and advancement, emoluments which he sorely needed, and popularity which he keenly relished, for the sake of causes and principles incomparably dearer to him than his own interest and advantage.

The change in his moral nature was silent and unostentatious; but, by the year 1778, some acute and friendly observers began to be aware what sort of man he had now become. Burgoyne's disaster, and the certainty of a breach with France, spread a panic through official circles. Lord North used the utmost diligence to attract to himself political support from outside his Government; and he was prepared to bid very high indeed for a young man who was already the favourite of the House of Commons. "Charles," (so George Selwyn was informed,) "eats, and drinks, and, though he never loses sight of the Treasury, confesses it is rather a distant prospect at present. A great part of the Opposition have had offers of coming in, but not on terms that they like; and I do think it does Charles great credit that, under all his distresses, he never thinks of accepting a place on terms that are in the least degree disreputable. I assure you, upon my honour, that he has had very flattering offers made him more than once of late, and he has never for a moment hesitated about rejecting them."[1] Fox explained the motives which guided him at this conjuncture in a letter to Captain Richard Fitzpatrick, who then was serving with the British army in Philadelphia; and his explanation is deserving of all credence, because those two young men had always been in the habit of writing to each other the plain unvarnished truth, even when that truth did not look well on paper. Fox now told Fitzpatrick that, according to general expectation, the Ministry would be driven to resign, but that he himself was firmly persuaded to the contrary. "People flatter me," (so he proceeded, with much underscoring of his manuscript,) "that I continue to gain, rather than lose, my credit as an orator; *and I am so convinced that this is all that I shall ever gain, (unless I become the meanest of men,) that I never think of any other object of ambition.* Great situation I *never* can acquire, — nor, if acquired, keep, — *without making sacrifices that I will never make.*"[2] Those were the convictions which inspired alike his House of Commons speaking, and his private talk; and not a few members of Parliament, who had hitherto regarded politics as a trade or a pastime, were brought to a consciousness of their public responsibilities by the force of his exhortations, and the influence of his example.

[1] James Hare to George Selwyn; June 1778.
[2] Fox to Fitzpatrick; February 1778.

Fox was popular with women, and stood high in the good graces of the best among them for reasons very honourable to himself, and to his admirers.   He was no lady-killer, and only too little of a fop.   The young Oxonian of nineteen, who had made himself talked about by travelling post from Paris to Lyons in order to select patterns for his fancy waistcoats, had already sobered down into the most plainly and carelessly dressed man, of his own age and eminence, in London.   He was not in, but above, the fashion; and the world, — over-stocked, as it always has been, with dandies and cox-combs, — liked Charles Fox all the better for his inatten-tion to outward appearance.   He possessed, in a remark-able degree, the rarest of social gifts, the power of being himself in every company.   Familiar, kindly, and expansive with high and low, — with the brilliant and the dull, the virtuous and the faulty, alike, — he united all suffrages; and his most loyal well-wishers were certain great ladies who had been satiated with flattery, and who knew no pleasure like that of being treated as intellectual equals, and trusty comrades, by one whose esteem and confidence were so well worth having.   They were no fair-weather friends.   In the very darkest period of his fortunes, — when English politics were dominated by an overwhelming reaction against the ideas of progress and the national traditions of liberty, — whoever else deserted Fox, those brave women remained loyal to him, and to the principles which he had taught them.   It was then that the Duchess of Devonshire expressed herself with a noble frankness to no less formidable a correspondent than Philip Francis, who had referred to the regard felt by the Duchess for Charles Fox in some sentences which, if style is any guide, most assuredly came from the pen of Junius. "The generous passions," (so he told her,) "are always eloquent, especially on a favourite subject.   You love him with all his faults, because they are *his*.   I wish I was one of them.   I should keep good company, and share in your regard."   Her reply ran as follows.   "As I am very sure you do not think that I, as a woman, ever was, could be, or am, in love with Charles Fox, you will allow that in fervour, enthusiasm, and devotion I am a good friend. . . . Would I were a man to unite my talents, my hopes, my fortune, with Charles's; to make common cause, and fall or rule with him!" That tribute to an unbroken intimacy of very long duration was paid in the year 1798, when the writer thought fit to call herself an old woman; but in the autumn and winter of 1777 the Duchess of Devonshire, and the Countess of Ossory, and Mrs. Crewe of Crewe Hall were all young together, and all sincerely attached to Fox. It was an example which others of their sex found it easy and agreeable to follow; for women could not meet Charles Fox without liking him. They became his sworn partisans. They canvassed for him at elections. They smuggled themselves under the gallery of the House of Commons on an afternoon when he was expected to speak his best. They studied political questions, although some of them had to begin with the rudiments;[1] and they took care that their husbands and brothers, if they called themselves Whigs, should give orthodox Whig votes. Throughout the whole of the struggle which convulsed Parliament, and London society, during the coming fifty months it was no slight benefit to Charles Fox that he had the women on his side.

[1] " Lady Melbourne," said Horace Walpole, "was standing before the fire, and adjusting her feathers. Says she: 'Lord! They say the Stocks will blow up. That will be very comical.'"

CHAPTER III

THE action of Parliament with regard to America entailed consequences of unspeakable gravity upon the British empire; but the British nation had been deliberately cut off from all effective cognizance of what was being said and done in its own House of Commons. No special accommodation had as yet been allotted to people connected with the newspaper press. Reporters and journalists sat in the Gallery among the crowd of strangers, and they could not be excluded from the House unless all the other visitors were excluded with them. That circumstance dictated the tactics which Lord North's Cabinet adopted. Charles Wolfran Cornwall, — and it is necessary to give his names at length in order to prevent his being mistaken for another Cornwall who was a much more respectable man, — was brother-in-law to a Lord of the Treasury. He drew a State pension of fifteen hundred pounds a year, and he sat at Westminster as one of the two representatives of a borough which contained only two genuine and available voters. On the fourteenth of March 1774, when Lord North was on the point of rising to introduce the Boston Port Bill, this gentleman interposed with a motion to expel Strangers from the Gallery. Ever since the House met on that afternoon the ministers had been whispering and bustling about among the private members who sat behind them, and Cornwall was the nearest approach to an independent politican whom they found willing to do them so odious a service. The unforeseen incident excited great surprise, and very general disapprobation. But Cornwall insisted on his right; the Speaker had no choice except to clear the Gallery; and, as soon as the lodge was securely tiled,

Lord North proceeded to explain the memorable Bill every clause of which lost England a colony. Cornwall was richly rewarded. He was taken on to the Treasury Bench; he received an office, and another office on the top of that; and, after the next Dissolution, he was put forward by the Government as Speaker, to the displacement of Sir Fletcher Norton, who, in his own rough fashion, had vindicated the interests of the nation against the encroachments of the Crown. But Cornwall lost in credit more than he gained in pelf. The man who had conspired with ministers to steal from British citizens the power of watching the conduct of their representatives in Parliament was popularly compared to a chimney-sweeper who had been lowered down the chimney to facilitate the operations of a party of burglars.[1]

From that day forward, whenever public business of great moment was under discussion, the proceedings in the Commons were, as a matter of course, withdrawn from public observation. On the second of February, 1775, the House resolved itself into a Committee to consider the papers presented by His Majesty's command, relative to the Disturbances in North America. A collection of documents more vitally serious, and more intensely readable, had never before been laid upon the table. The interest aroused was keen and universal, and people flocked to the entrance of the Gallery in great numbers; but none were admitted except such as were members of the Irish Parliament. The debate was worthy of the occasion. Lord North moved an Address, beseeching the King to take effectual measures for enforcing obedience upon the colonies; and Fox encountered the proposal by an amendment. There was no one present to take down his argument; and nothing remains of it except the bald record that "Mr. Charles Fox spoke better than usual, pointing out the injustice, inexpediency, and folly of the motion," and foretelling

---

[1] Walpole's *Last Journals.*

"defeat on one side of the water, and ruin and punishment on the other." [1] That is all that the world was permitted to know of a prognostication which came as near fulfilment as almost any prophecy that ever was uttered. Not many weeks afterwards Burke brought forward his Resolutions for Conciliation with America, and the Standing Order for the Exclusion of Strangers was again rigorously enforced. His speech has taken undisputed rank among the classics of the world. Posterity can read that noble composition, written out for publication by the hand of the speaker as Cicero wrote out the Second Philippic, and Demosthenes the Oration on the Crown; but the contemporaries of Edmund Burke, — unless they were rich enough to contest a county, or purchase the privilege of sitting for a rotten borough, — could not hear the accents of his voice, or so much as learn how and why his scheme of pacification had been rejected by Parliament. The light esteem in which Cabinet Ministers held the great body of their fellow-countrymen was expressed in the course of the Session by Rigby, "who spoke," (said the official reporter,) " with that rough and unpolished manner for which he is remarkable in his senatorial oratory. He begged to know by what claim those who were not members desired admittance. If one stranger had a right, every man in the kingdom had a right; and where were the people to be put?" [2]

The suppression of free reporting inflicted a twofold injury upon all persons who looked to the newspaper for information about what was passing in the House of Commons. They did not get what they wanted; but they got a good deal too much of that which they would gladly have been without. They had no opportunity of reading what was said by statesmen of influence and renown, and on the other hand they were at the mercy of any prosy senator who took the trouble to write out

[1] *Hansard's Parliamentary History;* volume XVIII, page 227.
[2] *Hansard's Parliamentary History;* volume XVIII, page 1327.

his own speeches, and communicate them to the press.
At the head of that class stood Thomas Pownall, who
had been Governor of Massachusetts, and afterwards of
South Carolina. He very probably knew more about
America than any other man in that Parliament; but he
was singularly incapable of imparting his knowledge by
word of mouth in a manner acceptable, or even endurable,
to his hearers, and he had no clear and settled ideas of
policy. Whenever Pownall, in default of any preferable
claimant, caught the reluctant eye of Sir Fletcher Norton,
no one could foresee on which side of the question he
would speak, but everyone was certain that he would
continue speaking until the impatience of his audience
compelled him to resume his seat. There is something
absurd in the contrast between the enormous space
which his speeches occupy in Hansard's Parliamentary
History, and the pithy official comments by which they
are accompanied. "Governor Pownall rose next; but
the House grew clamorous for the question." "Governor Pownall had been up several times before, but the
Chairman pointed to others." Such are some of the inter-
polations by which the long-suffering editor avenged himself on an orator whose written discourses he was reduced
to insert at full length in the dearth of more attractive
matter. Things came to such a pass that on the
occasion of a spirited debate maintained by a succession
of good speakers, which consumed a whole sitting,
Governor Pownall monopolised fifteen out of the
twenty-four pages of the report. And again, when
Mr. Burke introduced his plan for Composing the
Troubles in America, embodied in a Bill with preamble
and clauses, it is expressly stated that no Englishman,
whether reporter or otherwise, was admitted to the
Gallery, and that "the only Strangers present were four
women of quality, and a few foreigners." A notable
discussion ensued, culminating in a rhetorical duel
between the two best debaters in the House, — a performance with regard to which the general verdict was
that "Wedderburn shone, and Charles Fox outshone

himself." [1]   But the record of that brilliant and chivalrous passage at arms, with the fame of which all London
rang, is compressed into twenty ecstatic and most tan-
talising lines of print, while six long and solid columns
are devoted to Governor Pownall.   It was the very
burlesque of parliamentary reporting. [2]

As the American War progressed, and the situation
of public affairs changed continually from bad to worse,
the authority of the Government was on the wane
throughout the country, and declined steadily, though
less rapidly, within the walls of the House of Commons.
One signal result of the alteration in national opinion
was that the reports of parliamentary debates, in the
morning and evening papers, became more copious and
faithful than ever before.   A Standing Order forbade
the presence of Strangers ; but Sir Fletcher Norton, as
he more than once informed the House, did all in his
power to mitigate the rule, and, if ever he raised his eye
to the Gallery, he exercised his inherent and immemorial
right of seeing what he chose, and what he chose only.
The responsibility of putting the Standing Order in force
rested with private members; and it was abundantly
evident that any private member, who took upon himself to espy Strangers in the Gallery, would henceforward
have to reckon with the most formidable controversialist
in the House of Commons.   Charles Fox seized every
possible opportunity for denouncing the secrecy of debate, and enlisted in support of his view every conceiv-
able argument.   He expatiated on the advantage of
encouraging the attendance of young men of parts and
education, in order that they might become early habitu-

---

[1] Walpole's *Last Journals ;* November 16, 1775.

[2] " Mr. Fox," (it is recorded,) "was very severe upon Administration.   With infinite wit and readiness he gave a description of the Treasury
Bench, beginning with Mr. Ellis, and ending with Mr. Cornwall, by a
single epithet happily marking the characters of each.   The Solicitor-
General, in answer to Mr. Fox, defended Administration in a fine vein of
oratory. . . .   His speech was a restoration to the House; and, though
it was three o'clock in the morning, he awakened the attention of every
man."

ated to the conduct of political discussion, and to the management of State affairs; he claimed that every constituent had a right to hear in what manner his representatives discharged their duty; and he went so far as to assert that it was a breach of the constitution to hinder the public from obtaining accurate information about the proceedings of Parliament.[1] The dread of immediate and condign chastisement at the hands of Fox, and the prospect next morning of being held up to reprobation as a busybody and a tyrant by the London press, were quite enough to deter any man of ordinary courage from venturing to move that the Gallery should be closed.

There was one private member, however, whose stock of courage, moral or immoral, had hitherto proved equal to the most desperate enterprises. When Wilkes was excluded from Parliament in the spring of 1769, Colonel Henry Luttrell volunteered to contest Middlesex, to take a beating at the poll, and then to usurp the place of the rightful member in the House of Commons; and the man who had faced Wilkes at Brentford was capable of facing anything. On an occasion when Charles Fox moved for the production of papers relating to the military operations in America he was assailed by Luttrell with an acrimony which descended to the level of positive scurrility. The House was not in a humour for such an exhibition; and Luttrell was frequently called, and at last reduced, to order. Fox replied quietly and good-humouredly; Lord North followed in the same strain, and himself seconded the motion for papers which Fox had made; and so the storm blew over, and the matter to all appearance ended. But, two days

---

[1] *Hansard's Parliamentary Debates;* April 20, 1777. Rigby, who always took up the cudgels in defence of the Standing Order for the exclusion of Strangers, on this occasion made a fair hit at Charles Fox. "The Honourable Gentleman who spoke last," said Rigby, "is himself the strongest proof that a Gallery lesson in politics is not necessary to form a perfect statesman and orator; for, (if I recollect rightly,) that gentleman was elected into parliament under the age of twenty-one, before he returned home from his travels; and certain it is that he could not have been much schooled under that Gallery."

afterwards, Colonel Luttrell came forward with a complaint that a certain daily journal had taunted him with having incurred the censure of the House for unparliamentary conduct. That, (so the Colonel maintained,) was a gross misrepresentation on the part of the editor; and he accordingly announced his intention of moving that the Standing Order for excluding Strangers from the Gallery should be strictly carried into execution. Fox, as his habit was, passed very lightly over all that related to himself; but he expressed it as his mature conviction that the true and only method of preventing misrepresentation was by throwing open the Gallery, and making the debates and decisions of the House as public as possible. A brief and animated conversation followed. Burke spoke, and Conway; and Alderman Turner of York, a sturdy friend of the people, repudiated the very notion of an honest man saying in the House of Commons anything which he was ashamed, or afraid, that his countrymen should read. Rigby, whom nothing could abash, attempted to combat the almost unanimous sentiment of the assembly; but Colonel Luttrell, scared into penitence, allowed his motion to drop. The battle was won; and, from that day forth, the House of Commons ceased to deliberate with closed doors. It was the earliest among the splendid services which Charles Fox rendered to the cause of liberty. The reporters, who as yet were a feeble folk, had found a champion in one who not long since had been their most relentless persecutor. The young man, (according to the French saying,) had made his journey to Damascus, and had experienced a conversion as sudden in its operation as it was salutary and abiding in its effect.[1]

When Parliament met in the late autumn of 1777 the members returned to Westminster in a depressed and

---

[1] The insolence with which Fox, in his hot youth, assailed the freedom of the Press, and the richly merited punishment which he underwent at the hands of an indignant populace, are related in *The Early History of Charles James Fox*, in the last twelve pages of the Eighth Chapter.

chastened mood; for a belief prevailed that matters were going badly with Burgoyne's army. "It is not quite fashionable," said Horace Walpole, "to talk of America. The tone is just to ask, with an air of anxiety, if there is anything new, and then be silent." The Address in reply to the King's Speech was debated in a changed House of Commons. Opponents of the Government were no longer silenced by uproar, as in the days when the Ministerial *claque* was in a hurry to ruin Boston, and disfranchise Massachusetts. Henceforward, if a speaker was ill received, it was because he was a bore, and not because he was a Whig of the Opposition. Quiet and reasonable men, who had something of value to say, were heard with attention and respect; and Fox, who gave voice to the opinion of all on his own side of the House, and to the inward convictions of many who sat opposite, rose to a height of eloquence which he had seldom attained before. The main force of his attack was concentrated upon the American Secretary.

Ever since the day, (he declared,) that Lord George Germaine had manœuvred himself into Administration, the fortunes of the country had begun to decline. The King had placed that nobleman in the Cabinet as a recompense for the sinister ability with which he had dictated to the King's Ministers those deplorable measures that drove the colonists to declare their independence. Lord George had been entrusted with the conduct of the war which he himself had provoked, and that war he had fatally mismanaged. The instructions which he imposed upon General Burgoyne, — and then omitted, or forgot, to communicate to General Howe, — had brought a fine army into deadly jeopardy. It was not enough, (cried Fox,) that he should be ejected from office. It was not enough that he should be deprived of the power of sending better soldiers than himself to inevitable defeat, and probable captivity. He must be made to learn, by a sharper lesson, that a Minister is accountable to the nation for the orders which he gives, and for the measures which he advises.

Lord George replied in deprecatory, and almost humble, language, — defending himself with the ineffectiveness of a man who was only too well aware that the full strength of the case against him, in all its disastrous consequences, had not yet been made manifest to the world. Nor was his equanimity increased by a remark which he could not avoid overhearing, when Fox, in his easy fashion, paid a flying visit to the Treasury Bench, and was accosted by Lord North himself. "Charles," said the Prime Minister, "I am glad you did not fall on me to-day, for you was in full feather." Fox was well satisfied by the effect which he had produced on his opponents, as well as upon his followers. "I am clear," (so he wrote to Lord Ossory,) "that the opinion of the majority of the House is now with us. I cannot help flattering myself that *opinions* will, in the long run, have their influence on *votes*." But corruption, and servility, and perverted party-spirit, were still powerful enough to maintain the Ministerial numbers at their usual figure; and the Address was carried by two hundred and forty-three votes to eighty-six. Gibbon, who went with the majority, told Horace Walpole that, if it had not been for shame, there were hardly twenty men in the House who were not ready to vote for peace. "I did not," said Walpole, "think it very decent for so sensible a man to support the war, and make such a confession."

Fox had denounced Germaine on the very first evening of the Session, and a fortnight afterwards his justification came. When the House met on the third of December Colonel Barré summoned the American Secretary to declare, upon his honour, what had become of General Burgoyne and his brave troops. Germaine thereupon admitted that they had all been made prisoners, and begged the House to suspend its judgment on the conduct both of the General and the Minister. Barré vehemently protested against any insinuation that a portion of the blame might lie at the door of the General, inasmuch as the Minister, who had

contrived the plan of invasion, was alone responsible
for its failure. It was, (so Barré affirmed,) an inconsistent and impracticable scheme, condemned and all
picked to shreds beforehand by himself, and by every
soldier in either House of Parliament who understood
his profession ; — " a scheme unworthy of a British war
minister, and too absurd even for an Indian chief."
The House was terribly excited. It was one of those
sudden storms of passionate emotion when men of
high character and dignity are betrayed into actions
which they never afterwards love to remember. Burke
taunted the Solicitor-General with having accepted a
retainer as standing counsel for such a client as Lord
George Germaine ; and Wedderburn told Burke that he
did not know how to behave himself, and must be
taught to mend his manners. Burke walked out of the
House, making a sign for Wedderburn to follow ; and
their friends had some difficulty in averting a duel which
might have resulted in a catastrophe almost too serious
to contemplate. Fox, when his turn arrived, accused
the American Secretary of negligence which had been
nothing short of criminal, and hinted, in no covert
terms, that the culprit of the Minden Court-Martial
should once more be brought to the bar of Justice. The
suggestion displeased none except the occupants of the
Treasury Bench, as is shown in a familiar letter from
John Crawford of Auchinanes, the member for Renfrew-
shire, and a steady voter for the Government. " Charles
spoke with great violence," (so Crawford wrote,) " but
the House for this time went along with him. We were
not shocked at his talking of bringing Lord George to a
second trial. We were not shocked at being asked if we
could patiently continue to submit to see this nation
disgraced by him *in every capacity.*" The Ministers,
after the experience of that evening, did not care to face
another American debate until their own supporters
had recovered their composure and their docility. They
huddled up public business, adjourned Parliament
over Christmas for a recess of six weeks, and sent the

members away bewildered, rather than reassured, by a very positive official statement that the Courts of France and England had never before stood on a more friendly footing.[1]

Parliament separated in anxiety, and met again in gloom. France was armed to the teeth; and the disposition of her land and sea forces betokened an intention to commence hostilities by throwing an army across the British Channel. We had not enough troops at home to secure our arsenals and dockyards; and the open country to the south of London, in case of invasion, would be literally bare of defenders. Nor had the Cabinet as yet determined on any settled policy with regard to the prosecution of the war in America, — a problem which, at a time when two-thirds of our soldiers were on the other side of the Atlantic Ocean, had become a military question of the very first order. The Government was unwilling to recognise, and helpless to combat, the dangers which beset the nation; and Britain would have fared ill if stronger men, who did not share the responsibility of office, had refrained from taking the matter decisively and fearlessly into their own hands.

On the second of February the Duke of Richmond, — who, with his fiery industry, and his martial proclivities and antecedents, would have been an invaluable war minister at such a crisis, — addressed the House of Lords on the military situation. No effective precautions, (he affirmed,) had as yet been taken in order to meet as tremendous a peril as ever threatened the country. Some new regiments were in

[1] Mr. Crawford, who appears to have been an eye-witness of Burke's behaviour, states some particulars which are not incompatible with the account given by Walpole. "In the midst of Wedderburn's speaking," (Crawford wrote,) "Burke burst into one of his hysterical laughs. Unfortunately at that moment there was a dead silence in the House. Wedderburn, in a very angry tone, said that, if the gentleman did not know manners, he *as an individual* would teach th·m to him. This the other construed into a menace. . . . Burke was originally in the wrong, because nothing could be more uncivil than his laugh appeared to be, from the accident of the dead silence at that moment."

course of being raised by private effort; but the oldest
soldier in them was a recruit of a month's training,
and most of their officers were as yet little other than
civilians. Nothing had been done in the direction of
embodying the militia. It was idle to talk of recalling
troops from the garrisons of Gibraltar and Minorca,
which were far below their war complement; and
Ireland contained less than five thousand men with
muskets on their shoulders. The defence of Great
Britain rested exclusively on a few regiments of the
Line, ("the Old Corps," as the Duke called them,)
which were quartered within the confines of the island;
and the Returns of these regiments showed a force of
just ten thousand six hundred bayonets. Their strength
was barely sufficient to man the ramparts of the three
great fortresses, Plymouth, Portsmouth, and Chatham,
—the keys of England's power and security; and
those fortresses, within the course of a few weeks or
months, and London itself in a few days, would be in
the possession of an invader if we had not an army
powerful enough to hold the field. Those were the
circumstances under which the Ministry proposed to
keep in America fifty battalions of British infantry,
and to reinforce them from time to time by further
drafts from home. And yet even that force, immense
as it was in proportion to the military resources of the
country, had been pronounced by every competent
officer, from Lord Amherst downwards, to be totally
inadequate for the purpose of reducing the colonies
to obedience. When the Duke had thus stated his
case, he moved a Resolution to the effect that none of
the Old Corps, which still remained in Great Britain,
"could be spared for any distant service without
leaving the kingdom in a perilous condition, inviting
a foreign war, and exposing the nation to insult and
calamity."

It was a patriot's duty, manfully and calmly performed. "His Grace," (we are told,) "proceeded to
his task with candour, coolness, and precision, and

with a solemnity suited to the great interests which were to be taken into consideration."[1] He was met in a very different spirit by those members of the Cabinet who undertook to answer him. Lord Suffolk, quibbling like a third-rate attorney, disputed the existence of any evidence indicating, however remotely, that any rival Power entertained hostile intentions against the British nation. Lord Sandwich made a flippant and bragging speech, in the worst style of parliamentary raillery. He charged the Duke of Richmond with having exposed our military secrets to the gaze of the foreigner, — passing over the circumstance that all the Duke's facts and figures were extracted from Returns which the Ministers themselves had placed upon the table of Parliament for everybody to read. But it mattered little, (so Sandwich ventured to assert,) what force of troops we had on dry land as long as our fleet was irresistible at sea ; although how very far short of irresistible that fleet had become, under his own loose and corrupt administration, he knew better than anyone, and cared less. Lord Sandwich was followed by the Duke of Grafton, who disclaimed all idea of introducing jest and merriment into a discussion of such singular importance, and who expressed it as his earnest opinion that naval preparations, however formidable, were not a sufficient guarantee against invasion without a large army of defence, stationed upon English soil. The question, (he said,) did not admit delay. A war with France was swiftly approaching, and would be upon them within three months at the farthest, unless a stable peace with America was immediately concluded. When Grafton sat down the Peers divided, thirty-one for, and three times that number against, the Duke of Richmond's motion. It was a poor show; for the majority was largely made up by the votes of absent noblemen whose proxies lay ready for use in the Minister's pocket, as an acknowledgment for the pensions, and sinecure salaries,

---

[1] *Hansard's Parliamentary History ;* volume XIX, page 654.

with which their own pockets had been plentifully
lined.

On the same afternoon Charles Fox brought forward
the self-same motion in the House of Commons. The
interest excited by the anticipation of his speech had
permeated London society. A great crowd of people
assembled in the Lobby, and forced their way into the
Gallery in spite of the door-keepers. Among them was
a troop of nearly sixty ladies, headed by the Duchess
of Devonshire, and by Lady Norton, the wife of the
Speaker. Notice was taken of the presence of Strangers,
and the Gallery was cleared of men. The ladies, who had
no right to be there at all, were suffered to remain until an
ungallant member called for their ejection on the ground
that the business before the House was in a high degree
confidential, and that their sex did not specially qualify
them to keep State secrets undivulged.[1] "This," (so
the official report runs,) "produced a violent ferment;
the ladies showing great reluctance to comply with the
Order of the House, so that, by their perseverance,
business was interrupted for nearly two hours."[2] At
length Fox rose, in an assembly packed to suffocation,
which heard him with rapt attention. He spoke, according to his own reckoning, for two hours and forty
minutes; but there were few present who would not have
listened to him willingly for twice that time.[3] The
military statistics, on which he based his motion, agreed
in all points with those put forward by the Duke of
Richmond; for the uncle and the nephew had evidently
concerted beforehand what they should say upon that
branch of the subject. Most of the time which Fox had

[1] *The London Chronicle,* as quoted in *Hansard's Parliamentary History.*
[2] *Hatsell's Precedents ;* volume II, page 172.
[3] Coke of Norfolk, a young man who had plenty to amuse him outside
the House of Commons, relates how he once listened with pleasure while
Fox spoke, without notes, for five hours at a stretch. "During all that
time," (said Coke,) "he never hesitated for a word to convey his exact
meaning to his hearers, or paused to sift the arguments which poured
from him in an impassioned flow of eloquence." *Coke of Norfolk and his
Friends ;* volume I, chapter 8.

at his disposal was devoted to an historical retrospect of the whole American story, from the first outbreak of violence at Boston, down to the eve of the capitulation of Saratoga. Only the heads of his discourse have been preserved; for the reporters had been expelled from the Gallery, and Charles Fox was as little likely to transcribe a speech for publication as to preach a sermon. One of the audience appears to have written down from memory the substance of what must have been an unstudied and unadorned, but most convincing, peroration. "On the whole, Sir," said Fox, "it appears to me that, if gentlemen are not blind, they will see that the American War is impracticable, and that no good can come from force only ; that the lives lost, and the treasure spent, have been wasted to no purpose; and that it is high time we should look to our own situation, and not leave ourselves defenceless upon an idea of re-inforcing the army in America ; — an army which, after we have done all we can to strengthen it, will still be less strong than it was last year, when it produced nothing decisive, or in the least degree tending to a complete conquest."

A fine oration by Charles Fox exemplifies the doctrine laid down by the most consummate analyst of artistic processes that the world has ever known. What is ordinarily called the *style* of an artist, (so Mr. Ruskin wrote,) is, in all good art, nothing but the most direct and surest method of getting at the particular *facts* which the artist wants. "He catches at the best and easiest means to reach the end he sees and desires, and he has no time left for playing tricks on the road to it." If such is true of painting, it is tenfold the case with oratory. The stress of a great intellectual effort, con-ducted under the most trying conditions of publicity and grave responsibility, is fatal to affectation and artifi-ciality, and brings out, in all its force, the meaning of the phrase that "the style is the man." Fox habitually dealt with solid realities ; and, — while he never consciously arranged the sequence of his topics, or troubled himself

about the form of a sentence until he was half-way
through with it, — he always took infinite pains to have
his facts correct.[1] Moreover his nature was such that
he instinctively refrained from using in controversy
any argument which he himself did not believe to be
just and weighty ; and his fairness and sincerity carried
persuasion to others.   His power over the minds of men
was never more evident than on that second day of
February 1778.   When he sat down, he had the House
with him; and the Government was so cowed and
flustered that he remained unanswered.   Welbore Ellis,
perhaps the worst speaker on the Treasury Bench, and
Wedderburn, who certainly was the best, rose together,
and stood bowing and complimenting each other, to
the amusement of all who noticed their visible dis-
inclination for a thankless task.   Before they could
settle the matter between them, a division was called ;
and a wonderful division it was.   A hundred and sixty-
five members went into the Lobby with Fox, as compared with the eighty-six who had voted with him in the
previous November.   In a manipulated and subsidised
Parliament, on a strict party question, the minority
which opposed the Government had all but doubled
its numbers at a single bound.

Fox, writing to Richard Fitzpatrick in America, gave
a very modest account of his own performance.   He
had purposely avoided, (he said,) all considerations relating to the justice of the war, and had confined himself to the madness of continuing it.   His discernment
was rewarded; for his line of reasoning was in unison
with feelings and opinions which had by this time become prevalent in every quarter of the political world.
There exists an unpublished letter from a member of
Parliament who had hitherto been a consistent supporter
of Lord North's American policy.   " I feel with re-

---

[1] Many years afterwards, when an important debate was expected,
Sheridan offered Fox some good stories with which to illustrate his argument; but Fox would not have them unless they could be authenticated.
Sheridan went away grumbling that his leader was " so damned surly
about facts."

morse and sorrow," (so this gentleman wrote in December 1777,) "that I have given many mistaken votes, but never a wicked one, throughout this unhappy business. I thought the war both just and practicable. I think it is impracticable now, whatever it might have been if properly conducted. I know not what others mean to do; but I shall stop short. Not one drop more of human blood, or English treasure, will I vote away for ends which I now believe to be unattainable." In the same month Gibbon informed his friend Holroyd that there seemed to be "a universal desire for peace" among all parties. Gibbon himself voted with Fox on the second of February, and now began to talk freely against the American War in all companies, and to denounce Lord North, sometimes with cutting sarcasm, and sometimes in what, for such a master of irony, must be called the language of crude and violent invective. But none the less, before many months had elapsed, he accepted an appointment as a Lord Commissioner of Trade and Plantations; and thenceforward he again supported the war, and preserved a discreet silence about the Minister. There was retribution in store for him. In March 1781 the second and third volumes of The Decline and Fall of the Roman Empire were published; and, in the thirty-fifth chapter of that work, the malicious ingenuity of party-spirit soon unearthed a literary treasure. "The Armorican provinces of Gaul," (so Gibbon had written,) "and the greatest part of Spain, were thrown into a state of disorderly independence by the confederations of the Bagaudæ; and the Imperial ministry pursued with proscriptive laws, and ineffectual arms, the rebels whom they had made." It was long before Gibbon heard the last of his "Bagaudæ" at Brooks's, where it became a favourite amusement among the friends of Charles Fox to search for political allusions which the historian had inserted while he was an independent member, and had neglected to expunge after he became a placeman.[1]

[1] A certain "Lord John," who beyond any reasonable doubt was Lord John Cavendish, displayed much acuteness in detecting, or fancying that

The poet Cowper, — an acute judge of intellect, and not ill-read in history, — pronounced that the British Parliament, during the American War, contained "a greater assemblage of able men, as speakers and counsellors, than ever were contemporary in the same land."[1] The ranks of the Opposition, both in the Lords and Commons, displayed a very high average of talent and statesmanship, of public spirit and personal probity. It is true that the Whig leaders had not always exerted themselves to the utmost during the earlier stages of the American controversy. They were mostly wealthy peers, and great squires who held their heads as high as any baron or viscount; and they loved their ease too well, and detested London too heartily, to spend their winters in the Lobby instead of in the hunting-field, and their summers far away from their parks and gardens. But their apathy had at last been effectually dispelled by the news which arrived from Saratoga, from Philadelphia, and from Paris. The plight of Great Britain in the spring of 1778 was forcibly presented to Parliament by Mr. David Hartley, an honest and accurate speaker who had the ear of the House when it was not in a tempestuous mood. From thirty to forty thousand of our land forces, (according to Mr. Hartley's estimate,) as many of our available seamen, and a hundred of our ships of war, small and great, were engaged in fighting a rebellion three thousand miles away. The borrowing power of the country had been diminished by twenty-five per cent. since that rebellion commenced; and there was a very small margin of national credit left for the maintenance of a war with France, which was already upon us, and a war with Spain, which was imminent,

he had detected, passages where Gibbon " had thrown in sentences and sentiments when he was paying court to Charles Fox, and forgot to correct them after his change." Walpole to Mason; April 1781.

[1] William Cowper to the Rev. William Unwin; July 16, 1782. Cowper in this passage specially refers to "the Cabinet"; but it must be remembered that before July 1782 Lord North had fallen, and his former opponents, — Shelburne and Richmond, Dunning and Camden, Admiral Keppel and General Conway, — were now the Cabinet Ministers.

and all but inevitable. That, (said Mr. Hartley,) was
the price which we had paid in order to purchase the
loss of thirteen colonies, and to find ourselves stripped
of our national powers of defence at a moment when
the Ministerial policy had invited an invasion at home,
and had brought the seat of naval war to the coasts of
England.

If the eminent statesmen, who led the Opposition,
could have had their own way in the spring of 1774
there would have been no rebellion in America, and no
war with France; and therefore, in the spring of 1778,
they were able to face the arduous task which lay before
them with clean hands and a clear conscience, and with
a strong, a straightforward, and a practicable policy.
They urged the Ministry, — and, when Ministers would
not listen, they exhorted Parliament, — to end the dispute
with America, and reserve all the national energies for
the dispute with France. It was, indeed, almost impossible to hope that a war which imperilled the existence of the British empire, and the safety of the British
Isles, would be brought to a prosperous issue by the
same Secretaries of State, and Lords of the Admiralty,
who had failed to re-conquer America. The best
service that could be done to England was to get the
Government out of office; but that most essential
object seemed, for the present at least, beyond the
power of an Opposition to accomplish. The Peers
and Commoners, who acted with Lord Rockingham, were
not strong enough to defeat Lord North in Parliament;
but they did not on that account sulk in their tents,
or evade their full share of responsibility for the conduct of the French war. They were determined, as far
as in them lay, to mitigate the baleful consequences
of official improvidence and incapacity; to see that
prompt measures were taken for supplying the notorious
deficiency of battle-ships, and the absolute dearth of
regular troops; and to ensure that at all events the
story of Saratoga should not be repeated on English
soil. The Whig leaders played an honourable part,

and it was a part which they were singularly competent
to fill. Conway and Barré, Lord Frederic Cavendish
and the Duke of Richmond, had served with distinction
in former wars. They had kept their eyes open to everything which concerned the business of their profession
while they were fighting under such leaders as Prince
Ferdinand of Brunswick and Sir Jeffrey Amherst, and
against such adversaries as Marshal Saxe and General
Montcalm ; and the executive Government, distrustful
of its own sagacity, moved warily beneath the fire
of their criticism, and sometimes was incited to
vigorous and judicious action by their well-timed
advice.

Britain had need of all the military experience which
Parliament could supply, because inside the British War
Office there was little knowledge, and less zeal, and no
foresight whatever except in the shape of despondency.
That Department was administered by a conscientious
statesman whose conscience condemned the wisdom of
the quarrel in which his country was engaged. Lord
Barrington had long ago confided to the Prime Minister
his belief that " our undoubted right of taxation should
no more be exerted in America than in Ireland." The
author of Lord Barrington's biography, speaking with
the tenderness of a brother, and the authority in moral
questions of a Bishop of the Church of England, tells
us that, as soon as the Secretary at War "found that
the measures which he disapproved would be per-
severed in, he tendered his resignation ; but he did it
in that manly and consistent manner which became
Lord Barrington."[1]

The praise of consistency was in one respect deserved ;
for during the space of three livelong years Lord Barrington continued to tender his resignation at frequent
intervals, and in almost precisely the same terms. He
asked to be relieved from office in October 1775, and

[1] *The Political Life of William Wildman, Viscount Barrington,
compiled from Original Papers by his brother, Shute, Bishop of Dur-
ham.*

in June 1776. In the following September he told his Sovereign that he had his own opinions in respect to the dispute with America ; that he frequently gave them, such as they were, to his brother Ministers in conversation or in writing; and that next day he was forced to vote contrary to those opinions, as he could not bring himself to support an Opposition which he abhorred. "Your Majesty," (he went on to say,) " has condescended to be my patron. Be pleased to determine for me how, as a man of honour, conscience, and feeling, I am to act." For in that strange Cabinet the most vital and solemn of all constitutional axioms was habitually inverted ; and, instead of the minister being keeper of the monarch's conscience, the monarch claimed to keep the conscience of the minister. All through the years 1777 and 1778 Lord Barrington was still imploring King George to let him go, and plaguing Lord North to give him the Chiltern Hundreds. At length his importunity prevailed. On the sixteenth December 1778, — forty months after the Secretary at War had first petitioned for his freedom, and more than thirty months after he had let it be known, in specific language, that, as an honest man, he could not continue in office,— he received a letter informing him that His Majesty, though hurt by his desertion, would graciously permit him, in consideration of long and faithful service, to retire on a pension of two thousand pounds per annum. The whole story, from first to last, throws a searching light upon the private convictions of the more decent and thoughtful among those very Ministers to whose public policy we are indebted for the loss of America.

Brilliant results could not be expected from the labours of a minister whose mind was almost exclusively intent upon seeking political salvation by the abandonment of his office. In those battles over the Estimates, which are perpetually being waged inside every Cabinet, a Department must always be starved unless there is a man at the head of it who is not afraid of his colleagues, and who heartily believes in the value of the work which he himself is striving to accomplish. The rest of the Government paid very little attention to Lord Barrington's mild complaints that the army was not strong enough for the duties which had been imposed upon it. As early as January 1776 the regular infantry and cavalry, in England and Scotland, had been reduced to thirteen thousand men, all told ; and by December 1777 it was known in London that Burgoyne had been captured, and that nearly seven thousand fine troops had been lost to the country. The news produced a spirited rally in those districts where a belief in the military capacity of the Government still lingered. The townsmen of Manchester volunteered to enroll a corps at their own expense; Liverpool, Edinburgh, and Glasgow followed suit; and no less than six battalions were raised in the Scottish Highlands by noblemen and gentlemen of that country, not at their own cost, but by a generous exertion of their hereditary influence and popularity. The example of Scotland, and of Lancashire, was not imitated by the country at large.[1] Englishmen of both parties clearly perceived that the Ministry still extravagantly under-estimated the difficulty of subjugating America. A Tory member of Parliament, who had calculated the price of the policy which he wished to enforce, declared that " while he would part with reluctance with one shilling in the pound towards raising another army of ten thousand men for America, he would cheerfully pay ten shillings in the pound towards an additional army of sixty thousand men." But Lord North and his colleagues were as far as ever from rising to the height of the situation. They had no plan of action beyond a vague inclination to go on trifling over an attempt to suppress the rebellion with insufficient forces, under the leadership of generals hampered and bewildered with

---

[1] " Several independent companies, amounting to something about a regiment in point of numbers, were raised in Wales ; but the battalions, excepting those of Manchester and Liverpool, were all raised in Scotland." *History of Europe in the Annual Register for 1778 ;* chapter 5.

meaningless instructions conveyed across the ocean from
the remote latitude of Whitehall.

Before many weeks had elapsed a powerful and
profound emotion stirred the temper of our people.
It became known through the length and breadth of
England that we were on the verge of a French war,
provoked by France in spite of an exhibition on the
part of the English Ministry of long-suffering patience,
and scrupulous equity, which touched, though it did
not pass, the extreme bounds of what was consistent
with the dignity and self-respect of a great country.
The consciousness of an immense and sudden national
danger was intensified by a unanimous feeling of national
resentment.   Most men were sick of trying to coerce the
Americans, and all were on fire to resist and punish
the French.   King George, as interpreter of the general
sentiment, addressed an appeal to his Parliament, —
and, behind Parliament, to his subjects, — in terms
admirably worthy of a British sovereign.   His Majesty,
(so the message ran,) was persuaded that the good faith
of his conduct towards foreign powers, and the sincerity
of his wishes to preserve the tranquillity of Europe,
would be acknowledged by the world ; and therefore,
relying with the firmest confidence on the zealous and
affectionate support of his faithful people, he was
determined to exert, in repelling insult and attack,
" all the force and resources of his kingdoms."   Those
resources had been grievously impaired by four years
of civil warfare ; but one invaluable reserve of national
strength still remained intact.   At the height of the
Seven Years' War, while our regular army was winning
laurels abroad, Lord Chatham had confided the defence
of our island to the Militia ; and, under the fostering
care of Chatham, our Militia regiments were as efficient,
in proportion to their possibilities, as any branch of
the military or naval service.   Edward Gibbon, — as remarkable a captain, under several aspects, intellectual
and physical, as perhaps ever marched at the head
of a company, — tells us that the regulars and the

Militia, when quartered together on Winchester Downs in the summer of 1761, were heartily satisfied with each other as companions in arms. The regular regiments, while agreeably persuaded "of their own ideal pre-eminence," recognised the exact discipline of the best Militia battalions; and the worst among those battalions had improved their time and opportunities until "they were rather a credit, than a disgrace, to the Line." And now the King, in his utmost need, did not neglect that lesson of a thrice honourable past. On the twenty-third March 1778 he communicated to Parliament his intention of ordering the Militia "to be drawn out and embodied, and to march as occasion should require."

Lord Barrington had thrown, — or, to speak more accurately, had feebly dribbled, — cold water on the proposal to call out the Militia : but even Lord Barring-ton had admitted in a State Paper that the scheme had merits. "The Militia," he wrote, "when embodied in the late war, was officered by the first nobility and gentry, full of spirit, and fond of the thing. Their rank and authority had great weight with the common men." So it had been in the day of Britain's glory: and her cry of peril, in her present distress, evoked a response which proved that her sons had not degenerated. Before the close of the year 1778 threescore and ten battalions of Militia had been mustered, drilled, and disciplined. They were distributed over eight camps, — on Cox Heath to the south, and Warley Common to the east, of London; in the immediate neighbourhood of Bury St. Edmund's, Salisbury, and Winchester; at Portsmouth and Plymouth; and at Newcastle upon Tyne, where a Percy was in command.[1] Thirty of the colonels were men of title, from Duke to Baronet; and there were plenty of such commoners as Aclands, and Milbanks, and Herberts, and Herveys. Between thirty and forty members of Parliament were serving in the

---

[1] Two of these were almost exclusively cavalry camps: for the dragoons, who had been kept at home, were numerous out of all proportion to the regular infantry.

regiments on the south coast; and the greatest part of these gentlemen, (so the newspapers stated,) were "known friends to their country, and consequently no great supporters of the political measures at present adopted." A marked feature of that London season was the exodus of popular and fashionable Whigs from their accustomed haunts of pleasure and dissipation. Mr. Brooks, the most celebrated of club managers, had removed his establishment from Pall Mall, and had opened a new house in St. James's Street, " fitted up with great magnificence": but his vintages lay untouched in the cellar; the rattle of the dice-box was intermittent or silent; and in the drawing-room there seldom was anyone under forty years of age to hear George Selwyn's stories. The great men of the Opposition were at their post of duty. A Tory newspaper related, with honest appreciation, that the Duke of Richmond was the best marksman in England with a single ball, either from pistol or musket : and the Duke was continually riding between Lewes and Brighthelmstone, seeing that the Sussex militiamen learned to shoot straight, and working, (according to Edward Gibbon,) "like a Serjeant, a clerk, and a pack-horse." "Lord Derby," wrote Selwyn, "is the life of the camp at Winchester, where he keeps a constant table, and is indefatigable in training his regiment, which is one of the best. He scorns the luxury of travelling in a chaise, but performs all his journeys on horseback, generally on post-horses." The Duke of Devonshire, too, was out with his regiment, very busy when soldiering was to be done, but with no liking for the torture which then went by the name of punishment. It was noticed that his Grace retired to his marquee during the flogging, and came out of it in order to lift the fainting man from the halberts; and he was not on that account the less willingly and punctiliously obeyed as an officer.[1]

[1] Three men of the Derbyshire Militia, who were charged with insubordinate conduct, received each five hundred lashes. Public feeling, which always had been revolted by these ruthless sentences, became

" Why do I," (wrote a subaltern of Militia,) "who am
but a paltry commoner, presume to complain when I
see men who have filled the first places in the kingdom
going through the most fatiguing duties with alacrity
and cheerfulness ? In the foremost of these stands his
Grace the Duke of Grafton. The day before yesterday
he went the rounds at twelve at night, four miles on
foot, it raining hard the whole time. The propriety
with which he conducts himself has gained him the
admiration and esteem of the whole encampment."
Wet and tired as Grafton was, it may be doubted
whether he was not better pleased with himself, and
with his work, than in those days when, to his cost, he
occupied the exalted office of Prime Minister.

George the Third never showed to better advantage
than in his character of titular chief of the fighting services. In that department of State affairs he understood his duty thoroughly, he did it gallantly, and he
kept within it. He spared no pains to encourage those
among his subjects who were exerting themselves for
the protection of their native shores ; and his inquisitive
and intelligent supervision shamed into activity the
short-sighted administrators who had hitherto effected
little to prepare the country against such a formidable
crisis. In the early summer of 1778 there was no large
body of troops sufficiently advanced in their training to
face the ordeal of a royal inspection; but the fleet,

stronger than ever when many thousand Militiamen, who had lately been
civilians, were made liable to the penalties of martial law. The people
of Manchester had voluntarily contributed a regiment, recruited from
among their sons and kindred, to aid the forces of the Crown; and it is
stated that they "nearly killed an officer who flogged his soldiers cruelly."

Another instance of the methods by which discipline was maintained
at Cox Heath, though grim and rigorous enough, is less unpleasing. A
deserter had been condemned to death, and the brigade to which he belonged was drawn out to witness the execution. General Keppel, to the
relief of all present, announced that His Majesty had been graciously
pleased to pardon the prisoner, on condition that he did "as soon as
possible transport himself to Senegal, and there serve His Majesty for the
remainder of his life"; and the Duke of Devonshire, as officer of the
day, was then ordered to wheel the picquets to the right and left, and
march them off to their respective regiments.

though far smaller than the security of Great Britain demanded, and shockingly ill-equipped for serious operations, was already in a condition to make an imposing show on the occasion of a gala. After spending two days in a survey of Chatham Dockyard the King made his appearance at Portsmouth on the second of May, accompanied by the Queen, and several of the older Princes. Their arrival was awaited there with mingled feelings. The enthusiasm was overwhelming; but, on that very account, the resources of the district were so overtaxed that poor men, whose profession obliged them to be on the spot, found it difficult to subsist. The squires and parsons of all the south-eastern counties had flocked in to Portsmouth, bringing wives and daughters with them. Outward-bound vessels, in great quantity, had postponed their departure until their crews and passengers had caught a sight of the royal family. Thirty West Indiamen, and as many other great ships bound for Quebec and Halifax, were lying in the harbour. "Admirals," we are told, "were plentier than Captains in time of peace; and upwards of a thousand officers, and double that number of their dependents, had to be provided with fresh provisions every day." The inns charged so high that they were nicknamed the Spunging Houses; a lodging of three rooms let for twenty, thirty, or fifty guineas for the week; the butter was all sold within half an hour after the market was opened; the fowls had been bought up, straight from the farm-yards, at famine prices; and "the place was as bad as Jamaica, where a man cannot open his mouth under a dollar." The King entered Portsmouth amidst the acclamations of thousands of the neighbouring gentry, while the National Anthem was sung with infinite zest by a full chorus of shipwrights. His Majesty at once let it be known that he had come on business. He had received, (he said,) such contradictory accounts about the condition of his marine that he was resolved to look into the matter with his own eyes. Wherever he went, on land or water, Lord Sandwich was at his elbow, ex-

cusing deficiencies, and magnifying achieved results.
But, whatever the servant might say, the master contrived to get at the truth. His Majesty talked freely,
— and listened as often, and as long, as his expansive
temperament allowed him, — to naval officers of all
ranks, three fourths of whom distrusted and disliked the
First Lord of the Admiralty for reasons honourable to
them as sailors and patriots.[1] When he had done with
the battle-ships, the King disembarked from the royal
yacht, and turned his attention to the Dockyard. A
foolish poet, a precursor of Peter Pindar, — or possibly,
(for the dates permit it,) Peter Pindar himself, — detected
material for ridicule in the minute curiosity with which
His Majesty viewed the blacksmith's shop, the block-
manufactory, and the piles of timber which were season-
ing in the wood-yard. But George the Third had never
spent a couple of days more usefully than when he insisted on seeing his establishments for naval construction
in full swing of work. Glad as he would have been, (he
said,) to give his artificers a holiday, the times were such
that not a hand must be idle in the Yard, nor any necessary operation for the equipment of the fleet suspended
in consequence of his visit.

Before autumn ended the Militia had been brought
into shape, and welded with all the available battalions
of regular infantry into a compact army for home defence; and then George the Third once more discerned
an opportunity for usefulness. He played the King of
England with a judicious touch of dramatic effect, and
neglected nothing which could put heart into his people,
and teach them to meet the threats of the foreigner in

[1] King George had a hearty way with sailors, and they repaid him by
taking a friendly interest in his proceedings. A reporter " overheard two
honest tars disputing," — the one observing that the King had got leave
to stay at Portsmouth till Tuesday, and the other maintaining that he was
master of his own movements. But the first of them insisted that it was
" as necessary for the King to have leave of absence as for a fore-mast
man." On those rare occasions when he went pleasuring George the
Third had to get leave of absence from himself: and in that relation he
was the hardest of all taskmasters.

a spirit of gay and chivalrous defiance. Late in September 1778 he set out from Windsor at one in the afternoon, and reached Winchester, (for he loved to travel fast,) at half after five. Next morning he reviewed the force which was quartered on the downs, and dined in a gorgeous pavilion, erected on an eminence full in sight of the entire camp. Thence he passed on to Salisbury, and, after spending two nights with the Earl of Pembroke at Wilton House, he returned, through Stonehenge, by a westerly route to Windsor. All along his line of journey the houses were decorated with green boughs and garlands of flowers; the bells were ringing; and the streets of every town and village were crowded with a multitude of shouting spectators. In both the Cathedral cities which he visited he was harangued by the Dean and Chapter, and the Mayor and Corporation; and the best-born of the Winchester scholars addressed him in a Latin speech, and in some well-meant, but very ill-rhymed, English verses. The King replied, on each occasion, in a few plain but manly words; declaring himself proud of his just cause and his loyal people, and confident that the courage of his sailors and soldiers would render England secure against invasion. Three weeks afterwards he inspected Warley Camp, and was splendidly entertained at Thorndon Hall by Lord Petre, a great Roman Catholic peer, who welcomed an occasion for displaying his loyalty to the House of Hanover.[1] Again a few days, and their Majesties went to stay with Lord Amherst at his seat near Sevenoaks; a mansion which the valiant owner, with the best right in the world, had christened Montreal. Next morning the royal party repaired to Cox Heath, and, attended by a brilliant cavalcade, rode to and fro along the imposing array of battalions. Queen Charlotte, who at Portsmouth

---

[1] "Lord Petre," (according to the *Evening Post,*) "agreed to give his upholsterer five hundred pounds for making up a bed for His Majesty, has given his servants out of livery fifty guineas to purchase clothes suitable for the occasion, and has ordered the avenues to his house to be lined with silk." It was reckoned that the royal visit cost his Lordship three thousand pounds.

had been attired in blue and silver out of compliment to
the navy, now wore a scarlet habit; and the King, with
no affectation of a military seat, managed his charger to
the satisfaction of all beholders.[1] He then took up his
position opposite the centre of the line, and saw the
army, — fifteen thousand infantry, with fifty cannon, —
march past him in Grand Divisions. " The men," (wrote
a London journal,) "were exceedingly clean, and most
of them newly dressed. His Majesty is reported to have
said, ' Oh! Amherst; this is indeed a heavenly sight! ' "
In whatever terms George the Third may have expressed
his satisfaction, that particular sentence most assuredly
never issued from his lips.

The question of the Militia was vitally important to
the nation under its serious aspects; and it served the
idle world as a craze and a fashion until the novelty
had passed away. Those who are old enough to remember the Volunteer movement in 1859 and 1860
can imagine for themselves the flood of sense and
nonsense which poured from the printing press, and
eddied through clubs and drawing-rooms, during the
summer and autumn of 1778. "At Almack's," said
Gibbon, "the chief conversation is about tents, drill-
Serjeants, sub-divisions, and firings." The historian,
to his surprise and amusement, found himself revered
in London society as a veteran; and, when he visited
Cox Heath, he was received by the boy officers as a
"father of the old Hampshire Militia." The newspapers paid every regiment in turn an attention with
which its colonel would gladly have dispensed. Sometimes, (so one of these gentlemen complained,) he read
that his corps had been detached to one station when it
had all along been quartered at another. Sometimes he
learned that several of his companies had mutinied,

---

[1] George the Third, always to the front in the hunting-field, objected to
figuring as a bad horseman even in bronze and marble. It is worth while
comparing his equestrian statue at the East end of Pall Mall with the
effigies of other British monarchs, who look one less at home in the saddle
than another, even in cases where a sculptor, kinder than most, has provided them with stirrups.

that two or three duels had been fought by his subalterns, and that two or three dozen criminal assaults had
been perpetrated by his rank and file. Every corner
of the daily journals, — the matrimonial intelligence, the
theatrical reports, and, more especially, the advertise-
ment columns, — teemed with allusions to the Militia.[1]
The resident gentlemen of the southern counties, according to the London journals, were glad to see
military men seated round their tables; though hospitality was not always exercised irrespective of politics.
The Blues and Yellows, (we read,) were so fierce in
Maidstone that they could not meet at public entertainments; and an old gentleman of Whig opinions was
said to have given his daughter, who had a fortune of
ten thousand pounds, to a lieutenant in the Suffolk
Militia because that battalion wore yellow facings.
Lord Amherst, mindful of the time when he was a young
staff-officer on active service, always ready for a good
dinner, kept something like open house at Montreal,
where "the eating and drinking was wonderful, and the
desserts magnificent." And, within the precincts of the
camp, the wives of the Colonels, under the presidency
of the Duchess of Devonshire, instituted a ladies' mess
to which no officer was admitted except such as were
distinguished by regularity of conduct, and strict attention to their duty.

Cox Heath was not exactly a Valley Forge, and yet
the life in a militia-camp was sometimes very far indeed
from being a picnic. There were Government contractors who took good care for that. The ammunition
loaf was hard, and not of appetising colour; though pa-

[1] "Martial balsam" for the tooth-ache was recommended to all who
had to sleep under canvas on damp mattresses. Everybody who cared
for a good farce was advised to see "The Camp" at Drury Lane, where
the two principal actors, — a young spark of a lieutenant, and a Government contractor, who likely enough was the villain of the piece, — were
received night after night "with overwhelming applause"; and where
the heroine was a farmer's daughter who had followed her lover among
the tents under the guise of a recruit. "She was of a figure for the part,
and went through her exercises with an ease and address very extraordinary for a lady."

triotic journalists, who had not to eat it, discoursed finely
about Charles the Twelfth of Sweden, and his fondness
for black bread when he was with an army in the field.
"This camp," (wrote a Kentish correspondent,) "was
not built for show; and General Keppel is not a soldier
for sunshine. Educated beneath the famous Duke of
Cumberland he partakes of his temper, and has established the strictest discipline." We are elsewhere told
how certain of the junior officers, "thinking that birth
and title sanctioned everything, demeaned themselves
at first in a manner bordering upon maccaronism."
They came on parade with lapels unbuttoned; they
obeyed orders, or neglected them, as the humour took
them; and some of them had brought their mistresses
down from London. But Lieutenant General William
Keppel, though less celebrated than his two eminent
brothers, was a stern warrior of rugged character and
antique respectability, who had seen rough service.
He was not a man to take dandy ensigns and lieutenants
at their own estimate; and the young coxcombs had
soon been put under arrest, while their fair companions
were unceremoniously expelled from the neighbourhood.

Lamentations about the hardships of a military life
may still be read in private letters from Cox Heath, and
from Warley Common. Some of the subalterns out
of the rural districts, when their training began, seem
to have been very little better than so many Tony
Lumpkins in uniform. "I heartily wish," (Mr. Robert
Grimston told one of his relatives,) "that you may never
come to a camp as a soldier, for it is damnation upon
earth. Good God! What shall we come to at last?
General Pierson has given orders for all the Chaplains
to attend! Our ground upon Warley Common is by
no means cleared; and we are out exercising at five
o'clock in the morning, and then the men are set to
work stubbing the ground like day-labourers." A
gentleman from the North country, who spent two days
as a guest of the East Riding Militia, suspected that
many of the officers were heartily tired of Warley,

though none of them complained so loud as Mr. Robert Grimston. "He curses the camp, and himself for quitting two good houses, and every accommodation, to sleep in a tent, dine on coarse meat, and be confined like a pointer to his kennel." But discontent gradually exhaled itself in words. The grumblers became smart officers, and the private men were shaped into soldiers under a discipline which was often unnecessarily severe, but always scrupulously just. "General Keppel," said the Duke of Grafton, "had the merit of forming many raw corps into a formidable army." The praise was deserved; and there were other commanders who worked as hard, and almost as successfully, as Keppel. The House of Commons, in December 1778, voted pay for thirty-nine thousand Militiamen and Fencibles who, when they were stiffened by the presence among them of a few regular battalions, could look an equal number of the best French infantry boldly and confidently in the face.[1]

[1] Certain military and naval officers who had declined, on grounds of conscience, to draw the sword against Americans, now took service in the Militia. Among them was John Cartwright, Lord Howe's favourite among all his former officers, who had resisted a pressing invitation from his old commander to serve on board the Flag-ship against the revolted colonists. When the French war broke out Cartwright was appointed Major of the Nottinghamshire Regiment, and that corps, owing to his indefatigable pains, reached a degree of discipline which commanded universal admiration. He had a good sea officer's attention to detail, and a good sea officer's ingenuity for devising forms of punishment which were efficacious without being barbarous. When the battalion was sent southwards on garrison-service, Cartwright, "perceiving that, at first setting out on the march, the men were inclined to loiter in a manner inconsistent with military duty, assured them that he should find measures to prevent such irregularity in future. The offence was nevertheless repeated the next day; but, just as they came in view of their quarters for the night, the Major drew them up, and, ordering them to face about, without making any remark, marched them three miles back, thus adding six miles to the exercise of the day." It was a lesson which never needed repetition. He was inflexible where leniency was out of place. A private soldier, who had been sentenced to punishment, was advised to ask the Major for pardon, seeing that he had a vote for Nottingham, where Cartwright had been invited to stand as parliamentary candidate. "It will be of no use," said the man: "and for that very reason."

CHAPTER IV

It was well that England should be rendered secure at home, because for five years to come she had as much as she could do to hold her own on that element where the main source of her power and prosperity lay. During all those years no British and French forces, which could be dignified with the title of armies, met in battle on European soil. It was a maritime war on a vast scale, not unequally contested, and waged by our own country under enormous and unprecedented disadvantages. No hostile neighbour threatened the frontiers, and distracted the attention, of France; while England had many enemies, and no allies, with Portugal for her solitary friend, — until even Portugal was bullied into taking diplomatic action against her. Spain threw in her lot with France, not, as in Chatham's war, when France was already half beaten, but during an early and critical phase of the struggle. The quarrel with America, while it absorbed a large British army which otherwise would have been disposable for land operations against France and Spain, was not less injurious to British interests at sea. In the course of the last war eighteen thousand American sailors, according to the official computation, had shipped themselves for service on board of our fleets; whereas in this war at least as many were actively engaged against us. And, to complete the list of drawbacks under which our country laboured, her navy was in charge of an administrator who had long ago forfeited the confidence and esteem of the noble service over which he presided.

When the Earl of Sandwich became First Lord of the Admiralty his position was one which any statesman might have been proud to occupy. The hard-earned successes of the great French war had inspired our

navy with a quiet and unostentatious, but most legitimate, self-respect. Our ships and squadrons had then
been commanded by men in whom the best British qualities had been developed by favouring circumstances,
and by the wise and sympathetic attitude so long
adopted towards them in high quarters. Chatham
knew more about the navy than any ruler who ever
swayed the State; and his store of knowledge included
an accurate recognition of the limits beyond which civilian war-ministers should cease to interfere with the
responsibility of professional experts. His trusted ad-
viser was George, Lord Anson, a celebrated leader in
battle, and still more celebrated as a navigator, an administrator, and an equitable and sharp-sighted judge
of merit in others. When Anson was on the West
Indian station as a young post-captain, — and he attained that rank at a very early time of life indeed, —
he was described as loving his bottle and not hating
women, and as singularly handsome, well-bred, good-
natured, generous, and humane, "and so old-fashioned
as to make some profession of religion." A quarter of
a century of hardship and adventure, of arduous warfare, and unceasing care for the well-being and safety
of his crews, had called out all that was good in him,
and had corrected such defects as were unsuitable to
his advancing age, and to the high authority with which
he was invested betimes, and which he long retained.
He was First Lord of the Admiralty from 1751 till
1756; and, on the thirtieth of June 1757, he was re-ap-
pointed to the same office by Mr. Secretary Pitt. That
was a red-letter day in the calendar of the British navy;
for, during the glorious years which followed, Lord Anson made it his prime object, and his sole ambition, to
place the means of victory in the hands of the admirals
and captains who took our ships into action against the
national enemy. Simple, manly, and modest, he iden-
tified his own interests with those of his brother officers,
with the best of whom he lived on terms of close intimacy. The flower of the service had sailed under him,

in former days, on his expedition across the Pacific
Ocean; and a large group of young men who afterwards attained to eminence, — including such names as
Sir Charles Saunders, and Viscount Keppel, and the
Earl of Howe, and Sir Hyde Parker, — had served in
various capacities on board his flag-ship the *Centurion*
during that eventful voyage. The upper ranks of the
British navy, in the later period of the Seven Years'
War, constituted a true fraternity of colleagues whose
first and last thought was to do their duty by England,
and support each other in the hour of difficulty and
peril. Few of them were politicians, in the sense of
Whig and Tory; but, almost to a man, they entertained for Lord Chatham a strong personal feeling of
affection and loyalty.

That was the tone of the service when the Earl of
Sandwich entered upon his functions as First Lord of
the Admiralty. His type of character, and his previous
history, were not such as to recommend him to British
seamen. When the Court and the Cabinet were bent
upon satisfying their grudge against Wilkes, — and
when their arbitrary violence was foiled by the in-
vincible reverence for legality which the eminent Chief
Justice of the Common Pleas, who afterwards became
Lord Camden, brought to bear upon the case before
him, — they had recourse to darker and more tortuous
methods, and they found an instrument in Lord Sandwich. That nobleman, in days when the doings at
Medmenham Abbey were the scandal of society, had
been a brother-monk of John Wilkes, and a high-priest
in all the indecencies and blasphemies which constituted
the ritual of the Order. The House of Lords was therefore not a little astonished when Sandwich rose with a
solemn face, and the air of a John Knox or a Savona-
rola, holding in his hand a ribald poem which Wilkes
had written, and set up in type, for the private delecta-
tion of his boon-companions. He read aloud some of
the most outrageous passages, and called upon the
Peers to brand the production as impious and licentious.

The whole nature of the proceeding outraged the sense
of fair-play which was a dominant characteristic of that
hearty and downright generation of Englishmen; and
Lord Sandwich at once became, and ever afterwards
remained, the most unpopular man in the kingdom.
The only possible theory on which his conduct could
be defended was that he had sincerely repented of his
evil ways, and was now desirous to make such atone-
ment as lay in his power by denouncing the partaker in
his former sins and follies. But that theory was not
tenable; for his house continued to be, as it always had
been, a notorious centre of hard drinking and loose living. When he was fifty, and fifty-five, and sixty years
old his mistress lived at the Admiralty, with his large
family of illegitimate children round her, singing at his
concerts, and presiding at his table. She lent a ready
ear to the very few captains and lieutenants who stooped
to interest her in their prospects of promotion, and to
the much larger number of mercantile adventurers who
were on the hunt for a lucrative Government contract.
A wide-spread suspicion prevailed that her clients did
not approach her empty-handed; and Miss Ray, and
her influence over Lord Sandwich, filled many a column
in the poet's corner of the daily newspaper.[1] It was a
very sore subject in naval circles. Sailors are jovial fellows, and many of them in those times carried jollity
very far; but no civilian who has ever sat at the Board
of Admiralty can have failed to be impressed by the
habit of punctilious decorum which naval men, in their
official relations, observe themselves, and exact from
others. The resentment against Sandwich was deep
and bitter on shore and on ship-board; — in the Admi-

---

[1] In February 1776, (for one example among scores,) there appeared a
rhymed petition, imploring "the First Lady of the Admiralty" to distrib-
ute the contracts for Transport fairly among the whole body of ship-owners.
To this Miss Ray replies:
> "I do what I will with my swain ;
> He sings me a catch in return ;
> While such scribblers as you may complain,
> And the navy of England may burn."

ral's cabin, in the ward-room and the gun-room, and, (above all,) in the forecastle, where there was only one opinion about the man who, in order to curry favour with his superiors, had peached on an old comrade in his hour of trouble and distress.

The navy, as its best men in all ranks knew to their cost, was managed in the party interests of the Bedford connection. Political obsequiousness had become a sure road to professional advancement; and the fatal effect of such a system was already apparent in a service where high mental qualities are indispensable in peace and war alike. The tactlessness of John Montagu, a foolish Commander in Chief on the American station, had done much to fret and alienate the colonists during the earlier stages of the quarrel with New England; and the utter incompetency which, when the fighting began, was displayed by his successor, Admiral Samuel Graves, had contributed more than any other cause to bring about the loss of Boston. The spirit which guided Lord Sandwich in the disposal of naval patronage was unmistakably exhibited in a province of administration where a man of honour and feeling would have instinctively refrained from pursuing his own selfish advantage. He had the supreme control of an immense fund destined for the support and comfort of aged and disabled sailors of the Royal Navy, inasmuch as the revenues of Greenwich Hospital already had reached a total of sixty-four thousand pounds a year. More than a third of that great income was derived from the landed estates of the Hospital. Those estates were situated in the northern counties of England; but Lord Sandwich himself was a Huntingdonshire proprietor, residing in the outskirts of the parliamentary borough of Huntingdon. An exceedingly shrewd man of business, when he was acting on his own behalf, he often told his friends that he never would consent to employ a lawyer for his land-agent; and yet the Steward of the Greenwich Hospital Estates, who got his five per cent. on the gross rental, was a Huntingdonshire attorney, notable for his skill in the conduct of elections.

This personage had successfully carried through a scheme for creating a large number of forty shilling freeholds, which he made over to Commanders of the fleet, and departmental officers of the Admiralty, " on the implied condition of voting in the interests of Lord Sandwich." The two Chaplains, who were supposed to watch over and befriend the indoor pensioners of the Hospital, — few enough, at the best, among so many, — were both of them Huntingdonshire freeholders, and pluralists who had duties and emoluments elsewhere. The parish clergymen on the northern estates, according to an established rule of the service, were meritorious Naval Chaplains, who had served their time at sea ; but these veterans did not die fast enough to satisfy all the dependants of the Bedfords who were in need of Church preferment, and an additional living was accordingly purchased out of Hospital funds, and conferred on a parson who wrote letters to the newspapers, in defence of Lord Sandwich, under the signature of Anti-Sejanus. On the manors belonging to the Hospital there were more than thirty so-called gamekeepers, who, as a matter of fact, were local politicians, fond of carrying a gun, and not too scrupulous to act " as legal tyrants over the tenants of the Hospital estates," in order to ensure that, at county elections, those tenants would vote for the candidates whom Lord Sandwich favoured. But no game was ever seen on the tables of the Hospital, where it would have been an acceptable variety in the customary diet ; for the Master Cook, and all the contractors, exercised the license, — and, as far as Lord Sandwich could ensure it, enjoyed the impunity, — of political partisans. Bull-beef, supplied at the top market price of prime meat, was proved in court to have been served up to the pensioners twenty-seven times in the course of a single quarter. The veal was horrible, and its origin indescribable in print ; and the beer, which was conveyed to the dining-hall in rotten pipes, had frequently turned sour before it left the brewhouse. The worst of the delinquents was haled before the King's Bench, and severely punished by Lord Mansfield. That great judge, when a question of humanity came before him, was no respecter of person or party; and he commented with lively indignation on the treatment inflicted upon a helpless community of "oppressed old men," on the ignorance or corruption of the officials, and on the conduct of the Minister who had appointed them.

Our admirals and captains, who in essentials were the same as now, would have forgiven much to a First Lord of the Admiralty as long as he exerted himself to provide the country with an efficient fleet. They would have excused even the political favouritism by which they themselves personally suffered if the British navy had been in a condition to encounter the storm of war which was gathering in every quarter; but Lord Sandwich held a very different conception from theirs of patriotic duty. For seven years past he had administered his department as if England had no enemies in the world except the Parliamentary opponents of the Bedford clique; and, while he was jobbing and intriguing to secure for his own adherents the electoral representation of the Cinque Ports and the dockyard towns, the maritime force of Great Britain was going steadily downwards to rack and ruin. A deep anxiety prevailed among the survivors of those naval veterans whose skill and valour, under the auspices of Lord Chatham, had crushed the power of France and Spain. Such men as Hawke, and Hood, and Barrington, and Keppel were no vulgar panic-mongers and alarmists. They knew that the most extravagant expenditure in time of peace could not guarantee the country against chance and peril in war; and chance and peril, whenever a war broke out, they were cheerfully and resolutely prepared to face. But they knew likewise that our naval strength had been allowed to drop below the lowest mark which the most sanguine optimist could regard as the line of safety; and they confided their apprehensions to the

statesman who was best qualified to be their spokes-
man in Parliament. During the closing months of 1777
Lord Chatham twice warned the Peers, in plain and specific language, that our home ports contained scarcely
twenty ships of the line so completely manned, and so
thoroughly equipped, that an admiral, who had a care
for his reputation, would be willing to command them.
Lord Sandwich on the other hand declared, boldly,
roundly, and repeatedly, that five-and-thirty such vessels, with full crews on board, were ready to sail on a
moment's notice; that twenty others might be placed
in commission before two weeks had elapsed; and that,
if we were attacked by Spain as well as by France, our
Admiralty would undertake, before the end of a twelvemonth, to have ninety battle-ships at sea.   "My Lords,"
he said, "I am authorised to affirm, from what I have
now submitted to you, that your fleets are more than a
match for the united force of the whole House of Bourbon."   Three months afterwards, when the conflicting
statements of the Minister, and the ex-Minister, were
brought to the proof, it became evident that Lord
Chatham, so far from exaggerating, had under-estimated the denudation of our navy.

Admiral Keppel was a shining figure in his own
generation. He had led the enviable career of a
favourite of fortune during the culminating period of
a nation's greatness. As a lad of sixteen he sailed
round the world with Anson, and had the peak of his
cap shaved off by a Spanish bullet. He commanded
a frigate before he came of age; and, on the glorious
twentieth of November 1759, he headed the advance of
Hawke's column into Quiberon Bay, where he sank his
Frenchman, and was within a very little of going to the
bottom himself. Eighteen months afterwards he took
part in the siege and capture of Havannah. His eldest
brother, the Earl of Albemarle, commanded the land
forces; and his younger brother was a general on the
staff. Those who care to see how a noble Roman matron
must have looked, on the day when her sons obtained a

triumph, would do well to visit Sir Joshua's fine picture of old Lady Albemarle on the wall of our National Gallery. A true Roman triumph in all respects it was. The family divided between them an amount of prize-money equal to nearly twenty millions of sesterces;[1] and the list of promotions was extended so as to include Augustus Keppel among the Vice-Admirals of the Blue.

When New England rose in rebellion Keppel had attained the age of fifty; and his bright and prosperous life was soon clouded over with anxieties and troubles. He made no secret of a determination never to draw sword against his fellow-countrymen in America; and his attitude on that important question increased, rather than weakened, his immense popularity throughout the naval service. George the Third had long ago descried, more clearly than any of his ministers, the European complications towards which their American policy was leading them; and, as early as November 1776, he obtained from Keppel a promise that, if the proceedings of any foreign Court became such as to rouse suspicion, he would accept the command of " a fleet of observation" in the British Channel. And now in March 1778, when suspicion of the French intentions had developed into alarming certainty, Keppel was directed to hoist his flag, and take over the supreme charge of our naval forces in the home waters. Keppel assumed that arduous duty with grave forebodings. He frankly told the King that he was not on terms of acquaintance with the ministers, but that he relied for protection and support on His Majesty's well-known zeal for the public good; and, before leaving London, he warned his intimate associates in Parliament that he had no hope whatever of friendly, or even equitable, treatment at the hands of the Government, and that "the higher the command, the more liable he was to be ruined in his reputation." Keppel's acceptance was

[1] It was computed that Lord Albemarle got a hundred and forty thousand pounds, and his younger brothers twenty-five thousand apiece.

a godsend to the ministry, and the Earl of Sandwich made a characteristic use of it in debate. It was idle, (he affirmed,) for noble Lords to talk about the deplorable condition of the fleet, since he had found a man who was conversant with every branch of the navy, and who was willing to stake his credit upon its adequacy for all the purposes of war; — "a brave and experienced officer, as respectably connected, and as nobly allied, as any in the service;" and a man of whom he himself entertained the most exalted opinion.

It was the sort of language which Mr. Secretary Pitt might formerly have used to define his relations with Admiral Hawke and Admiral Boscawen; or which George, Lord Spencer, in the last few years of the century, might have employed when he was sending forth Duncan, and Jervis, and Nelson to victories with the means of winning which he had loyally and abundantly supplied them. What that language was worth in the mouth of Lord Sandwich the object of his crafty and insidious panegyric was not long in learning. "When I reached Portsmouth," said Keppel, "I saw six ships ready; and, on viewing even those with a seaman's eye, I was not by any means pleased with their condition." His indignant remonstrances shamed the Admiralty into a display of fevered and belated activity. The shipwrights and ropemakers were paid to do a day and a half's work in the twenty-four hours, — an arrangement which, according to the standard of industry then ruling in the dockyards, at all events secured for the nation something approaching the equivalent of a fair day's labour. No woman, who would take the sewing of flannel bags for cannon-cartridges, was kept idle within a circuit of several miles round the arsenal. The press-gangs exerted themselves to the utmost; and, amidst a great number of more valuable captures, they secured some very queer candidates for naval glory. Clerks and tradesmen who had repaired to the seaside for a holiday, mechanics travelling at a distance from their homes in search of employment, as well as the walking gentleman, and leading tragedian, in more than one company of provincial actors, were seized as lawful prize, and carried off to serve the King. The most likely among the younger convicts, who were undergoing a term of penal servitude, were transferred from the hulks to the lower-deck of a battle-ship.[1] It was a sorry prospect for a gallant officer whose early laurels had been won at a time when the British navy was administered by Lord Anson on a very different pattern.

What Keppel saw around him at Portsmouth was discouraging enough; but far more formidable were those unseen dangers which the Board of Admiralty, neglecting all the best traditions of our naval service, had taken no measures to detect and guard against. Lord Camden, who was good at epigrams, had recently told the Peers that the ministers had begun the American war because they supposed the colonists to be cowards, and imagined the French to be idiots. It was a true saying; for Lord North and his colleagues had entirely failed to recognise that France was now governed by very different rulers from those who, at the commencement of the last war, had allowed themselves to be forestalled, surprised, and discomfited by the audacious, if somewhat unscrupulous, alertness of the British Admiralty. That had been the case in the summer of 1755; but in the spring of 1778 the orders which issued from the Council-chamber of Versailles were marked by a foresight and a promptitude which were altogether lacking at Whitehall. Twelve ships of the line, and five frigates, with two strong brigades of infantry on board, lay ready for sea in Toulon Harbour under the

---

[1] In the late autumn of the same year "a petition was signed by a hundred-and-seventy young fellows sentenced to hard labour on the River for divers felonies, praying that they might be permitted to enter the Royal Navy; in consequence of which two lieutenants went on board the hulks at Woolwich, and took down the names of those fit for service, who exceeded the number by which the petition was signed. When the officers went away, the poor fellows gave them three cheers." *Morning Post* for November 1778.

command of the Comte d'Estaing. He sailed on the
fifteenth of April ; and on the fifth of June the naval
authorities in England learned, to their amazement and
confusion, that he was already well on his way across
the Atlantic ocean. Our West Indian islands, great and
small, would be at his mercy unless he was followed,
and caught, by a force more powerful than his own ;
and Vice Admiral the Honourable John Byron was
forthwith ordered off in pursuit of d'Estaing with a
squadron detached from the strength of the Channel
Fleet. Keppel rose to the occasion. He may not rank
in history as a strategist or tactician of the first order ;
but he was conspicuously endowed with that unselfish-
ness which is the noblest, and not the least valuable,
quality of a true warrior. Without hesitation or complaint he made over to Byron no less than fourteen
ships of the line, and gave him, out of his poverty, a
supply of provisions, of ammunition, and, (more especially,) of naval stores and fittings. The contents of the
Portsmouth magazines, which for a long time past had
been allowed to sink very low, were now exhausted ;
and " the tacks and sheets of the Valiant, and other
cordage rove in that ship, and in the Ramilies, then
under Keppel's command, were unrove, and given to
Byron's ships." The materials were scandalously bad ;
but there was no want of hands, and the work was
pushed forward with ceaseless industry. On the ninth
of June Byron weighed anchor, and started on his
voyage towards Western waters. He described his
vessels as wretchedly manned, carrying among their
crews " gaol-birds with gaol fever upon them, and
rigged with second hand, and even twice laid, rope,"
a most unsuitable outfit for an admiral whose ill-luck in
weather became a proverb in the British navy.

The tidings that d'Estaing was at sea fell like a
thunderbolt upon the West Indian interest in the
City of London. But Englishmen who understood the

operations of war found reason to apprehend a much more serious calamity than the temporary loss of Barbadoes, or even of Jamaica; for Sir Henry Clinton had not yet retired from Philadelphia, and his army, and Lord Howe's ships, were in a position of imminent danger. On the twentieth of May the French fleet, which already had got as far west of Gibraltar as Madeira and the Canaries, was hove to for an imposing ceremony. High Mass was performed on board the flag-ship; and then the admiral presented to his captains, assembled on the quarter-deck in full uniform, a passenger whom he introduced as Monsieur Gérard, the representative accredited by the King of France to the Congress of the United States. He announced, amidst rapturous applause, that the war had begun, and that every British vessel was thenceforward to be treated as an enemy. His language portended a headlong velocity of attack;[1] but the action which ensued was tame and tardy. If, within five weeks from that date, d'Estaing had reached the Capes of the Delaware, he would have entrapped Lord Howe's small fleet, and his immense convoy of overloaded transports, in the estuary of that treacherous river. If, on the other hand, he had made straight for New York, nothing could have preserved the city from capture; and, when New York was lost, nothing could have saved Sir Henry Clinton's army. The validity of d'Estaing's excuses for his slow progress across the ocean is still a subject of controversy among French historians. Most certainly, if offered by a British admiral, those excuses were not such as would have satisfied Mr. Secretary Pitt.

D'Estaing was opposed to an antagonist who knew the value of time, and who had been bred from a child on that element to which d'Estaing himself had been transferred at the age of thirty from an exalted position in the land army. When the first note of alarm reached

---

[1] " L'amiral lut à haute voix les instructions qui déclaraient l'ouverture de la guerre, et ordonnaient de courir sus aux vaisseaux de la Grande-Bretagne." Doniol's *Diplomatic Correspondence;* volume III, chapter 5.

Lord Howe his ships were in the Delaware river opposite the quays of Philadelphia, in the heart of a hostile district, with forty leagues of difficult navigation between the anchorage which he then occupied, and the comparative safety of the open sea. The crisis was of a nature to summon forth those capabilities which he possessed in unusual measure. Lord Howe was a bold and skilful leader in battle, and, (where Frenchmen or Spaniards were concerned,) a very willing fighter; but his special talent lay in planning and executing the details of extensive and complicated operations. In the course of the next few weeks a prodigy of labour was accomplished under his personal superintendence. He gathered in his cruisers from Chesapeake Bay, and from distant stations up and down the Atlantic coast. He recalled his ships of the line from New York and Rhode Island. He embarked on his transports, and on his hired merchantmen, three thousand Philadelphian loyalists, with the most valuable of their goods. He received on board the invalids, the wounded, the footsore, and, (in the instance of certain German regiments,) the faint-hearted, of the royal army. He filled up the space that remained with all the ordnance and commissariat stores which he could contrive to carry; and on the eighteenth of June 1778 he commenced his southward voyage. Howe was detained by calms and headwinds among the shoals of the lower Delaware during ten days of frightful heat; but, from the moment that he rounded Cape May, and issued forth into the Atlantic ocean, he came in for the weather he deserved. A favouring breeze carried him in forty-eight hours to Sandy Hook, where he was rejoined by Sir Henry Clinton, who had manœuvred and fought his way across country from Philadelphia at the head of sixteen thousand veteran infantry. Lord Howe ferried over the British army from the Jersey shore to the city of New York, and then fell to work upon his preparations for giving Admiral d'Estaing a suitable reception.

The problem before him was to protect an expanse

of water which, if he himself had been the assailant, he
would have insisted on regarding as an open roadstead,
against an enemy enormously superior to his own force
in weight of metal.[1] Lord Howe's arrangements for the
defence of New York Bay are still quoted as a model
by naval writers; and they found at the time a sincere
admirer in the Comte d'Estaing. On the eleventh of
July the French fleet appeared in view, and anchored
four miles to the south of Sandy Hook. There was
every prospect of a battle resembling those of Copen-
hagen and Aboukir Bay, but with a Nelson on the
defensive. "We expected," wrote a British eye-
witness, "the hottest day that had ever been fought
between the two nations." But when the New York
pilots, who swarmed around d'Estaing's flagship, learned
the draught of the French vessels, they declared that it
was impossible to cross the bar, which was only twenty-
three feet below the surface of the water. A French
lieutenant, who was sent out to take soundings, reported
that he could find nothing over twenty-two feet;
although every good seaman in Howe's squadron, from
the admiral downwards, knew that at spring tides there
were thirty feet on the bar, and that the spring tides
were then at their highest. But behind that bar Lord
Howe's weather-beaten vessels were anchored, at carefully chosen intervals, across the whole breadth of the
navigable channel; and d'Estaing came to the conclusion that, whatever the draught of his own ships was
now, some of them would lie very much deeper in the
water by the time they had spent half an hour within
pistol-range of the English broadsides. He lingered at
Sandy Hook ten days, the last three of which, in the
judgment of Lord Howe, presented conditions "favourable for forcing an entrance"; and then he stood out to
sea, and sailed away from his first, and his most propi-

---

[1] Lord Howe had six sixty-four gun ships, and three of fifty guns, as
against a ninety-gun ship, an eighty-gun ship, six seventy-fours, three
sixty-fours, and one fifty : which, in the number of cannon, made a disproportion of five to eight.

tious, opportunity of testing fortune in that naval battle for which France had been so long preparing.[1]

The well-laid scheme of the French Ministry for striking at the heart of the British power in America had been wrecked by the incapacity of their own agent, and the splendid qualities of the adversary against whom he was matched. The attention of d'Estaing was henceforward transferred to a subsidiary operation, the details of which had already been arranged in concert with General Washington. The large island, on which the town of Newport had been built, was held by a garrison of five or six thousand British soldiers. That island was of prime importance as a naval station. It forbade access by sea to Providence, the official capital of the State of Rhode Island; and it sealed up the entrance of Narragansett Bay, which flanked the line of ocean traffic from Europe to New York, and had been the nursery, and the sanctuary, of the most formidable American privateers which battened upon English commerce. It was, (wrote Admiral Rodney,) the best and noblest harbour on the Atlantic coast, where the whole royal navy could lie at all seasons in perfect security.

Major-General Sullivan was ordered to attack Newport at the head of a very small contingent of regular American infantry and a large host of local militia. It was a service for which Washington should have told off his best troops and his wisest general. Nathanael Greene ought undoubtedly to have been selected for the command of an expedition which he regarded as a crusade for the liberation of his native State. If the conduct of the campaign had been entrusted to that famous and popular New England soldier, the yeomen of Massachusetts and Connecticut, and most assuredly of Rhode Island itself, would have flocked to the scene of action in even greater numbers, would have yielded a more exact

[1] The naval operations on the coast of America, conducted respectively by Howe and d'Estaing, may be followed in the General Map of the American colonies at the end of this Volume.

obedience, and would have remained under arms in un-
diminished strength until the issue had been finally decided. And, again, it was most unfortunate for the
prospects of the Franco-American alliance that the citi-
zen-warrior of the young republic, with whom the French
military and naval authorities were first brought into intimate contact, was the impulsive and hot-headed Sullivan. But the buoyant confidence of the nation and the
army refused to admit even the possibility of disappointment and failure. Greene himself, in ordinary cases a
man of sober expectations, was elated beyond his wont
by the double patriotism of a Rhode Islander and an
American. " You are," (so he told Sullivan,) "the most
happy man in the world. What a child of fortune!
The expedition cannot, I think, fail of success. You
are the first general that ever had an opportunity of co-
operating with the French forces. I wish most ardently
to be with you." His desire was granted ; and he was
attached to Sullivan's army in the twofold capacity of
quartermaster-general, and military chief of a division
comprising half a dozen small battalions of excellent
Continental infantry.

A belief that nothing on that side the Atlantic could
resist the forces of the alliance appeared amply justified when d'Estaing's powerful and well-equipped fleet
brought four thousand picked soldiers of France to the
assistance of Sullivan's army. The besiegers, at the
outset of the affair, showed no lack of vigour and daring.
Two ships of the French line, under the guidance of de
Suffren, a much greater seaman than his admiral, ran
the gauntlet of the British batteries, and anchored in the
inner waters, on the north, and to the rear, of the threatened island. They were followed by several of their
consorts, and, (after a while,) by the entire fleet ; and
then the senior British captain, consenting to an inevitable sacrifice, sank or destroyed five frigates, and many
smaller vessels, which the royal navy, in an approaching
dearth of cruisers, could ill afford to spare. The attack
was pushed as briskly on land as on the water, and gave

promise of a like result. Nathanael Greene, who had planted his head-quarters within a few miles of the paternal forge and saw-mill, was an indefatigable, and most intelligent, provider for all the requirements of the siege ; — although on every third day he was called off from his administrative labours to take his turn as Major-General on duty for the space of twenty-four hours. A great store of intrenching tools had been rapidly and easily collected from a prosperous rural district where agricultural implements of the best quality were everywhere in use. The material wants of the American soldier at last were well cared for. Food was varied and abundant ; and, (what in those days was considered almost as essential as food,) there was a near prospect of rum. Reverting to homely phrases, amidst the associations of his old home, Greene reported in his official correspondence that he was as busy as a bee in a tar-barrel, and that everything would soon be in readiness " to give the enemy a cursed flogging." Sullivan, on the ninth of August, transported his nine thousand Americans across to the island where Newport stood ; while d'Estaing landed his French regiments, and confided them to the care of Lafayette. The British general, Sir Robert Pigot, who had distinguished himself at Bunker's Hill, did everything that any man could have accomplished in his place. But the situation was too hopelessly bad to be mended by the resources at his disposal, and it seemed as if nothing short of a miracle could preserve England from a disaster second only in gravity to the capitulation at Saratoga.

Miracles are always possible in war wherever professional knowledge, and native sagacity, are found in combination with irrepressible energy, and an inspiring sense of public duty. As soon as Lord Howe could ascertain the quarter towards which d'Estaing had sailed, he made signal to weigh anchor, and gain the open sea ; but the wind was dead in his teeth, and five days elapsed before he could cross the bar at Sandy Hook. The time, however, was not wasted, for his strength increased daily. Additional ships of the line, belonging to his own command, rejoined him from Halifax, and from the West Indies; and the first arrivals of Admiral Byron's fleet came straggling in, very much the worse for a heavy gale which had overtaken and scattered them during their voyage across the Atlantic. "Foul-weather Jack" had met with his usual barbarous treatment from that fickle element which his celebrated grandson loved in all its moods. On the ninth of August Lord Howe appeared off the mouth of Narragansett Bay, and the French admiral sallied forth to meet him. It was the right course for a sailor to pursue; but d'Estaing had so much of the military pedant still about him that he did not feel easy until he had re-embarked every man of his four thousand infantry. If it had come to a naval battle, there would have been a horrible butchery among that crowd of helpless landsmen; but sea-sickness soon reduced the poor fellows to a condition of physical misery and prostration which made it a matter of indifference to them whether they were sent to the bottom or not. Before the hostile fleets could come into action they were separated and dispersed by a frightful storm, which raged for fifty hours, damaging the British spars and rigging, and completely crippling the more unlucky, or less dexterously handled, vessels of d'Estaing. Lord Howe, driven far to the southward, took shelter in New York Bay, and used all diligence to refit his battered ships. He worked with such a will that he was out again in little more than a hundred hours; and then he returned to Rhode Island, eager for combat, only to learn that d'Estaing had already come and gone.

The besiegers were in evil case. Their camp had been devastated by the gale which, three quarters of a century afterwards, was still remembered at Newport as "the Great Storm." The windows of the town were encrusted with salt carried inland by the ocean spray; but the British were safely and comfortably lodged

behind those windows, while the Americans were exposed to the full fury of the tempest. The first gusts
laid their tents flat. Trees were falling in every corner
of the encampment. The rain came down in floods;
the provisions were drenched; and it was all that the
more careful soldiers could do to keep some of their
ammunition dry. "I saw for the first time," said one
who was present, "that men were more hardy than
horses." A very great number of animals perished
from exposure; but it took more than a high wind,
and a heavy downpour, to kill Yankee farmers. They
sat crouched on the lee side of the stone walls, which
in Rhode Island served as fences, until the hurricane
subsided; and, with the return of fair weather, their
spirits revived, and their hopes of victory were re-
kindled. When d'Estaing's great flag-ship, under three
jury masts, returned from her conflict with the Atlantic
waves, her arrival was hailed with lively joy by the
American generals; for, even if the French vessels
were not in a condition to manœuvre at sea in line of
battle, they could at all events make good the entrance
of Narragansett Bay against Lord Howe's fleet while
the allied infantry pushed on the siege by land. But
d'Estaing had looked in at Newport only to say he was
on his way to Boston, to repair damages, and repose
his crews; and, to the shame and chagrin of Lafayette,
and the blazing wrath of Sullivan, he announced that
he intended to carry away all his troops with him.

That craven resolve was the death-blow of the
expedition. The departure of the French fleet struck
such a panic among the militia and volunteers that,
(to use General Greene's expression,) they began to
desert in shoals. By the end of the week the full half
of them had gone home to their harvest-work. Those
who stayed with Sullivan were less numerous than the
garrison of the town which he was supposed to be besieging, and he accordingly withdrew from the vicinity
of the British lines to the northernmost corner of the
island. He was closely followed by Sir Robert Pigot;

and there ensued a sharp engagement, in which the Continental infantry, with Nathanael Greene to direct their efforts, maintained the credit of American marksmanship. Next morning came a message from General Washington conveying the intelligence that Sir Henry Clinton was on his way from New York with a reinforcement of British veterans equal in number to the whole of Sullivan's army. There was no time to lose if the Republican general, and all his people, were to avoid the necessity of an ignominious surrender. But the Americans, in the course of that intricate and arduous war, had advanced, or escaped, across more dangerous waters than those which now lay between themselves and safety; and Sullivan was fortunate enough on this occasion to command the services of Colonel Glover's regiment of New England mariners, who had practised their old craft to so much purpose in the retreat from Long Island, and on the night immediately preceding the battle of Trenton. Glover looked to the lading and despatching of the boats; Greene made himself responsible for seeing that no cannon, or stores, were left behind; and the entire force, together with everything which belonged to it, was rapidly and successfully transported to the mainland. Before the close of August the siege of Newport had been finally abandoned; and d'Estaing had anchored his fleet in the recesses of Boston Harbour, where he remained for ten livelong weeks, an unwelcome and unhonoured guest.

The sanguine imagination of the American people had greeted the French alliance as a sure pledge of swift and decisive victory on land and sea. Those fair hopes were already blighted; and the alliance itself seemed withered at the root. Each of the two parties imputed to the other the blame of a disgraceful failure to seize a unique opportunity. Those French colonels and majors who were in d'Estaing's confidence could not please him better than by regaling him with sarcasms uttered at the expense of the Republican army. Even the regular troops, (said one officer,) marched like a horde of Tartars. " I never," wrote another, "witnessed a more burlesque spectacle than the arrival of the militia. I could see plainly that these warriors had no mind to come to blows with the enemy, but had repaired to our camp for the sole purpose of helping us eat our victuals." Sullivan, on the other hand, who had far greater reason to be angry, was fairly beside himself with contemptuous indignation. He issued an Order of the Day denouncing the French admiral in language as forcible as anything in the Declaration of Independence ; and he asserted, roundly and plainly, that the time had come when Americans must show the world that they could hold their own without the assistance of an ally who had so basely deserted them. Those fiery words, which he would have done better to leave unwritten, embodied the almost universal feeling of his compatriots. The national antipathy against France and Frenchmen, which had formerly been more acute in the American colonies than even in the mother-country, was revivified in all its bitterness ; and that sentiment was nowhere more intense, and the expression of it nowhere more unrestrained, than in the city which d'Estaing had chosen as his place of refuge. French naval uniforms had never before been seen in Boston except when their wearers had been brought in as prisoners of war by one of Lord Chatham's frigates ; and the Bostonian populace did not relish the aspect of d'Estaing's officers and sailors parading the streets in the character of naval heroes,— a character which they had done so very little to sustain. Why, (it was asked,) were these Frenchmen idling in Massachusetts when they ought to have been fighting for the common cause in Rhode Island? If their fleet needed repairs, there were plenty of ship-carpenters, and riggers, and rope-makers, out of work in the town of Providence, who would have been only too glad to have been employed in refitting Admiral d'Estaing's vessels. He should have stayed at Newport, at the centre of danger, instead of seeking for an excuse to retire to Boston, two hundred miles further away from the muzzles of Lord Howe's cannon. That was the talk among the rough and outspoken frequenters of Hancock's Wharf, and Griffin's Wharf; and the quayside of Boston had always been a locality where, in a time of public excitement, words were speedily followed by actions. A fierce riot took place, and many French heads were broken, including that of a naval officer of very considerable distinction.

Lord Howe's task was now accomplished. "With the British positions secure, and superiority of force insured for the time being, he gladly turned over his charge, and sailed for home, burning against the Admiralty with a wrath common to all the distinguished seamen of that war." [1] Neglected, and to all appearance forgotten, by the Ministry at home, he had proved, — not for the last time in his glorious career, — that important successes may be obtained against great odds, and with a very small expenditure of gunpowder, by firmness of purpose, by magnificent seamanship, and by an evident readiness to come to close quarters with adversaries who themselves are not over-eager for battle. Lord Howe had begun by taking measures to save his own fleet from being intercepted and destroyed piecemeal. He had rescued the city of New York; he had foiled the attack on Newport; and he had preserved Sir Henry Clinton's army from imminent risk of capture. He

---

[1] These words are taken from the chapter by Admiral Mahan on the "Major Operations of the Royal Navy, 1762–1783," in Clowes's History.

Mahan's vivid and sympathetic narrative of Lord Howe's conduct in the summer of 1778 is an admirable illustration of his own doctrine about the value, and the limits, of hero-worship in the writing of history. "I believe enthusiasm no bad spirit in which to realize history to yourself or others. It tends to bias; but bias can be controlled. Enthusiasm has its place, not only in action, but in writing; quite as much as critical analysis, and judicial impartiality, have theirs. The moment of exaltation gone, the dispassionate intellect may sit in judgment upon the expressions of thought and feeling which had been prompted by the stirring of the mind; but, without this, there lacks one element of true presentation. The height of full recognition for a great event, or a great personality, has not been reached." The above passage occurs in that fine autobiography which bears the inadequate title, "From Sail to Steam."

had, indirectly, and without intending it, accomplished a still greater service for his country. The mutual suspicions and jealousies, which were engendered by the miscarriage in Rhode Island, had taken the heart out of the cordial understanding between France and the United States ; and, for three years to come, no combined operation on a great scale against the military power of Britain was so much as attempted by the land and sea forces of the two allies. At the end of that period George Washington, and French generals and admirals of very different quality from the Comte d'Estaing, united in a well-conceived and vigorously executed enterprise against the army of Lord Cornwallis. The Earl of Sandwich, to the sorrow of England, still remained in office ; and on this second occasion there was no Lord Howe in command on the coast of America, to repair the improvidence, and redeem the blunders, of the Government at home. The event ran its course ; and a signal and irreparable disaster to the British arms proved, beyond all possibility of excuse, that the most negligent administrator who ever sat at the head of the table in the Admiralty Board-room had trusted to chance once too often.

CHAPTER V

THE BATTLE OF USHANT. KEPPEL AND PALLISER.

On the twelfth of June 1778, three days after Admiral Byron sailed from Portsmouth, Keppel himself put out to sea with twenty ships of the line. He was burdened with an immense responsibility. War had not yet been declared between France and England ; and Keppel, as commander of the Channel fleet, was vested with an unlimited discretionary power of action by a government which, if things went wrong, would not scruple to disavow him. His judgment was soon put to the test, for he fell in with a parcel of French cruisers which drew near with the evident intention of watching his movements, and ascertaining the number and rating of his ships. Keppel hoisted the signal for a general chase. The Belle Poule, a French frigate of the most formidable type, made off towards the coast of Brittany with the Arethusa at her heels ; and an engagement ensued the memory of which has attained mythical dimensions in the songs and legends of the two navies. The result of the combat was prophetic of the fighting which took place, all the world over, during the first forty months of that confused and unsatisfactory war. The rigging of the Arethusa was so shot to pieces that she was towed back to the fleet by two of her consorts, while the Belle Poule struggled home to a port of refuge hulled through and through, and her decks strewn with dead and wounded.

Two other French frigates were seized and detained by Keppel. The papers found on board of them, and the particulars elicited from the talk of their officers, threw an unexpected light on the dangers of the situation. Keppel had been specifically informed by the authorities at Whitehall that the Brest fleet consisted of no more than seventeen sail of the line fit for service. " How-

ever confidently that assurance was given," (so he told
the House of Commons,) " I measured them in my own
mind at twenty-four sail; and, in that opinion, I was
determined not to avoid them." But he had failed to
make due allowance for the shortcomings of the Intelligence Department in an Admiralty over which Lord
Sandwich presided. Two and thirty ships of the line,
in far superior condition to his own short-handed and
woefully provided vessels, lay in Brest harbour prepared
to sail at a moment's notice. Even victory, gained by
superhuman prowess against such an overwhelming
inequality of force, would have left the remnant of
Keppel's ships so dismantled and unseaworthy as to be
incapable of further effective action. And a defeat
at sea, — if such an ill-omened word is admissible, —
would have entailed consequences of almost inconceivable gravity; inasmuch as that result, (so a contemporary author wrote,) "owing to the courage of our
commanders, and the urgency of the occasion, could only
have been accomplished by the absolute destruction of
the British fleet."

Everything was at stake for England. Her militiamen had not as yet been converted into soldiers; and
five thousand trained infantry could by no possibility
have been collected to screen London from an invader.
" The protection of the commerce of Great Britain, the
defence of her extensive coasts, the security of her vast
capital, her dockyards and arsenals, — those invaluable
reservoirs of her naval power, in which were included
her present strength and her future hope, — all these
immense objects were committed to the defence of
twenty ships." [1] That was a true statement, but it
was not the whole story; for, (shameful and humiliating to relate,) Admiral the Comte d'Orvilliers had ten
or a dozen frigates to Keppel's three; and two great
fleets of merchantmen from the West Indies and the
Levant, which were expected daily in the Bay of

---

[1] *History of Europe* for 1779; chapter 4.

Biscay, would be at the mercy of the French cruisers if the British ships of the line were temporarily disabled in battle. In the face of those circumstances Keppel subordinated personal inclinations to patriotic duty, and sailed back to Portsmouth with the intention of gathering together every available particle of England's naval strength before, (in the most literal signification of the phrase,) he " tried conclusions " with her adversary. He subsequently declared that he never experienced so deep a melancholy as when he found himself obliged to turn his back on France. His courage, (he said,) had nowhere been put to such a trial as in that retreat; but he was firmly persuaded that, by the course which he then took, he had saved his country.

His country was not unintelligent, nor ungrateful, although no effort was spared in official quarters to distort his motives, and blacken his honour. His reputation was given over to the scurrility of those hireling newspapers which, " from the circumstance of their abuse having been so frequently the prelude to the downfall and disgrace of officers, were considered as having the sanction of authority for their censure and condemnation." [1] " Nauticus," and " Nearchus," and " Richard Forecastle," and a whole tribe of sham-sailors who would have been sea-sick before they got as far down the river as the Isle of Sheppey, jeered at Keppel as an impostor and a poltroon, likened him to Admiral Byng, and threatened him in brutal language with that unlucky officer's fate. But the great majority of Englishmen never for one moment lost faith in his tried valour, and his professional experience and insight. The Government itself was by no means unanimous in distrusting and condemning him. Sandwich, indeed, represented to his colleagues that " party intrigue had so thickened the medium around the Admiral " that he saw double when he was looking at the French fleet; but no one believed his statement of the case. The

[1] *History of Europe.*

King had used his eyes during his recent trip to Portsmouth, and he now laid the blame on the right shoulders. Lord George Germaine, who could not afford to go shares in an unpopularity which did not properly belong to him, let it be generally known that he had exhorted the Cabinet to keep the Admiralty on a level with its duty, and that the consequences which had resulted from his advice being neglected "did not lie at his door." In their secret correspondence, and their intimate talk, the supporters of Government frankly admitted that Keppel's course of action was prudent, and that the cry against him was factitious. "Some one or two merchants," (so a specimen letter runs,) "scheme against Keppel; but the voice of the nation is with him. Lord Sandwich says he is to blame, and that his apprehensions of the superiority of the French fleet are ill-grounded. Keppel stands to his accounts; and I believe *them*."[1] Keppel bore himself with admirable temper, and imposed silence upon the generous indignation of the captains by whom he was surrounded. He gave his whole mind to urging forward his preparations; and he was aided by the hearty support of dockyard officers who were proud to work for him, and by the zealous obedience of his own crews, impatient to be once again on blue water. During the first week of July the simultaneous arrival of the Mediterranean, and the West Indian, merchant fleets replenished his muster-rolls with prime sailors; and on the ninth of the month, a short fortnight after his return to harbour, he put out to sea with thirty ships of the line, determined not to revisit Spithead until he had fought, and gained, a battle.

Our fleet was arrayed in three divisions, of equal force. In the van was Vice Admiral Sir Robert Harland, a veteran who, thirty years back, had wound up the naval operations of a long French war by a splendid feat of arms; and who, twenty years back, had taken part in Boscawen's smashing victory on the southern coast

[1] Lieutenant Colonel Edward Smith to William Eden, July 8, 1778. *Steevens's Collection of Facsimiles* in the British Museum.

of Portugal. Rear Admiral Campbell commanded in the centre. He had been Hawke's flag-captain at Quiberon Bay; and he now had Keppel with him on board the Victory, the only vessel in the British fleet which mounted a hundred cannon. The eighty-gun ship next her in the line carried no less a captain than John Jervis. The rear was in charge of Vice Admiral Palliser, who first went to sea when he was twelve years old, and had been under fire in more actions than he could well remember. A battle was in immediate and certain prospect; for the French had been keenly irritated by the seizure of their frigates, and the circumstances of the combat between the Belle Poule and the Arethusa had stirred their national enthusiasm, and had excited, for the first time for many years, a legitimate pride and confidence in the fighting qualities of their navy.[1] Louis the Sixteenth and his Ministers responded to the demand of public opinion by sending the Comte d'Orvilliers to sea; although they were not very clear as to what they intended him to do when he got there. They had provided him with two separate papers of instructions, one of which, if there is any meaning in words, commanded him to fight, while the other recommended him to run. D'Orvilliers was worthy of serving employers who knew their own minds better, and he did his utmost to reconcile his contradictory orders in the spirit of a gallant man. The last letter which he wrote before leaving harbour informed the minister at Versailles that he should not return to Brest until a full month had elapsed. "Till then," (he said,) "I shall not abandon the field to Admiral Keppel, whatever his strength may be. If he is much my superior in force, I shall endeavour to avoid an engagement on too disproportionate terms; but I am well aware that,

---

[1] Doniol's *Correspondence;* volume III, chapter 40. The crew of the Belle Poule received two months' extra pay; and the widows, who were many, were allotted a provision for life. A rain of promotion fell on the officers; and the Paris journals gave details of their gallant conduct in paragraphs which were copied into the London newspapers.

if the enemy is resolved on fighting, it will be very difficult indeed to baulk him." [1]

Then, and for several years to come, the French fleet was a powerful, and most manageable, instrument in the hands of an able commander. A high standard of seaman-like efficiency, coupled to a manly, and remarkably disinterested, type of character, was very general among the officers. The crews were drawn, under a system of naval registration as equitable as the conditions of enforced service would permit, from hardy mariners employed in the fisheries and in the coasting-trade of the Atlantic sea-board. The cannon were loaded and pointed by marine artillery-men, kept up to their full strength of ten thousand men, and regularly drilled at gun-practice even in time of peace. The French ships of the line were larger than our own vessels of the same class, and built on a better model; and they were taken into action, or kept out of it, with a skill which extorted a tribute of praise from more than one baffled and disappointed British admiral. The most eminent of all naval historians has pronounced that "the superior tactical science of the French" imparted to the War of American Independence those features which specially suited their own national methods of fighting. "The general chase and the mêlée," (so Admiral Mahan writes,) "which marked the actions of Hawke, Boscawen and Anson, were for the most part succeeded by wary and complicated manœuvres, too often barren of decisive results as naval battles." One advantage, however, England still retained, which, in the last resort, was worth all the others together. When they stood to their cannon, stripped from the waist upwards, in a blinding and choking fog of powder-smoke, and on a deck slippery with blood, her sailors almost invariably proved themselves the tougher fellows. The truth was well put by a contemporary journalist of remarkable power. "If our ships," he wrote, "are not, for the whole time

[1] *Histoire de la marine Française pendant la guerre de l'Indépendance Américaine, par E. Chevalier, Capitaine de Vaisseau.*

of engaging, yard-arm to yard-arm, the French will always be found to fire as well as we can; nay, perhaps better. But, when our muzzles are close to their port-holes, they cannot be kept to their guns. We can never expect to take a French ship until we have been some time alongside, and within pistol-shot."[1]

Keppel sighted the French fleet at a point about a hundred miles to the west of Ushant; and the signal for a general chase was thenceforward kept flying at the mast-head of the Victory. During four successive days the British ships, each of them sailing her very best, continued to beat up against the wind in pursuit of an enemy who, if so minded, might have chosen any hour of that time to bring on an engagement. At last, on the morning of the twenty-seventh of July, Admiral d'Orvilliers recognised that battle could no longer be avoided, and he accepted the obligation in handsome style. The hostile fleets sailed past each other in parallel lines, and in opposite directions, discharging their broadsides as fast as they could load and fire. "The ships," (so a contemporary writer observes,) "were frequently changing their antagonists in the course of their progress. If a French ship found herself mauled by a ninety-gun, or a seventy-four gun, vessel she bore it patiently, consoling herself by the certainty of soon sailing past her, perhaps to encounter a sixty-four in her room; and at the worst she knew that, if her sails held, she must soon have run the gauntlet of the fleet." D'Orvilliers lost more men than his adversary; although there were fewer killed and wounded in all his vessels together than on board a couple of French ships in more than one of Nelson's battles. The British men-of-war, on the other hand, were badly damaged in their ropes

[1] Letter of Aratus in the *Evening Post; August* 3, 1778. The horrors of a sea-fight below decks in a closely-packed line-of-battle ship with wooden sides were a severe test of courage. John Adams, when he sailed for Europe in 1778, noted that the frigate which carried him was not furnished with pistols; "which," he said, "she ought to be, with at least as many as there are officers, because there is nothing but the dread of a pistol will keep many of the men to their quarters in time of action."

and sails; and several of them lay in a cluster to lee-
ward, temporarily disabled from action. D'Orvilliers,
well pleased by the success of his march past, directed
the admiral in charge of his van to tack about, and
place the rear of the English line between two fires.
The admiral in question was that Duc de Chartres
who afterwards became Duc d'Orléans, and ended as the
Philippe Egalité of the Revolution. Prince of the
Blood as he was, the liquid which coursed through his
veins was not warmed by the prospect of coming to
closer quarters with an enemy. He paid no attention
to the command, and the hour or two during which
Admiral Keppel might have been taken at a disadvantage soon passed away. Labouring with warlike
ardour, and workmanlike dexterity, the British had
repaired their damages by four o'clock in the afternoon;
and quite enough of a summer's day was left to begin,
and finish, a second battle. Keppel ordered his lieutenants to re-form the line, and renew the combat.
Harland eagerly responded to the call; but Palliser,
to the astonishment of his superior officer, gave no
indication whatever of having perceived the signal.
After another hour had elapsed Keppel sent across to
him a frigate bearing a peremptory summons to bring
all his vessels into action without a moment's delay.
No notice was taken of that urgent message; and the
Commander in Chief, having at length exhausted a
forbearance which had already been unduly prolonged,
signalled the captains of the rear division to leave
Admiral Palliser to his own devices, and take up their
posts in the line of battle. But darkness, which now
closed in, forbade a fight, while it favoured a retreat,
and by daybreak on the twenty-eighth July only three
French ships could be seen from the quarter-deck of
the Victory. The rest of them had disappeared over
the eastern horizon; and, forty-eight hours afterwards,
Admiral d'Orvilliers was once again safe in Brest
harbour.

Palliser was no coward. The Formidable, which car-

ried his flag, had on that very morning been more closely
engaged, and had lost a larger proportion of her crew,
than any other ship in the fleet.   He was as little afraid
of a cannon-ball as Lord George Sackville at Minden
had been afraid of a cavalry-sword or a horse-pistol;
but, like that perverse and ill-advised officer, he had a
fit of the sulks at the most critical moment in the whole
of his career.   Palliser was a member of the Government, who had gone straight from the Treasury Bench
in the House of Commons to serve under a political opponent whom he silently, but bitterly, disliked.   A Lord
of the Admiralty, admitted to the familiarity of Sandwich
and Rigby, he had caught the tone of the Bedfords when
they were abusing Keppel in their cups; and his en-
mity was the more dangerous because the object of it
was unconscious of its existence.   When Keppel, nearly
a quarter of a century back, returned to England after
laying down his command on the North American station,
he had taken his passage home on Palliser's frigate; and
he had ever since regarded himself and his brother-officer
as a pair of loyal comrades, united by a bond of common
memories, and mutual good services.   Augustus Keppel
was never a friend by halves, as his despatch reporting
the circumstances of the battle of Ushant still remains
to testify.   His secretary has described how, "in pen-
ning the letter upon that affair, the admiral and himself
had much trouble in wording it so as to relate facts without conveying any censure upon Sir Hugh Palliser; a
man whom the admiral considered as his friend, and of
whose courage he had no doubt."   Keppel's ink did not
flow as profusely as Burgoyne's.   The whole story of
that eventful week, as he narrated it, was compressed
into a single page of the London Gazette; and the sole
allusion to Admiral Palliser was a word of hearty admiration for his spirited behaviour under fire.

The officer who took Keppel's despatch home carried
a verbal message with it.   "Give my compliments to
Lord Sandwich," (so the admiral charged him,) "and
tell him that I have more to say to him than I think it

proper to put in my public letter." But Sandwich appeared to think that no explanations were required. He wrote to Keppel announcing, in the most explicit terms, the King's full approbation of his conduct; and, on the next occasion when he spoke in public, he assured the House of Lords that, although the French fleet had not been destroyed, " the consequences of the battle were, in every beneficial respect, equal to a victory." The enemy, (he said,) had been cowed and paralysed; and our own commerce was effectually protected, while that of our foes would be almost entirely ruined. Such indeed was the case. Until the ill-omened day arrived when Keppel was ordered to strike his flag, the Channel once more became, and continued to remain, a British water. When he put into Plymouth to refit his fleet, before going once more in search of an adversary who took good care never again to meet him, he was greeted, by high and low, with an enthusiasm which proved that he retained his hold upon the affection of his compatriots. The general feeling was pleasantly expressed in a letter written by the wife of the peer whose beautiful domain overlooked that noble harbour. Lady Mount Edgecumbe professed herself delighted to think that, as long as the ships lay at Plymouth, it would be her duty to attend upon Admiral Keppel, and a score of his post-captains. " I feel proud," as she told a friend, " to be sutler to the fleet. This place is thrown open to them every day; and, if the last blade of grass would comfort the lowest of their men, he would have it. I wish with all my heart you was here at this moment; — thirty sail of the line now lying under a terrace of shrubs, as if only to ornament our park. Whenever our fleet sails again I shall remain on my knees as long as they are in sight in prayers for their success." Lord Mount Edgecumbe, (the lady added,) was so busy attending to the wants of his brother-officers that she could not get at him to frank her letter.[1]

[1] Lady Mount Edgecumbe to the Countess of Harcourt; August 2, 1778.

While Keppel was looking around on the high seas for the enemies of England his own detractors were hard at work in London. All recipients and expectants of ministerial favours were sneering at his tactics, and whispering reflections on his valour; and all newspapers in the pay of the ministry abounded with paragraphs cleverly and craftily framed to discredit the reputation of the Commander in Chief by pointing to Sir Hugh Palliser as the real and only hero of the recent battle. It was a method of controversy which did no good to Palliser; for it ran directly counter to that public opinion of the naval service by which, on questions of professional merit and demerit, the national judgment is ultimately guided. These misdirected eulogies, and malicious insinuations, were intensely distasteful to hundreds of officers who had fought at Ushant; and there were those among them who gave expression to their resentment. The true story soon got abroad in the world; and Palliser, who had not Keppel's self-control, was hurried by the consciousness of his unpopularity into a grave breach of discipline. He sent his commanding officer a prepared document, which he required him to sign and publish, asserting, as a matter of fact, that his calling Admiral Harland, and Admiral Palliser, into his wake on the evening of the twenty-seventh July was not for the purpose of renewing the combat then and there. When this extraordinary proposition was rejected, Palliser inserted in a morning journal, under the authority of his own name, an account of the battle which, if uncontradicted and generally believed, would be ruinous to the honour and career of Keppel. On the second of December, 1778, the subject was raised in the House of Commons, and was treated by Keppel briefly, and with studied moderation. He confessed to have been greatly surprised when an officer under his command, against whom he had made no accusation, addressed the public through the newspapers in a manner which tended to render him odious and despicable in the eyes of his countrymen; and he informed the

House that the signal for coming into the Victory's wake was flying, unobeyed by Palliser, "not in the evening only, but from three in the afternoon until eight at night." He had refrained, (he added,) from bringing any charge against the Vice-Admiral because he had manifested no want of the courage which was the most essential quality of a British seaman; but he begged to inform the Noble Lord, who presided over the Admiralty, that he never could again sail in company with that gentleman until the matter in question had been thoroughly and satisfactorily explained.

The opportunity for explanation came in a most unexpected shape. On the eleventh December Sir Hugh Palliser informed Parliament that he had taken steps to vindicate himself, not by demanding an enquiry into his own conduct, but by bringing his superior officer to trial "for having lost a glorious opportunity of doing a most essential service to the State, and for having tarnished the honour of the British navy."[1] He had, (he said,) in the course of that morning exhibited five capital articles of charge against Admiral Keppel; and the Board at Whitehall had in consequence ordered a Court-Martial. Keppel, in the discussion of the previous week, had requested the House to let him read from a written paper, because he was in poor health and out of spirits, had seldom before spoken in public, and could not trust his memory. But he needed no preparation now. In a few sentences, — every one of which, according to the official report, was followed by "an almost general plaudit," — he begged his well-wishers in the House of Commons to throw no difficulties in the way of the trial. The charge, (he said,) attacked both his life and his fame; and he must insist upon its being brought to an issue, although he lamented the mischiefs that it might occasion. Thank God, he was the accused, and not the accuser! He had been called out to serve his country at a very critical period; he had performed his duty

[1] Those were the exact expressions used in the short paragraph which summed up the list of charges.

to the best of his ability; he could not think of voting on a question which so nearly concerned himself; he declined to say a syllable more; and he should forbear, and retire from the debate.[1]

All who heard him were strangely moved. His friends, (we are told,) had not given him credit for such powers, and were surprised by the majesty and grace with which he spoke; and those who were least his friends admired the dignity of his action, "and thought his homely figure was shot up into heroic stature."[2] Keppel walked out, and left Palliser face to face with a crowded House of Commons where every man's hand was against him. He had better have been in his flagship the Formidable, alone and unsupported, in the middle of the French fleet. "He had the mortification," (so a contemporary relates,) "to hear his conduct openly, and without reserve, condemned by every gentleman, of whatever side and party, who spoke on the occasion."[3] But the attention and wrath of the assembly were after a time diverted to another quarter. Admiral Pigot, a veteran of forty-four years' standing, confessed his wonder at a Court-Martial having been sanctioned with such precipitation in the case of an officer of Mr. Keppel's rank, services, and professional character. Thereupon Lord Mulgrave, speaking for the Government, asserted that the Admiralty had no choice in the matter; because, whenever a complaint was preferred, the Board was constitutionally bound to receive it, and to give the necessary directions for proceeding with the trial. Pigot, on behalf of the navy, exclaimed against the notion that if a discontented post-captain, — and indeed, according to Lord Mulgrave, if a foolish lieutenant, or a paltry midshipman, — thought fit to trump up an accusation of cow-

---

[1] *Parliamentary History;* volume XX, page 57.

[2] *Last Journals;* 11 December, 1778.

[3] *History of Europe in the Annual Register.* "We had yesterday," (wrote Richard Fitzpatrick to his brother Lord Ossory,) "the most interesting debate I ever remember to have heard. The House was violently disposed to Keppel, who spoke like a man inspired; and no tool was bold enough to venture a word in favour of Palliser."

ardice, or neglect of duty, against the greatest naval
commander of his day, that officer must be brought
home at the first convenient opportunity, and placed on
trial for his life.[1] Sir William Meredith, who formerly
sat at the Board of Admiralty, assured the House that
he, for his part, had without hesitation quashed a frivo-
lous and malicious charge brought by a quarrelsome
subordinate against his own captain. General Conway,
and General Keppel, protested that the theory of an
obligatory Court-Martial, as propounded from the Treasury Bench, would be subversive of all discipline if applied to the army. Burke denounced the monstrous
doctrine on grounds of public policy and natural equity;
and Dunning, the greatest practising lawyer then alive
in England, summed up an argument of rare lucidity
and precision by declaring himself amazed to hear such
absurdity obtruded upon the good sense, and the discernment, of the House of Commons. There was not
an educated man inside or outside Parliament who, on
the evidence before him, had any doubt whatever that
the whole plot had been concocted between the Naval
Lord of the Admiralty, who laid the accusation, and the
First Lord of the Admiralty, who granted the Court-
Martial. The common people took a short road to the
same conclusion, and at once, and with one accord,
rushed to the belief that "Jemmy Twitcher," who told
tales against Wilkes, had put up one of his underlings
to tell tales against Keppel.[2]

The action of the Government was fraught with mani-

[1] Wedderburn, who had recently become Attorney-General, on this occasion concurred in Lord Mulgrave's view of the law ; but, three months
afterwards, he confessed to the House of Commons that he had been entirely in the wrong. "He was now," (he said,) "as ready to acknowledge that the Board of Admiralty had a right to direct, refuse, or delay
Courts-Martial as he was, when the question was first agitated, to state his
doubts, and give a conditional opinion that no such power existed."

[2] Lord Sandwich had never lost the nickname earned by his betrayal
of Wilkes. According to an anecdote which, half a generation after that
occurrence, was going the round of the newspapers, "a man of learning
and abilities, when dining with Lord Sandwich, asked him why he was
called Jemmy Twitcher. 'Why, for no reason in the world,' answered his

fold scandals and dangers; and the most disastrous of all its consequences was the disturbing effect produced upon the temper of our navy at the outset of a naval war of formidable character, and of vast dimensions. A cruel and treacherous wrong had been inflicted upon a man who was the idol of the service. Keppel was a good ship-mate, without a taint of jealousy or self-seeking; hospitable, and generous to profusion; a true aristocrat, homely and unpretentious in manners, and with a kindly heart. Those are the qualities which sailors love; and Keppel's brother officers, who were no fair-weather comrades, were profoundly moved by a sincere apprehension that he stood in peril of his life. Some few days before the Court-Martial sat at Portsmouth a London newspaper which was believed, (and with good reason,) to be in the secrets of the Ministry, pointedly reminded its readers that at the beginning of the last war our affairs bore an unpromising aspect; but that, as soon as Admiral Byng had been brought to his account, we speedily became victorious in every quarter of the globe. Keppel's friends had been ill-pleased with his report upon the battle of Ushant. They had reckoned it " obscure and weak, and dictated by his extreme tenderness and desire of saving Palliser," and they were all the more shocked when the man whom Keppel, at imminent risk to his own reputation, had shielded from deserved punishment, stepped forward as his accuser.[1]

The patience of our naval officers, which Sandwich had long and sorely tried, was at length exhausted. Their sense of justice was revolted, and their self-

Lordship. 'Nay, my Lord,' said the divine, 'I am sure there must be some reason; for I see you so named every day of my life.' Relief most opportunely arrived in the shape of a pudding, of which his Lordship put a large slice on the parson's plate, saying : 'Eat your pudding, Doctor, and hold your tongue.'" Whatever the story may be worth, it is typical of the method usually employed by Sandwich for stopping the mouths of the clergy.

[1] This feeling was characteristically expressed by old Admiral Campbell. "The rascal!" (so he styled Palliser). "He knows that Keppel has his head in his pocket."

respect wounded. "Seamen," so Walpole remarked, "by the element they live on, are less exposed than others to the corruptions of the world ; and those simple men discovered a manly integrity that startled the Court." Lord Hawke, (so the story ran,) had been requested to preside at the Court-Martial ; but he replied that he would sooner cut off his hand than be accessory to such a trial. With courage hardly inferior to that which he exhibited at Quiberon Bay he handed in a memorial to the King, embodying a thoughtful and powerful remonstrance against the course taken by the Board of Admiralty. Twelve senior admirals, several among whom were warm supporters of Lord North, affixed their signatures to the document. The Ministerial journalists, writing after their kind, railed at them as Quakers and old wives ; but the list of names included the most famous fighting men of two glorious wars. Another petition, to the same effect, was circulated among the post-captains, and subscribed by many of their number, until Keppel imposed his veto on the project, insisting that, as the matter had now gone so far, his conduct must be fully investigated, and laid before the public in its right colours. His friends, more uneasy about him than he was himself, lost no opportunity of testifying to the value which they set upon his welfare and safety. Admiral Pigot represented to Parliament that Keppel, (who indeed was seriously ill,) would run a risk of life if the Court-Martial was held in the crowded and stifling cabin of a man-of-war, to and from which he would be conveyed in an open boat, day after day, during a long portion of the most inclement season of the year. Pigot's view was earnestly enforced by Lord Howe, who was now back in England from New York and Rhode Island ; and a Bill, enabling the trial to take place on land, was rapidly carried into law. The Ministers indicated their dislike of the proposal; but the feeling was such, both in the Commons and in the Lords, that they did not venture to call for a division in either House. It had already been brought home to

Keppel's enemies that, if a hair of his head was touched, there were hundreds of thousands of Englishmen, of all ranks and classes, who would know the reason why.

No stupider thing had been done by any Government since the impeachment of Doctor Sacheverel. For five livelong weeks the attention of the whole country was concentrated upon the chamber in the Governor's House at Portsmouth where the Court-Martial held its sittings. Reports of the trial filled the newspapers to the exclusion of other topics; and the demeanour of the judges, and the character and credibility of the witnesses, were handled with a freedom which showed that the Opposition journalists had no fear of a Contempt of Court before their eyes. Keen and universal as was the public interest, there was little difference of opinion, or divergence of sympathy. "The whole stream of all men, and all parties, runs one way;" wrote Edward Gibbon; and that way was in favour of the accused, and execration of the prosecutor. Keppel's friends rallied round him to the neglect of their own affairs, and with a supreme indifference to their own comfort and convenience. Lord Rockingham, and many of his leading adherents, lived in lodgings at Portsmouth all the time that the trial lasted. The town contained so many members of both Houses that, according to Lord Shelburne's calculation, a respectably sized parliament might have met for despatch of business on board one of the three-deckers. The Dukes of Cumberland and Gloucester, of Portland, Richmond, and Bolton, were assiduous in their attendance in court; and a greater man than any Royal Highness, or ex-Prime Minister, did not once leave Keppel's side until the protracted ordeal was over. "I went to that place," (said Edmund Burke,) "in an agony of mind at so strange a thing so strangely appointed upon so meritorious and beloved a friend; but I went in resignation, and the fullest trust in the Almighty defence of the innocent." [1]

[1] Burke's regard for Keppel was not a transient sentiment. Seventeen years afterwards, in the *Letter to a Noble Lord*, he once more described

No precaution was neglected to avert a catastrophe which would have thrown half the kingdom into mourning. Counsel were not allowed to examine witnesses, or to address the Court; but Admiral Keppel was assisted by legal advisers who were no ordinary practitioners. His general line of defence was carefully planned by Dunning himself, aided by another notable Whig barrister, "honest Jack Lee," with his strong parts and rough manners, who still wore the stuff gown, inasmuch as the title and rank of King's Counsel were exclusively given by political favour. The every-day details, and the unexpected turns and incidents, of the proceedings at Portsmouth were watched by the Honourable Thomas Erskine, a young advocate who had recently elevated himself from briefless obscurity to great employment, and to a reputation which already was nothing short of fame. His career had been assured by a single speech before the Court of King's Bench, in which he had exposed the abuses of Greenwich Hospital to public reprobation, had bearded Lord Sandwich, and had respectfully, but resolutely and successfully, disputed the ruling of Lord Mansfield. It is related in Lord Campbell's Lives of the Chancellors how, "from the first day to the last of Admiral Keppel's trial, Erskine exerted himself for his client with unabated zeal and with consummate discretion. He suggested questions, which were put in writing, and he composed the speech which Lord Keppel delivered on the merits of the case."

The trial began on the seventh of January 1779, before a court composed of five admirals and eight captains. All the approaches to the Governor's House

his state of mind during the Portsmouth trial. "I ever looked on Lord Keppel as one of the greatest and best men of his age; and I loved and cultivated him accordingly. He was much in my heart; and I believe I was in his to the last beat. With what zeal, and anxious affection, I attended him through that his agony of glory!" And then Burke went on to say that "if, to the eternal disgrace of this nation, things had taken a different turn to what they did," he should have attended Keppel through the final scene on the quarter-deck with no less good will, and more pride than he felt at his triumphant acquittal.

were thronged by sailors, who greeted Keppel with lusty and reiterated cheers. On the benches inside long rows of Earls and Viscounts were packed shoulder to shoulder with such Commoners as Charles Fox, and Sir George Savile. But the scene was no holiday spectacle; for the accuser was in fierce earnest, and his train had been carefully laid. One of the judges discovered, by a happy chance, that some leaves had been extracted from the log-book of the Formidable, and a doctored account of the battle inserted in their place between the covers. All trace of the signals from the mast-head of the Victory in the afternoon of the twenty-seventh July had consequently disappeared from the official record of the vessel which carried Admiral Palliser's flag. This drastic falsification of essential evidence had been engineered by the Master of the Formidable, unknown to his own captain, but with the cognizance of the prosecutor, and of the prosecutor's solicitor and advising counsel; and, as the trial advanced, it was ascertained that the log-books of other ships in Palliser's division had been treated in the same fashion. The Master of the Ramilies, on being closely questioned by the Court, found no better excuse to offer in the case of that vessel than a suggestion that the missing pages had been probably torn out by some of the young gentlemen on board. None of the captains were privy to the conspiracy except Alexander Hood of the Robust, who admitted that, after he heard talk of a probable Court-Martial, he had struck out of his log-book all allusions to Admiral Keppel's signals for re-forming line of battle in the wake of the Victory.[1] A pitiless cross-examination, conducted by such masters of the art as Lee and Dunning, would have dragged the whole black story to light, and involved all the accomplices, high and low, in shame and humiliation; but Keppel had no mind to defend himself by branding and ruining others. He haughtily refused, as Commander

[1] Captain Alexander Hood afterwards became Viscount Bridport. He was the younger brother of Samuel, Viscount Hood.

in Chief, to engage in a contest of wits with the Master of a man-of-war; and he listened to the confession of the captain of the Robust with sorrow rather than with resentment. "Mr. President," he said, "as that alteration in Captain Hood's log-book affects my life, I shall ask him no more questions;" and, with singular generosity, he expressed his personal belief that the mutilation of the record had been undertaken for the purpose, not of criminating him, but of exculpating Sir Hugh Palliser.

Keppel lost nothing by his magnanimity; for his judges, with sailor-like directness, took the management of the case into their own hands. When the prosecutor complained that they put leading questions to his witnesses, several of them called out together that they had come to do justice, and, under the help of Heaven, they would see that justice was done. Over the space of twenty days a long procession of captains from the Channel Fleet appeared before the Court; and all of them spoke out like men of feeling and honour. Captain Marshall, the first witness whom Palliser called, was asked whether the accused had performed any act unbecoming a flag-officer. "No, as God is my judge!" was the instant reply. Next came Sir William Burnaby, who volunteered the statement that Admiral Keppel had always pressed sail, and given every proof of a desire to bring the French to action. If such was the evidence for the prosecution, it may well be believed that the witnesses for the defence were not backward. Sir Robert Harland, when interrogated as to what would probably have occurred if he had been ordered by Admiral Keppel to renew the battle without waiting for Palliser, replied bluntly that he should have obeyed the signal, and that the French would have deserved to be hanged if they had not captured him, and the whole of his division. Harland was then asked whether the British fleet gave any appearance of flying from the enemy. "Oh, fie! No!" was the veteran's answer.[1]

[1] In the *Last Journals* this exclamation is erroneously attributed to Admiral Campbell.

The case was clenched by the testimony of an officer whose established character for professional science and capacity gave sure promise of a brilliant future. Captain Jervis, of the Foudroyant, declared it as his opinion that, during the whole time the French fleet was in sight, Admiral Keppel had displayed a naval skill, and a bold enterprise, which would be the subject of his own admiration and imitation as long as he lived. He indicated, not obscurely, his view of Palliser's conduct on the afternoon of the twenty-seventh July ; — conduct which indeed stands out in notable contrast to the support long afterwards received by Jervis himself from that Commodore Nelson who led his rear ships in the battle off Cape St. Vincent. There could be only one end to such an investigation. On Thursday the eleventh of February the Court unanimously and honourably acquitted Admiral Keppel of the several articles contained in the charges exhibited against him, and gave him back his sword, with the expression of a hope "that he would ere long be called forth by his Sovereign to show it once more in the defence of his country."

As soon as the verdict had been pronounced, Keppel, standing between the Duke of Cumberland and Sir Robert Harland, showed his sad and pensive face to an enormous multitude which was fairly beside itself with delight. A banquet, with a ball to follow, was improvised in his honour by the Captains of the men-of-war in harbour; and the members of the Court-Martial attended the festival as willing guests. There was hearty rejoicing among the shipwrights in all the Government establishments. Since the day when Keppel took over the command of the Channel Fleet they had come nearer being overworked than ever before in the course of their easy lives; but none the less they loved and admired their taskmaster. Plymouth, in particular, commemorated his acquittal by a pageant on such a scale as the dockyard had never witnessed. A perfect army of artisans and mechanics tramped along in endless files, with gilded mallets, and saws and axes painted blue, (for blue was Keppel's colour,) escorting a model of the Victory carried shoulder-high, and singing in triumph to the music of bands interspersed in the procession.   When night fell, the vicinity was ablaze with torches and rockets; and the special feature of the occasion was a huge bonfire built of bundles of chips from Government timber, one of which formed the daily perquisite of every workman in the yard.   As the news travelled through the kingdom a roar of exultation went up from the inland cities and market-towns, and from many of the larger villages.   Exeter and Gloucester, York and Norwich, led the way; while Bristol, Newcastle, Whitby, Fowey, and Monkwear-mouth, — and all other ports, small or large, where sailors congregated, with the solitary exception of Liverpool, — vented their gladness and relief after the accepted English fashion.   Everywhere the windows were decked, and the streets illuminated, and the cathedral-bells and the church-bells rang their merriest peals; and the regiments of the line were drawn out in parade to fire a volley, and display their sympathy with the sister service.   There was roast beef and strong beer for all comers, and " a genteel entertainment" provided by the Mayor and Corporation, or by the officers of the Militia, where "the principal inhabitants" drank to the health of the Admiral, the prosperity of the Navy, and the expectation that Malice and Cowardice would for ever be banished from this Kingdom.   The items of the programme varied in the several localities; but Sir Hugh Palliser was always hanged, and afterwards burned, in effigy with a log-book tied to his neck; — sometimes alone, and sometimes with Captain Hood and Lord Sandwich dangling in his company.   If more noise was made in one place than another, it was in the borough of Windsor, which Keppel represented in Parliament, and where cannon boomed, and horns sounded, all through the hours of darkness.   The principal inhabitant of Windsor, fortunately for himself, was out of hearing, fifteen miles away in the Queen's House at the end of the water in St. James's Park, — the house which now goes by the name of Buckingham Palace.

Palliser, foreseeing the result of the Court-Martial, drove out of Portsmouth at five in the morning of the eleventh February; but the tidings reached London before him, and it was with difficulty that he escaped from the rough attentions of an angry group of by-standers, and sought sanctuary in his official residence behind the railings of the Admiralty. At midnight, as if by magic, the whole city was lit up at lavish expense, and with startling effect; for most of the great London mansions belonged to friends of Keppel; and even people who cared little about him knew better than to leave their windows dark. Every pane of Lord George Germaine's glass was broken; and the mob stormed the house in Pall Mall where Sir Hugh Palliser had recently dwelt, but which now contained no inmates to be frightened, and not much furniture to be destroyed. A story runs, (which no Whig has ever been strait-laced enough to question or to contradict,) that Charles Fox, and the Earl of Derby, and two or three other young men of quality, who had been drinking deep at Almack's, suddenly bethought themselves of making a tour of the streets at the hour of three in the morning. They fell in with a stray Duke, a supporter of the Government, who on this occasion had placed fun before politics, and was enjoying himself as much as any glazier or tallow-chandler in the crowd. The whole party made for Whitehall as fast, and as straight, as they could walk. Refusing to be conciliated by a row of lamps with which, as a concession to public sentiment, the screen of the Admiralty courtyard had been decorated, they burst in the gate, and proceeded to assail Sir Hugh Palliser's windows. There was terror and perturbation inside the building; and Lord Sandwich, and his mistress, escaped half-dressed through the private door which, up till a very few years ago, afforded access from the

Admiralty garden to the Horse Guards Parade. A more dangerous class of rioters visited Downing Street, and forced their way into the Prime Minister's house; but they were taken in rear by the military, and a dozen or two of the ringleaders were captured, and hauled away to prison.[1]

During a full week to come the citizens wore blue favours, and the livery-servants went about with blue shoulder-knots; while night after night the bonfires flared as brightly, and the cannon in front of Sir George Savile's house in Lincoln's Inn Fields thundered as loudly, as ever. Quiet people began to think that they would never get to sleep before four in the morning again. The Londoners, it is true, were in high good humour, and there no longer was a prospect of any serious disturbance. Elderly gentlemen, who remembered the Excise mobs, and the Wilkes mobs, declared that the Keppel mobs were " so tame that you might stroke them." Lord Weymouth and Lord George Germaine, however, who took a grave view of the situation, called out the Footguards, and implored King George to remove himself and his family to the comparative security of his house in Kew Gardens. It was pleasant, (said Horace Walpole,) to see those Ministers, who had condemned so many American towns to the flames, terrified out of their composure by a few squibs and crackers. In a great capital where there existed no drilled police force to stand between the excesses of popular violence, and the terrible remedy of a military execution, it was of immense importance that the

[1] Earl Russell, writing with a twinkle in his eye, relates that the Honourable Thomas Grenville, who subsequently was known as the most staid and decorous of statesmen, was, a partner in the frolic. Two years afterwards Lord North brought the story up against Charles Fox in the neatest style of House of Commons raillery. " Had the Honourable Gentleman," (the Prime Minister asked,) " forgot the temper of the times when the trial of Admiral Keppel was over ? Had it totally slipped his memory that the town was in disorder for three nights together? Had the Honourable Gentleman forgot that he and his friends were obliged to go out early in a cold, raw, February morning, to endeavour to quell the tumult, and disperse the mob?" *Parliamentary History;* Feb. 1, 1781.

authorities responsible for the preservation of order should not be susceptible to panic; and most fortunately, — as was soon to be made manifest during the Gordon riots, a much more alarming crisis in the history of London tumults, — there was not a man living who possessed a cooler head, and firmer courage, than the King of England. His Majesty, with a touch of scorn which well became him, laughed at the notion of running away from an imaginary revolution, and ordered his Guards back to barracks. One wretched lad was singled out from all the culprits to be tried on a capital charge as having been present at the attack on Sir Hugh Palliser's house; but Charles Fox pleaded for him in Parliament with the eloquence of undisguised and unabashed sympathy; and Lord North, who was good nature itself, directed his Attorney-General to enter a *Nolle Prosequi.*

The thanks of the House of Commons were voted to Keppel "for his distinguished courage, conduct, and ability in defending the kingdom, and for effectually protecting its trade, as far as his command extended." A Ministerial newspaper reported that, when the question was put, "the ayes were thundered with such a combination of voices as made the affirmation sound like the assent of some interposing deity."[1] Four days afterwards the Peers unanimously expressed their appreciation of Admiral Keppel's services in the same form of words; and on that afternoon he arrived at his town-house amidst a prodigious concourse of spectators, who lined the whole road from the suburb of Kensington to Audley Square. The crowd repeatedly attempted to unharness his horses, and drag him in triumph through London; but his carriage was driven "with such velocity and judgment as to defeat all their efforts." Soon after his return he put forth a handbill proclaiming his extreme desire that the further continuation of the illuminations should be stopped, as being burdensome

---

[1] *Morning Post;* February 13, 1779.

and expensive to many worthy people. His attitude
on this point was quite in character. Keppel was a
sturdy Whig; — and considering how the Government had
used him, he could not very well be anything else : — but
he regarded himself as the servant of his country, and
was not ambitious to be the figure-head of a party, or
an idol of the multitude. He had no wife to await his
home-coming; but his mother was at hand to greet him.
Lady Albemarle, who was the daughter of the first Duke
of Richmond, and therefore grand-daughter of Charles
the Second and grand-aunt of Charles Fox, was still,
at seventy-five years of age, a bright element in private
society, and a graceful and imposing figure on occasions
of public ceremony. She had watched the career of
Augustus Keppel, since he first "went foreign" as a
boy of ten, with ever increasing pride and satisfaction;
although the mother and the son had seen much less
of each other than they both desired. His trips on
shore, (so his biographer relates,) had been almost
limited to the brief intervals of hauling down his pennant
on one ship, and hoisting it on another. Lady Albemarle was very miserable while the Court-Martial held
its sittings. She was not greatly moved by the peril of
death in which, according to the Government journals,
her Admiral stood ; for to that form of anxiety she was
well accustomed. There had been long periods of time,
in the course of the last forty years, during which she
had never opened a *London Gazette* without the knowledge that one or another of her sons, and sometimes all
three together, had their lives in jeopardy from bullets
and cannon balls. But she had been tortured by her
fear lest the verdict of the Portsmouth Court might
inflict a slur upon the family honour. That apprehension was now dissipated. Keppel's reputation had
been cleared, and his popularity established as a
national article of faith. After the lapse of three
more years his mother had the immense satisfaction
of seeing him appointed First Lord of the Admiralty
in substitution for the Earl of Sandwich.

Keppel sent John Lee two bank-bills for five hundred guineas each, and the same to Dunning; but the money was returned in both cases, accompanied by letters assuring him that his friends asked no reward except the privilege of serving him. From Erskine, who was of an age to be his son, Keppel would take no denial. The young advocate had been living very sparely ever since he joined that English bar of which he was destined to be the most brilliant ornament; and he made no secret of his exultation over his great fee of a thousand guineas, and his heart-felt gratitude to the most generous of clients. Henceforward, (he said,) he could speak in Court without seeming to feel his little children plucking at his robe, and crying, "Now, father, is the time to get us bread." Keppel commissioned Sir Joshua Reynolds to paint four portraits of himself, and gave them to Burke, Dunning, Lee, and Erskine; nor is that circumstance the only link between the Portsmouth Court-Martial and contemporary British art. The Wedgwood manufactory was then at the summit of its renown; and the two principal managers were keen opponents of the Ministry, and ardent partisans of Keppel. The Admiral was persuaded, after a display of characteristic reluctance, into giving them permission to reproduce his bluff and benevolent features for the contemplation of his fellow-countrymen; and the Wedgwoods found no difficulty in disposing of thousands upon thousands of busts, and cameos, and seals, — and copies of a medallion, in high relief, inferior to hardly any specimen of modelling in blue and white which ever issued from their famous workshop.[1]

It was brought to the King's knowledge that Charles Fox had prepared a Resolution, called by the curiously

[1] Mr. Bentley told Mr. Wedgwood that he intended to present a ring, or polished seal, of Keppel's head "to each of the thrice-worthy Court-Martial." *Privately published Letter from Thomas Bentley to Josiah Wedgwood;* Etruria, February 25, 1779.

One of the four presentation portraits of Admiral Keppel is now in the long English room of our National Gallery. It ought by rights to be hung close to the picture of his mother.

inappropriate title of a Humble Address, requesting that His Majesty, "in consideration of the honour of the British navy, and in order to prevent those jealousies and animosities which must necessarily arise among his officers whilst they were liable to be associated in service with a person judged guilty of a malicious and ill-founded accusation, would be graciously pleased to remove Sir Hugh Palliser from all his military employments." Sandwich, alone among his colleagues, proposed to fight the matter out in Parliament; but George the Third insisted that his Ministers had been sufficiently discredited already, and that Palliser must be thrown overboard.[1] The King acknowledged that the cry against the unhappy officer did not proceed only from a faction, but that moderate men of all parties were naturally shocked at his having brought a capital charge without the smallest appearance of being able to justify his grievous allegations.[2] Lord North, accordingly, informed the House of Commons that Sir Hugh Palliser had resigned his Lieutenant-Generalship of the Marines, his Lordship of the Admiralty, and his Governorship of Scarborough; that he had vacated his seat in Parliament; and that, as there were several circumstances of a criminating nature against him, the Government had directed an investigation by Court-Martial. The trial was conducted on board the Sandwich man-of-war in Portsmouth harbour. Keppel refused to act as prosecutor, and earnestly, though vainly, begged to be excused from attending as a witness. The First Lord of the Admiralty, unless he was greatly belied, took infinite pains to pack the tribunal; but the case was so strong against Palliser that he had a narrow escape from ruin. There was a division of opinion among his judges with regard to the

[1] " I believe," (the King wrote,) " you will find no one but Lord Sandwich against this step. As it seems inevitable, I own I think it wiser to do it spontaneously than to be drove to it." George the Third to Lord North; Feb. 13, 1779.
[2] George the Third to Lord North; Feb. 19, 1779.

verdict, and visitors had to be turned off the deck of the Sandwich in order to prevent them from overhearing the clamour of angry voices in the cabin below. The dispute ended in a compromise, and Palliser's acquittal was announced to him by the Court in very grudging terms. Little interest was shown in the trial by the public at large. The English people had broken Palliser's windows in his character of an informer; but they felt no desire whatever to have him, or any other of their admirals, shot. Palliser applied to be reinstated in all the offices which he had resigned under pressure from the Cabinet; but to grant such a request, made by such a petitioner, was beyond the courage of any Prime Minister. It was as much as the House of Commons could endure when, as a solace for his disappointment, he was made Governor of Greenwich Hospital; and there, — among Lord Sandwich's contractors, and meat-inspectors, and hangers-on of various ranks and occupations, — he passed the remainder of his days in congenial company.[1]

[1] Fox moved a Resolution censuring the appointment, which was likewise condemned by Burke in an animated and closely reasoned speech. They took a hundred and fifty members into the lobby with them.

CHAPTER VI

BRITISH COMMERCE.   FOX AND SANDWICH.   THE
ENEMY IN THE CHANNEL.

THE immense unpopularity of Lord Sandwich was
undoubtedly aggravated by the notorious scandals of
his private life, and by his disregard for the rights, and
the self-respect, of other men with whom he came in
contact; but England had a heavy account against him
in a matter more intimately connected with the national
welfare.   Since the Colonial rebellion broke out, in the
early part of 1775, the American privateers, and the
cruisers of the United States Navy, — which were little
larger than privateers, and quite as intent on the main
chance, — had made prize of more than a thousand of
our trading vessels.   After the European Powers took
part in the conflict the annual average of our losses by
capture rose to nearly six hundred ships; and, before
the war ended, almost exactly three thousand British
merchantmen had fallen into the hands of an enemy.[1]

The   full   signification   of   such   figures   may   be
estimated from the effect which a single misfortune of
this class produced upon the most stable and flourishing
of all our industries.   "Trade in these parts," (wrote a
citizen of Leeds in September 1778,) "has received a
severe shock by the capture of the Duchess of Tuscany,
a vessel belonging to Hull, which was principally loaded
with goods of our manufactory to the amount of at least
fifty thousand pounds, the property of the merchants
here.   An accident of such magnitude as this has thrown

---

[1] This statement is founded on the figures which the Secretary of Lloyds'
supplied to Mr. Laird Clowes, for the purposes of his great work.   They
may be found in the note on page 396 of the Third Volume of *The Royal
Navy, a History from the Earliest Times to the Present.*   Eight hundred
of the three thousand vessels are entered as "Re-taken or Ransomed";
but, under both those heads, a very considerable money loss fell upon the
merchant and the ship-owner.

such a damp on the spirits of our merchants that none will dare export, but rather suffer what few goods they have on hand to lie in their warehouses, and await the chance of home consumption. This accident has occasioned great want of employ to many hundreds of industrious manufacturers. Waste, misery, and the approach of winter, fill up the whole prospect. The dejection in the countenances of the unemployed manufacturers is not to be described." These manu-facturers, (as they were styled in the language of the day,) were the artisans who worked at the looms ; and the employers were in as bad a case as their employed, with less hope of recovering themselves if ever times mended. The non-importation agreements in the American colonies had hit all the Yorkshire clothiers very hard ; and, when the American War supervened, the credit of many leading firms was brought in sudden destruction to the ground.

People of every class who subsisted on the profits of sea-carriage, from a merchant-prince to a labourer in the docks, were in such distress as had never before been experienced. The wharfingers of London, according to a Ministerial newspaper, were supposed to be the great-est of all the sufferers, since very little business indeed was done on the water-side.[1] A picture of the desolation which had overtaken British commerce was sketched in bold strokes by an eloquent and well-informed journalist. The great bulk, (he wrote,) of the profitable trade with America and the West Indies was gone from us. The natural and legitimate traffic in commodities with the colonist and the foreigner, upon which the prosperity of Great Britain mainly depended, had dwindled, and almost disappeared ; and shrewd and pushing men preferred to seek a livelihood out of the produce of those Govern-ment loans and taxes which were draining the vitality of the nation. Our merchantmen were being converted into troop-ships and commissariat store-ships, and our

---

[1] *Morning Post* of June, 1778.

merchants were turning themselves into army and navy contractors. "Some of them, in their desperation, had resorted to the business of privateering, like a bankrupt citizen who takes to the highway in the hope of repairing his broken fortunes;[1] while all other traders, not connected with the trade of war, were sinking into silent ruin." It was a melancholy contrast, (said this able writer,) to the flourishing condition of Great Britain during the height of the recent war with France and Spain. Before that war had run half its course the power for mischief possessed by each of our antagonists had been annihilated by the vast superiority of our navy. Their trade had been driven off the ocean; while, under the protection of regular convoys, our merchant fleets carried British products to all quarters of the globe. Millions of industrious customers in America purchased and consumed our goods, and were more beneficial to our manufacturing industries than if they had been settled in the heart of our island; many thousand American sailors served on board our ships of war; and more than a hundred American privateers scoured the seas, with hostile designs upon the commerce of France and Spain. That was the work of Mr. Secretary Pitt, who had loyally and confidently appealed to the spontaneous patriotism of the American colonists, instead of employing towards them, after the fashion of his unwise successors, the language of dictation and compulsion.

Very different was the plight in which England had now been landed by those fatal Ministers who, (as was wittily said,) could not be satisfied until, like idle children with their toys, "they had broken up the

---

[1] Privateering was a poor resource for British ship-masters. Only eighty American merchantmen were captured during the thirty months which followed the outbreak of rebellion. A member of Parliament told the House of Commons that letters of marque were hardly worth taking out. "They were of little service, unless those who had them fell in with an American tobacco ship; and that was as much a matter of chance as the obtainment of a ten, or twenty, thousand pound prize in the Lottery." After the European war began, our captures of hostile vessels rose to about two hundred and fifty in the year.

empire to see what it was made of." [1] The Earl of
Sandwich, as a member of the Cabinet, had been a
prime instigator of the policy which had brought about
the American Rebellion ; and it was his personal duty,
as First Lord of the Admiralty, to prepare the country
for that European contest which was inevitably bound
to follow. He was closely questioned in Parliament
by eminent peers, who endeavoured to get from him
a clear and definite statement of the provision which
his Board had made for the security of British commerce in the event of a war with France. In the
spring of 1777 Sandwich admitted, in answer to
Lord Chatham, that no fewer than eighty-seven of our
cruisers were operating against the rebels on the other
side of the Atlantic ocean ; but he jauntily observed
that, if danger arose nearer home, he could easily find
eighty-seven others to replace them. A year afterwards, — flinging about his figures at random, as was his
custom in debate, — he talked about having at least
half a hundred frigates ready.[2] Before many days had
elapsed the matter was brought to the proof. In April
1778 the Governor of Jersey applied at Whitehall for a
guard-ship to protect the Channel Islands, and was
informed that there were only three frigates at the
disposal of the Admiralty, one of which had already
been borrowed for special service.

The commercial world very soon awoke to the consequences of the levity and improvidence which had so
long prevailed in high quarters. Towards the middle of
May forty-five ship-owners and masters, whose vessels
could not put out from Portsmouth because the very
slender convoy, which had been promised them for
their protection, was not ready for sea, signed a letter
to the Board of Admiralty unfolding their grievance in

[1] Walpole to Mason ; July 4, 1778.
[2] In that same month Lord Sandwich laid on the table of Parliament a
memorandum placing the number of available frigates at thirty-four ; all
but eleven of which, (it was authoritatively contended,) ought more
properly to have been classed as sloops and schooners.

no measured, or even respectful, terms. " Is not this shameful usage, my Lords," (so the remonstrance was worded,) "thus to deceive the public? There are two hundred ships loaded with provisions waiting at Spithead these three months. The average expense of each ship amounts to one hundred and fifty pounds monthly, so that the expense of the whole West Indian fleet since February amounts to ninety thousand pounds." The discontent was immense, and the case very pressing. Up to the summer of 1775 the West Indies had drawn their main supplies of food, and other necessaries of life, from New England and Pennsylvania; and those supplies were entirely cut off as soon as the American War commenced. Instead of trading-vessels laden with cattle and cereals our revolted provinces henceforward despatched to the Bahamas and the Antilles a multitude of privateers which, in a very short space of time, starved and impoverished our unhappy dependencies. In the course of the first twelve months salt beef and pork had reached famine prices; and Indian corn, the chief article of diet for the negroes, had risen no less than four hundred per cent. West India sugar, and West India rum, when sold on the spot, had fallen to two-thirds of their former value. The cost of insuring a ship, bound to London or Bristol, already touched twenty-five per cent. on the vessel and the cargo; and it was estimated that these combined causes inflicted upon the British planters a loss of sixty-six pounds in every hundred that they were earning before the war. Yet, with all this, the West India merchant fleet, after assembling by the date, and at the place, which the Admiralty itself appointed, had still to wait many weeks for convoy during the most favourable period of the year for an outward voyage.[1]

From that time forward, whenever a trading-fleet from Hindostan, or the Levant, or Jamaica, was expected in the Channel, manufacturers, and insurers, and

[1] The story is admirably told by Admiral Mahan in chapter 31 of Clowes's Naval History.

bankers, whose fortunes were at stake, lived for weeks together in a condition of suspense and apprehension little short of agony. It was a new and humbling feeling for the great London merchants, who once had ruled the commerce of the world in peace and war alike, to know that they could not rely for safety upon the resources of the British navy, and that their only hope lay in the blunders of the enemy, and in some happy chance of wind and weather. " Fortune," wrote Horace Walpole in the autumn of 1779, " has smiled on us by conducting home our West Indian fleet. Huffed, rebuffed, and driven off as she has been, she is likely to be our best ally. The rest, as ill-treated, are not so forgiving."

But Fortune at last grew weary of repairing the errors committed by Lord Sandwich. In the third week of August 1780 a notice was issued by the Admiralty to the effect that our outward-bound East Indian and Jamaica merchant-fleets, sailing in company, had fallen in with a very powerful force of French and Spanish men-of-war, and there was the gravest reason to apprehend that nearly the whole of the convoy were taken. "In the memory of the oldest man," (we are told,) " the Change never presented so dull and melancholy an aspect as on that Tuesday afternoon. No instance, we believe, has been known in the annals of this country where so many ships have been captured at once, nor above a fourth of the value." Seven-and-forty West India merchantmen and Government transports were taken, with cargoes valued at six hundred thousand pounds, together with two thousand sailors, eight hundred passengers, twelve hundred soldiers, and eighty thousand stand of arms. The same fate befell five large East Indiamen, the contents of which, — in coin, bullion, and private ventures, and carefully selected goods belonging to the Company, — were estimated at a million sterling. And, last but not least, the French laid hands upon an abundant supply of naval stores, sent out from English dockyards for the repair and re-equipment of the squadron commanded by Admiral Sir Edward Hughes, who was engaged in an obstinate and dubious struggle with the Bailli de Suffren for the supremacy of the Eastern seas. It was a terrible blow to the West Indian trade. Next morning the Jamaica merchants were offering a premium of fifty per cent. for the insurance of their homeward-bound fleet; but the underwriters, who had lost near three-quarters of a million, were afraid to back any more policies.[1] The public opinion of commercial and naval circles laid the blame at the door of the Government. Our Channel fleet had escorted the unfortunate merchantmen as far as Cape Finisterre, and then, acting on orders from the Admiralty, had returned to port without seeing them safe past Cadiz, where thirty-six hostile war-ships were lying in wait for their prey. Young Lord Chatham was captured upon this occasion while going out to rejoin his regiment at Gibraltar. The enemy treated him like a royal personage, complimented him with a parole of honour, and sent him home to reside quietly at Burton Pynsent until he could benefit by an exchange of prisoners. He would have been secure enough on board an English transport in the days when his father was Minister.[2]

It was not the fault of the British navy. Our frigates, few and very far between, patrolled the seas like solitary policemen in the dangerous quarter of a populous city,

---

[1] This overwhelming misfortune, (so a City correspondent prophesied,) over and above the loss of property, and the sailors made captive, " will be the cause of keeping the goods, expected from both the Indies in return, twelve months in the West, and two years in the East, longer than they would have taken to make their way to Europe in the usual course of trade." Such was the complicated and wide-spreading dislocation of British commerce produced by the war.

[2] In the same month of the same year tidings reached England which still further illustrated the well-considered policy of Mr. Secretary Pitt in protecting our merchant convoys through the zone of danger which surrounded the point of departure, and the point of arrival. The London newspapers reported that " the Quebec fleet of fifteen ships had been met off the Banks of Newfoundland by an American frigate, and two brigantine privateers, who took twelve ships, — a very serious loss to the Quebec troops and people."

— avoiding opportunities of battle which, if they had had consorts to support them, they would have seized with joyful alacrity; or fighting against tremendous odds, sometimes to their own destruction, but never with any loss of honour. For the heroism of our officers, and the staunchness of our sailors, had seldom been more conspicuous than in these ill-matched encounters. Our frigates were not scared off their cruising ground by the proximity of French line-of-battle ships; and the commanders of our smaller vessels snatched at any fair occasion for showing that they were fit to be promoted to the charge of frigates. Almost every week brought home the story of some combat which proved that, whatever might be the case with England's war-ministers, her mariners at all events had not degenerated. In October 1778, (as a fair sample,) a Frenchman of superior force was captured by a British sloop carrying fourteen four-pounder guns, and something over a hundred men. " On our side," thus runs the account in a London newspaper, "six were killed, and twenty wounded. The action lasted three hours. While the French captain lay wounded in his cabin, there was an explosion of cartridges on board, and he overheard talk of hauling down the colours. ' I beckoned,' so he said, ' to the people near me to run up on deck, and hoist the colours again; and, if that was impracticable, to spread them out on the quarter.' Our own commander was shot through the left breast, and through the throat. He gave Midshipman O'Brien orders to board; but, on account of the narrowness of the forecastle, we could not at first mount sufficient men to support him. Here we suffered most, and, (what was more unfortunate,) the prime of our men. After the engagement Mr. O'Brien threw overboard twenty-three dead Frenchmen."

There were certain classes of the home-staying British community which now, for the first time in recent history, tasted the inconveniences and alarms of war in an unaccustomed shape. In June 1778 the crew of a large American corsair landed in Banff, and plundered a gentleman's residence situated in the Gordon country. That was not the first instance of the sort, nor the most notorious. Two months earlier a party of privateersmen stole into Whitehaven at dead of night, and set fire to the shipping in the harbour with a design to destroy the town ; but their purpose was baffled by the coolness and activity of the citizens. A few days afterwards the same vessel appeared off the coast of Kirkcudbrightshire. Thirty stout fellows, who represented themselves to be a British press-gang, and were dressed and accoutred for the part, surrounded Lord Selkirk's mansion. Three of them, each with a brace of pistols in his belt, walked indoors, and asked to see the mistress of the house. They told her, " with a mixture of rudeness and civility," [1] that, if Lord Selkirk had been at home, they would have taken him on board as a hostage; and they carried away the plate, which their captain subsequently ransomed out of his own pocket, and sent back with his compliments to Lady Selkirk. They belonged to the Ranger privateer, mounting eighteen cannon, with a complement of a hundred and fifty men, hailing from New England, and commanded by Captain Jones. " His real name," wrote an Edinburgh correspondent, " is Paul ;' though he assumes that of Jones, to veil in some measure his crimes, for he has been guilty of two or three capital offences in different parts of the British dominions." [2] The news of these exploits made unpleasant reading for Scotch and English householders who dwelt near the coast. It was all very well to talk of Captain Paul Jones as a criminal; but George the Third's Ministers had established an awkward precedent when they issued orders to burn the New England trading towns and fishing villages, from which these privateersmen came, as a lawful and proper mode of warfare. It was borne in upon the perception of the King himself that rough and high-spirited people, who had been so sorely provoked, were

[1] Letter of May 1, 1778, in the *Morning Post.*
[2] *Annual Register for* 1778 ; Chronicle of the Year, pages 176, 177, and 185.

only too likely to retaliate now that the negligence of the Admiralty had left our own shores defenceless against a raid from the sea. " I believe," he wrote to Lord North, "in the American project of harassing our coasts, which the want of frigates almost disables us from preventing."

There might have been some excuse for the short-comings of the Board of Admiralty if Parliament had showed any disposition whatever to starve the navy. But the case was far otherwise. Both Houses were full of men who took an intelligent, a responsible, and a most sane and reasonable view of the military necessities of Great Britain on sea and land, as proportioned to the pecuniary resources of the country. They voted money generously ; and they knew on what services that money ought to have been spent a great deal better than the Ministers themselves. The accurate and weighty criticisms, which came from the Opposition benches, were met on the part of the Government by flimsy generalities, and magniloquent and fallacious assertions ; while the Parliamentary papers which emanated from the Admiralty Office were so cooked and doctored that they had ceased to command the confidence of readers who were familiar with the subject. On the thirteenth of February 1778, in a debate on the Naval Estimates, Mr. Temple Luttrell, a private member of industry and capacity, laid stress upon the enormous sums which had been granted for constructing vessels that never were constructed, and for refitting vessels that were never refitted. He instanced the case of four ships of the line, for the repair of which, in the course of the last four years, Parliament had voted close upon a hundred and twenty thousand pounds ; an amount of money which, according to his calculations, would have more than sufficed to build them anew from the keel upwards. They should, (he said,) have been ready for sea long before the difficulty with France had reached an acute stage ; whereas they were still lying, untouched and in a rotten condition, in the inmost recesses of Portsmouth harbour. Lord Mulgrave, who answered on behalf of the Government, was driven to admit that not one single shilling had been laid out on the repair of those four vessels, because the money had been applied to other naval objects. Lord Mulgrave's confession brought Burke to his feet, with a vehement exclamation that the House of Commons was contemptuously treated when it was presented with a fine bound and gilt book of Estimates, calculated to a farthing, for purposes for which the money granted was never meant to be applied. According to the official report " Mr. Burke, in the warmth of his indignation, threw the book at the Treasury Bench, which, taking the candle on its way, nearly struck Mr. Welbore Ellis's shins." It was an anticipation of the dagger-scene as played by the same famous actor in the earlier days of the French Revolution ; except that in this case the incident was unpremeditated, and the missile was a real book of Estimates, and not a stage-property.

The vigilance and foresight of statesmen out of office, who had no access to special information, and no call to exertion beyond the patriotism common to all Englishmen, were in strange contrast to the indolence and indifference of the Minister to whose care the efficiency and honour of the Navy had been committed. Throughout the whole period of Chatham's war Lord Anson had always been on the spot to receive reports, and to issue orders ; and the best traditions of the British Admiralty were afterwards revived, and maintained, during our protracted struggle against the French Republic and the French Empire. It is on record that Mr. Marsden, the First Secretary, never ventured to sleep away from his official residence between May 1803 and November 1806 : and he was still at his desk, at one o'clock in the morning, when the news of Trafalgar reached London. He stepped across the corridor into his chief's bed-room, and drew Lord Barham's curtains; the clerks sat up all night ; and at a very early hour the story had been communicated to the King, the royal princes, and the Cabinet Ministers; had been sent to the Mansion House; and had been posted up in Lloyd's Coffee-room.

Those were not the habits and customs of the Admiralty under the rule of Lord Sandwich. When Keppel's messenger arrived in the last days of June of 1778, bringing the momentous intelligence that the British fleet had retired from before Brest, and had got back to Portsmouth, neither the First Lord, nor the Secretary of the Admiralty, could be found to unseal the despatches. A letter from the pen of David Hume relates how, at a serious conjuncture of the American War, Lord Sandwich was at a country-house near Newbury with three or four friends, and two or three ladies of pleasure, fishing in

> The Kennet swift, for silver eels renowned.

" He had been catching trout," (wrote Hume,) " which gave him incredible satisfaction; and they sent by the London fly from Bath a good cargo of Soles and John Dories, which would render their happiness complete. I do not remember in all my little, or great, knowledge of history such an instance, — and I am sure that such an one does not exist, — that the First Lord of the Admiralty, at a time when the fall of the British Empire is in dependence, and in dependence on him, finds so much leisure, tranquillity, presence of mind, and magnanimity as to have amusement in trouting, during three weeks, near sixty miles from the scene of business, and during the most critical period of the year. There needs but this single fact to decide the fate of the nation." [1]

---

[1] Hume to Strachan; Bath, May 10, 1776.

Lord North and his colleagues, throughout the American War, religiously observed the custom of the week-end, which had long been a cherished Parliamentary institution. Horace Walpole was writing in 1770 on the European situation. " I shall," he said, " let all this bustle cool for two days; for what Englishman does not sacrifice anything to go his Saturday out of town?" Mr. Speaker Onslow used to relate that the

The pastimes of Lord Sandwich in his Berkshire retreat were innocent and Arcadian as compared to his
ways of life at Whitehall. There he spent his idle
hours in a course of shameless dissipation the memory
of which was handed down with disgust and resentment
from generation to generation of Admiralty officials.[1]
His more serious energies were meanwhile devoted to
extending and fortifying his own electoral and parliamentary influence, or to thwarting and persecuting naval ·
officers of character and renown, who had done good
service to the nation, but who did not choose to enroll
themselves among his political adherents. The most
eminent of them was Lord Howe, who had saved the
British fleet and army in America from an imminent
catastrophe, and who was requited after a strange
fashion. He was copiously and systematically abused
in the Government newspapers ; and his conduct, (to
employ his own words,) was publicly arraigned in pamphlets written by persons in high credit and confidence
with Ministers.[2] While he had been busily engaged, on
the other side of the Atlantic ocean, in rescuing the city
of New York and relieving Rhode Island, certain strong
supporters of the Ministry in the House of Commons
attacked him with railing accusations and specific
charges ; and no one on the Treasury Bench was at the
pains to defend him. When Lord Howe came back to
England, and took his seat at Westminster, he told
Parliament frankly that "a thorough recollection of all
that he had suffered induced him to decline any risk of
ever returning to a situation which might terminate in
equal ill-treatment and mortification." Such, (he said,)

Saturday holiday was due to Horace's own father, who wanted to be sure
of his day's hunting; but it must be remembered that Sir Robert Walpole,
during the first four-and-twenty years that he governed the country, took
good care not to be a war-minister.

[1] More than forty years ago, when, after a change of administration, a
new Civil Lord was inducted into office, he was shown the very room in
which the Bedfords had held their revels, and was told anecdotes about
their proceedings which are entirely unsuited for the publicity of print.

[2] Hansard's *Parliamentary History;* volume XX, pages 720 and 721.

was his motive for declining any future service so long as the present Ministry remained in office.

Those words were uttered in March 1779. In March 1782 North fell from power, Keppel succeeded Sandwich at the Admiralty, and Lord Howe was forthwith invited to hoist his flag on board the Victory. In the following autumn intense and increasing anxiety began to be felt about the critical position of the heroic garrison in Gibraltar. General Eliott had defeated all attempts to get possession of the Rock by force. None the less he was narrowly blockaded on sea and land; his store of powder, which he had put to such notable use, had fallen very low; and his magazines, — supplying, as they did, the civil population as well as the soldiers, — had not been re-victualled over a space of eighteen months. But Lord Howe was at hand to save the situation. In the presence of a hostile fleet much superior to his own in numbers, by a succession of daring manœuvres, and a small amount of judicious fighting, he contrived to throw into the place a sufficiency of ordnance stores, and a positive superabundance of provisions. The ablest, and the best informed, seamen of every nation have always quoted the relief of Gibraltar as an example of rare professional skill, and lofty personal attributes; and their opinion has been embodied in telling phrases by a French naval historian of deserved repute. "This operation," writes Captain Chevalier, "one of the finest in the war of American Independence, deserves to be accounted as equal in merit to a victory. If the English squadron was favoured by circumstances, — and fortune goes for something in every prosperous enterprise, — it was Lord Howe's unerring perception, his sound judgment, and his rapidity of decision which mainly assured success." Such were the powers of leadership possessed by an admiral of whose services Britain was wantonly deprived during three years as perilous as any in her history.

Viscount Howe was not the only distinguished officer who had bitterly unpleasant experience of Lord

Sandwich. There was no British commander whose services in the local warfare against the naval forces of the revolted colonies could bear comparison for a moment with those of Sir George Collier. He crowned a long series of victorious operations, conducted with signal address and valour, by utterly destroying a large New England war-fleet in Penobscot Bay, on the coast of the district which is now the State of Maine. It was the solitary British success, of any real importance, gained during the last three years of the war through-out the whole immense region which lay north of the Carolina border.[1] Collier reaped nothing from his exertions except vexation and disappointment. He was superseded in his American command; and on his return home he was left unpromoted, unemployed, and un-noticed, devouring his heart in idleness, and attributing the extinction of his brilliant career to the personal en-mity of Lord Sandwich. And again, after the war with Holland had broken out, Admiral Hyde Parker came back from the battle of the Dogger Bank, so honourable to both antagonists, boiling over with his grievances against a Minister who had sent him out to fight the Dutch with a handful of unseaworthy and undermanned vessels. King George, who had a liking for the gallant

[1] Sir George Collier's official report of the proceedings in Penobscot Bay, as published in the *London Gazette*, is modest almost to a fault ; and the full story can best be learned from American sources. Sir George, whose squadron carried only two hundred guns, and fifteen hundred men, burned, sank, or captured nearly a score of war-ships. They constituted what was probably the strongest and finest naval force furnished by New England during the Revolution, — mounting three hundred and twenty-four cannon, manned by two thousand soldiers and sailors, and built and equipped at an expense of a million and three-quarters, not of paper dollars, but of pounds sterling. General Lovell, who on this occasion commanded the land forces of Massachusetts, was an eye-witness of the scenes which took place when the American Commodore fled before the onset of the British, and made a fruitless attempt to escape up the Penob-scot river. "To give a description," he wrote, "of this terrible day is out of my power ; — to see four ships pursuing seventeen sail of armed vessels, nine of which were stout ships ; transports on fire, men-of-war blowing up, and as much confusion as can possibly be conceived." *The Original Journal of General Solomon Lovell, published by the Weymouth Historical Society,* 1881.

veteran, intimated to Parker that marks of the royal favour were in store for him; but Parker replied, with the surly freedom of a septuagenarian, that he would accept no title or reward which came to him through the channel of the Earl of Sandwich.

The same was the case with other zealous and capable naval officers who had opposed a ministerial candidate at an election, or whose elder brothers voted against the Government in the House of Peers. Lord Robert Manners wrote to the Duke of Rutland in November 1779 that he had been repeatedly baulked of his promotion, and, — which he liked still less, — had been beguiled, and befooled, by the First Lord of the Admiralty. "Lord Sandwich's character," he said, "is too well known for any man of higher understanding than an idiot to put confidence in his promises. . . . I hope to God some time or other to have it in my power to show my displeasure." The end of the story is told in a letter to the Duke of Rutland from the surgeon of the ship which Lord Robert Manners commanded in Admiral Rodney's epoch-making victory on the twelfth of April 1782. "The Resolution," (so this gentleman wrote,) "sustained a severe fire from nine or ten of the French ships, in breaking through their line. Your Grace may guess my feelings when I saw Lord Robert brought down wounded, the first man. His behaviour on this, as on every other occasion, was heroism itself. A cannon-shot had wounded both legs, and at the same instant he received a compound fracture of his right arm, I believe by a splinter. The left leg was in such a state as to preclude all hopes of saving it, and accordingly I took it off immediately by his own desire. It will scarcely be credited not only how undaunted he appeared, but how perfectly he seemed to possess himself during an operation always dreadful, and in that situation particularly so, making jocular remarks with a smiling countenance during its most painful steps." Lord Robert died ten days later on, and was buried, like a seaman, in blue water.

The discontent prevailing throughout the royal navy, on account of the treatment dealt out to able and popular members of the service, was brought to a head by the manifest complicity of the First Lord of the Admiralty in the plot against Keppel. Sir Robert Harland resigned his command, and indicated, in no obscure terms, that he would not continue to serve under the auspices of a Minister on whose good faith it was impossible to rely. The Channel Fleet was then offered to Admiral Barrington, an excellent officer, and a brother of the nobleman who had lately been Secretary at War in Lord North's Cabinet; but Barrington gave it to be understood that nothing would induce him to take the chief command, although he was ready and willing to go to sea under any officer senior to himself, save and except Sir Hugh Palliser. An epidemic of anger and uneasiness spread through the higher ranks of the entire service. It was reported and believed that no fewer than twenty of the most experienced and distinguished captains in the navy were on the point of throwing up their commissions in a body on one and the same day; and they were with difficulty recalled to the path of duty by the earnest remonstrances of wiser friends. Men of honour and probity, who could not bring themselves to be flatterers and satellites of Lord Sandwich, felt painfully conscious that their reputations were not safe in his hands. If they consented to undertake posts of danger and responsibility he was only too likely to treat them as he had treated Keppel, and none of them had Keppel's immense personal popularity to shield them from the fatal consequences of ministerial treachery and disloyalty.

The betting-book at Brooks's Club affords a striking testimony to the estimation in which Augustus Keppel was held by his associates and admirers. There were no crowned heads so august, no family relationships so sacred, no personal questions so delicate, or so indelicate, that these audacious companions refrained from making them the subject of a wager; and their favourite matter of speculation, among all others, was the verdict which the jury would return in a sensational trial on a capital charge. And yet those thickly scored pages contained not one single bet with reference to the finding of the Portsmouth Court-Martial so long as the life and honour of their beloved friend were at stake. But as soon as the acquittal was pronounced, and Keppel was beyond the reach of danger, there was brisk and lively betting as to the probabilities of an event towards which every man's eyes were set. Ten guineas, and twenty-five guineas, were given and taken freely between Dukes, and Earls, and Commoners of political eminence, on the question whether, at the date of one calendar month, or two calendar months, after the decision of the Portsmouth Court, the Earl of Sandwich would still be First Lord of the Admiralty. No time was lost in bringing that question to an issue. On the third of March 1779 Charles Fox moved a resolution to the effect that the sending of Admiral Keppel to sea in the previous June, with a squadron of only twenty ships, at a time when the French fleet was in far superior strength, had been "a measure greatly hazardous to the safety of the kingdom."

It was a parliamentary field-day of the first order. The official report states that not a seat was unoccupied in the body of the House, while upwards of fifty members, for whom there was no room below, were obliged to seek accommodation in the galleries. They did well to put themselves to some inconvenience, for seldom had an orator been better worth hearing. Fox began by a powerful justification of the right inherent in a deliberative assembly to pass judgment on the management of a war. His argument was based on broad and sound principles, and illustrated by apt and telling historical examples. No nations, (he asserted,) had been more formidable as belligerents than those in which the great mass of the people had a share in the national counsels,—in which the power was delegated by the people, and wielded by the executive authority as the

agent of the people, answerable to the people for the
success, or the failure, of a military policy. England
herself, the England of Marlborough and of Lord
Chatham, would remain a monument to the end of time
of the fortunate and irresistible exertions of a mixed,
a free, and a constitutional government. In such a
government the executive power had ample latitude
to make peace and war, to enter upon alliances, to
equip armaments, and to direct campaigns by land and
sea, on the sole condition that a minister, in the last
resort, was responsible to Parliament for his conduct.
"If," (said Fox,) "the Ministers act negligently, cor-
ruptly or traitorously, they do it at their peril; while in
arbitrary governments, where men are subject to the
same failings and vices, they are not exposed to the
same liability of being called to account by their fellow-
countrymen for what they do amiss."

The general doctrine, as laid down by Fox, commanded the respect and assent of the whole assembly;
but the storm began when he proceeded to apply that
doctrine to the case of Lord Sandwich. His speech
was interrupted by a furious altercation, and a large,
a tumultuous, and a very close division on a contested
point of order. Lord North was betrayed into language of
such unwonted vehemence that Fox moved to take down
his words; but the uproar had been so great that
the Clerk at the Table had failed to catch the exact
expressions, and no two members were agreed in their
recollection of what the Prime Minister had said. The
main debate was resumed amidst intense excitement.
The House, which was in no mood for trifling, would not
listen to specious or shallow party talk on either side
of the question, and reserved its attention for those
who could discourse on naval matters with practical
knowledge, and recognised authority. Keppel, who
had found his tongue at last, spoke no less than three
times with convincing force and persuasive fervour;
and Lord Howe, in a few sentences weighty with the
common-sense of the quarter-deck, cut the Government

case to ribbons. Lord Mulgrave, who undertook to defend the Admiralty, was unequal to the task ; and the current of feeling ran so visibly and so violently against Lord Sandwich that the Prime Minister, "observing strong marks of defection, particularly among that part of the country gentlemen who supported administration," [1] thought it necessary, in explicit terms, to stake the existence of the Government upon the issue of the vote. If it was criminal, (he said,) to send out Admiral Keppel with twenty ships, it was either a crime in common to all the Cabinet, or no crime at all. To whatever determination the House might come, it must be clearly understood that there was no possibility of directing the intended vote of censure against any particular minister without involving all his colleagues in the consequences. Lord North's announcement brought many of the waverers to heel, and the resolution which Fox had moved was defeated by a narrow majority. Sixteen months previously, when both parties mustered their strength in a stand-and-fall debate, the Government had won by two hundred and forty-three votes to eighty-six; and four months previously, under similar circumstances, they had a majority of two hundred and twenty-six to a hundred and seven: [2] whereas on the present occasion Fox was beaten by only thirty-four in a House of three hundred and eighty members. That was a sweeping and a most significant turn-over of votes within a very short space of time, and in a Parliament where the Ministerial ranks were kept in obedience by lavish bribery, and a strict and inquisitorial discipline.

Six weeks afterwards the whole world was again talking of Lord Sandwich. A lieutenant in the army named James Hackman, who possessed a fine voice and an ear for music, while stationed on recruiting duty in the town of Huntingdon had occasionally been invited

---

[1] *Parliamentary History;* volume XX, page 204.
[2] *Parliamentary History;* volume XIX, pages 442, and 1365. Charles Fox acted as teller in both cases.

to bear part in the concerts which Lord Sandwich gave
at Hinchinbroke.   Hackman there fell in love with Miss
Ray, and proposed to marry her; but, (as the newspapers phrased it,) "a tie of children by a noble lord
high in office, well known as her protector, put a bar to
their union."   The lady moreover told her young lover
pretty plainly that in any case she had no mind to be
the wife of a subaltern in a marching regiment; and he
accordingly chose what he regarded as the shortest and
surest road towards bettering his prospects.   "Being
led from his intimacy with Miss Ray, and her influence
with Lord Sandwich, to expect great preferment in the
clerical way, he left the Army for the Church."   He took
orders, and was appointed to the charge of a parish;
and it may at all events be said for him that he was not
the most disreputable among the loose-living divines
who looked up to the First Lord of the Admiralty as
their patron.   He continued to press his suit; but
Miss Ray remained deaf to his solicitations, and his passion gradually deepened into despair and frenzy.   On the
night of the seventh April, as the unfortunate woman
was stepping into her carriage at the door of Covent
Garden Theatre, Hackman shot her dead, and made an
unsuccessful attempt on his own life with a second pistol.

Lord Sandwich was at the Admiralty, expecting
Miss Ray home to supper, when the dreadful news
arrived; and his sorrow was undisguised, deep, and
lasting.   His reputation suffered terribly from the
revelations which came to light during Hackman's trial.
The domestic arrangements at Hinchinbroke and Whitehall were no new story to men of the world in London;
but many thousands of quiet people in the provinces,
whose daily business lay outside the sphere where
fashionable gossip circulated, now learned for the first
time that a nobleman over sixty years of age, in high
Cabinet office, had for a long while past been living with
a mistress permanently and openly established in his
house.[1]   Hackman's fate was not long in abeyance.   The

[1] There is an observation to this effect in the fair and discriminating

proceedings were summary in the case of a murderer who had been taken red-handed; and he was hanged within the fortnight. Connoisseurs in crime and horrors, who then were a numerous tribe, did not neglect so rare an opportunity for courting emotion and gratifying curiosity. George Selwyn, indeed, was absent from London; but the cleverest of all his led parsons took care to send him full and accurate accounts of the tragedy; and a fine lady, who knew his tastes, supplied him with some interesting details about the execution.[1] James Boswell got himself introduced to the condemned man in his cell at Newgate, accompanied him to the gallows, and was noticed by the reporters as having taken an affectionate leave of him when he entered the cart. "The poor assassin," (wrote Horace Walpole on the twentieth of April,) "was executed yesterday. The same day Charles Fox moved for the removal of Lord Sandwich, but was beaten by a large majority; for in Parliament the Ministers can still gain victories."[2]

The crisis which Lord Chatham had long ago predicted was now close at hand. During the opening months of 1779 there had been an intense and sinister activity in the diplomatic circles of Europe. King George's Government, which was without an ally, or even a friendly informant, among the leading Powers, possessed no trustworthy clue to the network of intrigues which had its centre at Versailles; but, at the very least, it was as good as certain that Spain would enter the lists before the summer was over, and that the war would be a naval war in the strict sense of the term, — unless indeed France could contrive to

article on Lord Sandwich by Sir John Laughton in the *Dictionary of National Biography.*

[1] Letters to Selwyn from the Countess of Ossory, and the Reverend Doctor Warner. "I called," wrote the clergyman, "at the Shakspeare Tavern in order to see the corpse of Miss Ray, and send you some account of it; but I had no interest with her keepers, and could not get admittance for money."

[2] Walpole to Mann; April 17, 1779. The postscript of the letter is dated Tuesday the 20th.

disembark an army upon English or Irish soil. To enter upon such a war with Lord Sandwich as our chief naval administrator was a prospect appalling to every sensible and patriotic man; and the Opposition regarded it not as a party, but as a national, duty to take measures against his continuance in what had now become the most important department of the State. Fox, on the date mentioned in Horace Walpole's postscript, moved that a Humble Address should be presented to His Majesty praying that he would be graciously pleased to remove John Earl of Sandwich from the office of First Commissioner of the Admiralty on account of the general ill state to which, under his administration, the Navy had been reduced. The debate soon turned, as debates do, towards the personal side of the question, which in this case was one of its most serious aspects. A succession of speakers bore their testimony to the fatal effects produced upon the efficiency of the service by the proscription of every officer whose politics were not those of Lord Sandwich, or who, apart from politics, was known for his independence of character. Colonel Barré, in particular, enlarged with characteristic vigour upon the treatment dealt out to Howe and Keppel. Those two admirals, (he said,) besides all their great and good qualities, enjoyed a species of professional popularity among their brother officers more perhaps than any two men ever experienced at any time in this country. Nor was that popularity confined to officers alone, — nor even to the crews which had served under their immediate orders, and beneath their flags. It was universal in every quarter of the globe where a British sailor was to be found. He firmly believed, (so the veteran boldly asserted,) that, if the whole Royal Navy was united in one squadron, or two squadrons, which "Black Dick," and "Little Keppel," were to command jointly or severally, such was the confidence and affection in which they were held by the common seamen that the exertions of the press-gang would on such an occasion be hardly needed. And those, (observed Barré,) were the two officers whom the First Lord of the Admiralty had inveigled into active service for certain temporary purposes, and whose reputation and career, after those purposes were answered, he had conspired to ruin.

In the same week the same Resolution was brought forward in the Upper House by the Earl of Bristol, Vice-Admiral of the Blue, who as Captain Hervey had earned a fine record in the late war against France and Spain. His health was broken by arduous and continuous work in many climates; but he had kept in close touch with his profession, and his store of knowledge about the navies of the world was supposed to exceed that of any man then living. In a speech of vast detail, — which, sure of the accuracy of his facts and figures, he afterwards published as a pamphlet, — he contended that the British fleet, in numbers and condition, stood far below the point where it ought to stand as compared with the fleets of France and Spain, and that the fault lay with the Board of Admiralty, and not with the House of Commons. He calculated that since the year 1771, when Sandwich became First Lord, the money granted for naval purposes had exceeded the amount expended by Lord Anson, during an equal period of time, by seven millions of pounds. The British fleet, he maintained, might have been augmented by at least one half if a due proportion of that money had been properly applied to ship-repairing and ship-building; whereas the vessels of the line now fit for service were actually fewer than those which had been handed over to Lord Sandwich by his predecessor, Sir Edward Hawke. Sandwich, in his reply to Lord Bristol's indictment, said much that was jocular, and much that was irrelevant, but very little that could be called explanatory or reassuring. He repeated, in identically the same words which he employed when answering Lord Chatham twelve months previously,

an off-hand assertion that our navy was more than a
match for the whole House of Bourbon ; and the Peers
had to be content with what satisfaction they could
derive from that hackneyed, and much disputed,
formula.   But the First Lord of the Admiralty was free
to adopt any tone he chose in addressing Parliament,
for he was well aware that he had no longer anything
to fear from the result of a division.   The Minister
in charge of the House had brought down a copious
handful of proxies ; and the public spirit of the Episcopal
Bench rose, or sank, to the occasion.   John Hinchcliffe
and Jonathan Shipley, alone among their Right Reverend brethren, protested against the retention of the
Earl of Sandwich in a place of authority among the
rulers of the British people.   They were the Bishops of
Peterborough and of St. Asaph, and at Peterborough
and St. Asaph they remained until their lives ended ;
for George the Third was not in the habit of mincing
matters when the question arose of translating a prelate
who had voted in the House of Lords against the point
of view which His Majesty favoured.

The motion for an Address was lost in both Houses
by great majorities.   Lord Sandwich had escaped a
pressing danger ; and there exists no doubt whatever as
to the quarter from which his salvation came.   George
the Third knew his House of Commons by heart, and
he could read the signs of the political weather better
than any of his Cabinet.   He was too strong a man to
under-rate the abilities of those whom he disliked ; he
recognised the extraordinary powers of Charles Fox;
and he was not blind to the growing influence of one in
. whom he had long seen an antagonist, and now began
to foresee a rival.   Moreover he sct great store on
Sandwich, who was a statesman exactly to his mind.
Subservient in the Closet, masterful and overbearing in
the Cabinet, and a fearless bully in debate, the First Lord
of the Admiralty was always ready to accept the King's
views on policy, to impose them upon his own colleagues,
and to champion them against all comers in Parliament.

Such a Minister was too precious to be thrown away or abandoned, however unseemly his private life, and however deplorably mismanaged might be the public department committed to his care. George the Third had been greatly alarmed when Fox so very nearly carried his first vote of censure on the third of March. As soon as the master learned that a servant, whom he highly valued, had only been saved from a crushing condemnation by a small margin of votes, he at once resolved upon sharp and uncompromising action. The division had taken place late at night; and the next morning, before most of those who bore a part in it had left their beds, King George was already expressing to Lord North by letter his indignation at the number of Ministerialists who had shamefully failed in their duty, and his determination to adopt any means, which he could personally take, in order to suppress such irregularities in the future.[1] " The list of the House of Commons," he wrote, " has I trust been so accurately prepared that there will be no difficulty in knowing whose attention must be quickened. I trust Lord North will not let his usual good nature accept excuses upon this occasion. It is the good of my service that calls forth severity." Severe enough, in all conscience, His Majesty showed himself. He left it to the Prime Minister to see that all defaulters in civil employment were " strongly spoke to;" and meanwhile he took into his own hands the officers of the Army, who abounded in the House of Commons, and who for the most part shared the feelings of the Navy with regard to Lord Sandwich. The King desired the Acting Commander in Chief of the Forces to call to account the colonels, captains, and subalterns; and he stated it as his decided opinion that generals, who held those governorships of fortresses which were the special

[1] George the Third to Lord North ; Queen's House, March 4th, 1779 ; fifteen minutes past eight, a.m. Suetonius tells of Augustus Cæsar that " he was extremely precise in dating his letters, and in putting down the day, the hour, and the moment at which they were despatched." In that respect, no less than in his admirable bodily temperance, King George resembled the Roman Emperor.

prizes of the service, should lose them for opposing the wishes of the Crown.   That trebling of the Government majority, which took place on the second vote of censure, affords a remarkable indication of the multitude of place-men who then sat in Parliament, and a measure of the King's industry and dexterity in manipulating a division-list.   His strength of will was seldom more effectually displayed than when, with public sentiment almost unanimously against him, he kept Lord Sandwich safe in office on the morrow of a flagrant personal scandal, and on the eve of a fresh naval war.   England was con-demned to encounter Spain, as well as France, in mortal combat, with that Old Man of the Sea triumphantly and irremovably mounted on her shoulders.

It was high time for those who had no confidence in the existing administration of the Navy to let their views be known in Parliament.   On the twelfth of April 1779, — the day week before Charles Fox moved his Resolu-tion for an Address to the Crown,— France and Spain had signed a secret Convention, which the contracting parties called " an amicable and reciprocal engagement," and which was in fact a treaty of alliance for waging in union a war against England.   In coming to that mo-mentous decision the Spanish Government was actuated solely by considerations of expected national advantage, and supposed national honour.   Madrid felt none of that enthusiasm for liberty, and for the general interests of humanity, which prompted and dignified the American sympathies of such Frenchmen as Lafayette and Turgot. Spaniards looked upon the people of New England as a par-ticularly objectionable form of heretics, and disapproved of them as turbulent and disloyal colonists whose rebel-lion against their rightful master set a very dangerous example to the inhabitants of their own vast, immensely valuable, and loosely attached dependencies in the West-ern Hemisphere.   Count Florida Blanca, and the other Ministers of His Catholic Majesty King Charles the

Third, cared not one jot for the rights, the welfare, or
the good opinion of any American citizen from George
Washington downwards.   The one object of their policy
was to utilise the season of England's weakness and distress in order to avenge the defeats which she had inflicted upon Spain in many previous wars, and to gain
for themselves accessions of territory, and fresh sources
of wealth, at the expense of their hereditary enemy,
and, (to a still greater degree,) at the expense of the
United States.   It was expressly stipulated, in the
Convention between the two Powers, that the whole of
Florida, as well as the important town, and still more
important bay, of Mobile, on the coast of what is now
the State of Alabama, should be added to the Spanish
empire.   It was agreed, moreover, that, if France succeeded in obtaining possession of Newfoundland, all foreigners except Spaniards were to be excluded from the
fisheries, which would be a severe blow to Great Britain,
but nothing short of ruin to the mariners of Rhode
Island, Connecticut, and Massachusetts.   The most emphatic and explicit clause in the whole compact was that
by which His Catholic Majesty, and His very Christian
Majesty, bound themselves respectively not to lay down
their arms until the Rock of Gibraltar was once more a
Spanish stronghold.   That clause, however, had been
pre-ordained by fate to be null and void ; and Spain, in
the course of her endeavours to carry it into fulfilment,
was destined to get a great deal which she had never
bargained for at the hands of Eliott, and Curtis, and
Howe, and Rodney.

The allied monarchs proposed to secure the conquests
at which they aimed, not by distant and detached expeditions into out-lying regions of the globe, but by a direct
and sudden thrust at the heart of England's power.   As
early as the month of February 1779 a plan of attack
had been concerted between them, and had been carefully arranged in outline, and in all the more important
details.   The Spanish Ministers had long entertained a
hankering for an invasion of Ireland, where they be-

lieved, truly enough, that much discontent with the then existing state of things prevailed. They sent, as a special commissioner to conduct an enquiry on the spot, an ecclesiastic who had received the promise of a mitre if his errand proved fruitful. This singularly chosen emissary soon discovered that the mass of the Catholic population was reserved and silent on the burning questions of the hour; that many of the Catholic gentry were frank in their condemnation of the American rebellion ; and that the admirers, and would-be imitators, of the New England insurgents were to be found among the fiery Presbyterians of Ulster, who, if the Spanish agent had gone among them in his character of a Roman Catholic priest, would probably have ducked him in the Bann. It was further ascertained that the Episcopalian protestants, — though they were engaged in a hot, and very loud, agitation for commercial freedom, and for the removal of a mysterious instrument of tyranny entitled the Poynings' Act, — would undoubtedly turn out to a man in opposition to a foreign invader; and Irish protestants, when it came to fighting, had always shown themselves redoubtable fellows.[1]

The Comte de Vergennes, — who was the foreign Minister of France, and the guide and inspirer of her national action throughout the whole succession of these great events, — found other, and very sound, reasons for declining to concur in an attempt upon Ireland. The scheme of aggressive strategy, which the allied Powers ultimately decided to adopt, was expounded in an able Memorial drawn up in Madrid, but suggested and dictated by the French Minister. Vergennes had conceived a design of landing troops on the Isle of Wight, capturing all the shipping "in the roads of St. Helen's and Spithead," and destroying the dockyards and ar-

[1] Mr. Bancroft's *History of the Common Action of France and America for the Independence of the United States;* chapter 11. Letters from the Comte de Vergennes of February 12, and July 2, 1779, as given in the text and notes of Doniol's History.

senals of Portsmouth.[1]   The army was to be provided
by France; while Spain contributed a sum of money
calculated on the expense of the regiments which she
would otherwise have been under obligation to supply.
A junction of the two navies was to be effected, at a
fixed date, in the neighbourhood of the ports of Vigo
and Corunna; and the combined fleet, in overwhelming
strength, would then sail eastward to achieve the mastery of the British Channel.   In the middle of June,
when the programme had been settled, and all the preparations were complete, Spain declared war against England.   Our Ministers were taken by surprise, and all
the more because they had of late been deep in a friendly
negotiation with the Spanish Foreign Office.   Charles
the Third, — simulating an ardent love of peace, and a
genuine goodwill towards Great Britain, — had voluntarily offered himself as an impartial mediator to bring
about a reconciliation between King George and King
Louis.   It was an act of deliberate treachery; and, in
their dealings with England, there was little to choose,
on the point of common honesty, between the governments of France and Spain.   Two imposing and elaborate manifestoes from the monarchs of the two nations
were published in parallel columns, in an elegant pamphlet, by the Royal printing establishment in Paris, and
were circulated broadcast throughout Europe.[2]   These
twin productions, — which resembled each other so
closely, in spirit and in substance, that they might very
well have been written by the same hand, — displayed
no little adroitness, and an utter absence of scruple.
The charges which the allied governments adduced
against the British Cabinet were based upon falsified
statements and distorted facts.   Many of their complaints and grievances were nothing better than trumpery; and the real and true motives, which impelled

[1] *Traduction de l'écrit de la Cour d'Espagne à celle de France.   Du
Pardo*, 26 *Février*, 1779.   *Doniol; tome III, annexe IV du chapitre 11.*
[2] A facsimile of the title-page of this publication is given in Doniol's
third volume.

them to plunge half the civilised world into strife and misery, had no place whatever in those disingenuous pages.

Lord North and his colleagues took the judicious step of issuing a counter-appeal to the public opinion of Europe ; and their choice of an advocate showed good sense, and sterling originality. Edward Gibbon, as a member of parliament, and a Lord of Trade, was versed in practical politics ; and he expressed himself in French, (it is hardly too much to say,) more easily and naturally than in English. His first printed book, the *Essai sur l'étude de la Littérature*, had been widely read on the Continent, while a translation of the work into very indifferent English had fallen dead in London.[1] His early love-letters had been indited in the pure and classical French of the Pays de Vaud ; and on various occasions he had published in that language dissertations, and monographs, and prefaces more than sufficient to fill a good-sized volume. In the early autumn of 1779, at the instance of Lord Chancellor Thurlow and Lord Weymouth, Gibbon drew up, in the best of French, a vindication of his own country, and a scathing exposure of her wrongs, compressed into the space of thirty pages, and losing nothing by its brevity. Compact, lucid, powerfully and fairly reasoned, and glowing with the eloquence of indignant patriotism, it was a composition which, in its own line, has seldom or never been surpassed. The author brought out in strong relief the damning circumstance that France and England, by the First Article of the Treaty of Paris, were under " a sacred engagement to give no succour or protection, direct or indirect, to any who should act to the prejudice of one or another of the High Contracting Parties." He related, concisely and convincingly, in a few strokes

---

[1] " In Britain," wrote Gibbon, " it was treated with indifference, little read, and speedily forgotten. The bookseller murmured that a small impression was slowly dispersed ; and the author, (had his feelings been more exquisite,) might have wept over the blunders and the baldness of his English translation."

which betokened a master of narrative, how, in insolent
contempt of that solemn promise, the Ministers at Versailles had assisted the American colonists with arms
and money, had entertained their envoys, harboured and
sheltered their privateers, and provided them with a
market where they might dispose of those British ships
and cargoes which they had captured in European
waters. Gibbon concluded his argument by a fine
denunciation of the Spanish government for pretending to intercede between France and England in the
assumed character of a pacific and neutral umpire.
" Spain," (he wrote,) "has now openly commenced
hostilities which she is unable to clothe with the most
feeble appearance of equity ; and she has thereby made
it manifest that her resolution to join the ranks of our
enemies was taken long ago, under the inspiration of
the French Minister, who had counselled her to hold
back her declaration of war for the sole object of striking, beneath the mask of amity, a mortal blow at the
honour and interests of Great Britain." Whatever the
moral victory might be worth, it had been won by England ; for Gibbon, with a single broadside, had blown
the case of the allied powers out of the water.

The confederates were amply provided with the material means required to prosecute their unjust quarrel.
France, which had not an enemy, or even the threaten-
ing shadow of an enemy, on the Continent of Europe,
was at liberty to disgarnish her eastern and northern
frontiers, and draw down the whole flower of her army
to the shores of the British Channel. Fifty thousand
thoroughly drilled and well-appointed soldiers had been
collected at Havre and St. Malo before the end of May.
Their commander-in-chief was the Comte de Vaux, who,
ten years previously, had defeated General Paoli by
hard fighting, had driven him into exile, and had an-
nexed Corsica to France. It was the current belief in
the camps which lined the coasts of Normandy and
Brittany that, with such a general, and such an army,
one island would be as easy to over-run and subdue as

another.   The officers, high and low, were affected by
that airy and voluble self-confidence which was a customary mood with French military men in the eighteenth century ; and the most exalted among them was
their Quarter-Master-General, the Marquis de Lafayette.
That young nobleman, after a perilous voyage, had arrived in his native country for a short holiday ; had reported himself to the War Office ; and had been placed
in arrest for a week, which he was allowed to pass under
his father-in-law's roof in the company of his wife and
children.   When the period of seclusion was over he
went to Court, where he was solemnly rebuked, heartily
forgiven, and graciously complimented ; and then, for a
short while, he surrendered himself to the whirlwind of
applause, and to the demonstrations of enthusiastic affection, which greeted his re-appearance in Parisian society.[1] His solid position, as the connecting link between
France and the United States, was creditable to himself,
and invaluable to both of the governments which he
served with equal zeal, and equal fidelity ; but it cannot
be denied that, at this point of his career, his head was
somewhat turned by a popularity as widely diffused, and
as hardly and honourably earned, as ever was enjoyed
by a man of one-and-twenty.   The earliest editors of his
correspondence, who were members of his own family,
showed a wise discrimination in suppressing most of
what he wrote after he had joined the army of invasion,
and while he was still fresh from the intoxicating atmosphere of Paris and Versailles.   Those letters have of
late been brought to light ; and we may read how Lafayette's blood "boiled in his veins," and how in imagination he was already riding with the advance-guard
along the high-roads in the South of England.   Two
thousand soldiers, (he said,) were all that an officer of

[1] Lafayette was kissed by all the ladies.   The same would have happened to him, if he had permitted it, after the Paris Revolution of 1830,
in spite of his seventy years.   Three such spontaneous and blameless
ovations, — if we include his progress through the United States in 1824,
— were never granted to any other man but him in the course of the long-
est life-time.

his rank in the French service would be entitled to command, although he had led three times that number to battle in America; but he was willing to go into action against the British at the head of fifty dragoons or grenadiers, provided only that his men were staunch, and that his small party was allotted the post of danger. He would never rest satisfied, (so he passionately declared,) unless he was the first to plant the standard of France on the shores of the most insolent of nations.

Four hundred transports were in readiness to convey the French army across the Channel, as soon as the coast was clear, and the passage safe. The Ministers at Versailles had the advantage of knowing, with exact precision, the weakness of their adversary;[1] while the real strength of the allied fleets was an impenetrable secret to the Admiralty at Whitehall. The great mass of our frigates, and the best of our smaller vessels, had long ago been sent away across the Atlantic ocean to form a cordon of cruisers along seven hundred miles of the American seaboard; and their vacant places on stations nearer home were still unsupplied. There remained far less than enough of them for the protection of our commerce, and few, or none, to spare for scouting. In the previous summer the Comte d'Estaing had sallied forth unperceived from Toulon harbour, and had reached the Straits of Gibraltar, on his way to New York, before he was sighted by a British war-vessel; and the case was no better now. Lord Sandwich had left himself without the means of ascertaining the numbers, the condition, and the movements of the Spanish navy. England, (said the Earl of Bristol in Parliament,) had nothing in the Mediterranean except a poor old sixty-gun ship, with two or three frigates, creeping about from port to port, while the French were ranging

---

[1] " Pour cela, on suppose d'après ies dernières nouvelles d'Angleterre que cette puissance pourra, tout au plus, avoir sous voile dans le cours de l'été prochain trente-six vaisseaux de ligne dans les mers de l'Europe." *Le Plan d'Opérations;* 26 *Février,* 1779. Doniol's Correspondence; vol. III.

those seas with a squadron seven times the force of ours.[1]

On the eleventh of June 1779 the Comte d'Orvilliers duly kept his appointment at the island of Cisargas, off Corunna; but the Spaniards left him waiting there for five livelong weeks, consuming his provisions and his drinking-water, and losing the prime of the summer weather. They arrived at last; and the united fleets then attained the enormous total of sixty-six vessels of the line, and fourteen frigates. Sailing in double column, they covered four and a half miles of sea from van to rear; and the merc list of their names, and their gun-power, fills two closely printed pages in the naval histories. The British fleet lay, off and on, fifteen leagues to the south-west of the Scilly Isles. It was commanded by Sir Charles Hardy, the Governor of Greenwich Hospital, — a respectable veteran coming from a family of admirals who had done faithful and honourable service for more than a century past. He had with him what, under the circumstances, might be called a forlorn-hope of five-and-thirty ships, which were the most that could be scraped together from every available quarter in that hour of national peril. Such was the worth of the ministerial announcement that, when hostilities commenced, our naval strength would be found a match for both branches of the House of Bourbon.

The French and Spanish commanders occupied five more days in agreeing upon a common code of signals, and in teaching it to the fleet; — an elementary precaution the need for which had apparently never before occurred to them. On the thirtieth of July they turned their bowsprits northwards; loitered for a while in front of Brest, exchanging messages with the Ministry at Versailles; and then, — giving a very wide berth to Sir Charles Hardy, who had no more conception of their whereabouts than if they had been in the Pacific ocean, — they entered the British Channel, and

[1] *Parliamentary History;* XX, 435.

made their appearance at the mouth of Plymouth Sound. It was a bad moment for the menaced town when " the bloody flag," which signified that an enemy was in sight, was hoisted on the steeple of Maker Church.   No man knew what had become of Sir Charles Hardy, or what misfortune might not have befallen him.   Nothing was certain except that the most powerful armada that ever walked the waters had inserted itself between the British fleet and the British arsenals and dockyards. The military and naval officers, who were responsible for the safety of Plymouth, had the gravest cause for anxiety ; and the helplessness of their situation was brought home to their minds when the Ardent, a fine ship of sixty-four guns, was cut off and captured, within view of the ramparts, after a gallant resistance against preposterous odds.   The sea-front of the place was strong ; for most of those works which guarded the harbour had been constructed, and armed, under the personal care of Lord Amherst, the Lieutenant-General of the Ordnance, than whom no man was more competent to select the site for a battery.   But there were weak points in the circuit of wall on the land-side which were accessible to a sudden attack by an enterprising assailant.   The town contained a dangerously large number of French prisoners, violently excited by the sound of French cannon, and the proximity of a French fleet.   The reserve of cartridges for the great guns, which for many months had been constantly drawn upon for the needs of our fighting ships, was at a very low ebb ; and the garrison, consisting of four thousand men, all told, was sadly insufficient for the defence of such extensive fortifications, and such incalculably precious national possessions.   England had never been so near to an immense, and possibly an irredeemable, disaster since the day when Admiral de Ruyter broke the chain at Chatham.   But the Comte d'Orvilliers, and most assuredly Don Luis de Cordova, were not de Ruyters.   They paced the quarter-deck, trying to summon up their courage, and gazing dubiously at the long rows of thirty-two pounder guns which peered from the embrasures on Drake's Island and at Cawsand Bay. They dallied just too long with wind and weather; and, within the short space of forty-eight hours, their chance had come and gone. They had caught their first sight of Plymouth on Monday the sixteenth of August; and on Wednesday the eighteenth a gale blew from the east which swept them out of the British Channel, and only abated its fury when it had driven them into the Atlantic ocean fifty leagues to the west of Lizard Point.

The Plymouth garrison was not lulled into a false security by this abrupt departure of the enemy. Their preparations for defence were pressed forward to completion; and their exertions were loyally seconded by the people of the western counties, who showed abundance of public spirit and martial ardour. At first, as was sure to be the case, there had been some slight and transient symptoms of a panic; and timid householders removed their families up-country in such a hurry that the hire of a post-chaise and pair rose to a guinea a mile. But the main stream of travellers flowed in the opposite direction; and those who had their faces turned towards Plymouth were more numerous, and much more serviceable for military purposes, than those who deserted it. Armed men, and men eager to carry arms, — and, (which was not less important,) men as skilled in the use of the spade and pick-axe as any population in the world, — flocked in from Devon, and Cornwall, and even from remote parishes in Somersetshire. In an astonishingly short space of time after the news of the French fleet got underground in the neighbourhood of Liskeard eight hundred Cornish "tinners," with their local capitalists, and their captains of industry, at their head, marched in continuous column through the town gate of Plymouth; and, by the end of another week, six times as many were drawing rations, and labouring in gangs under the direction of officers of the Military Engineers. They formed a corps, or rather an

army, of sappers and miners ready made ; and they
raised parapets, and excavated trenches, and cleared
away houses and plantations which obstructed the
line of fire from the redoubts and batteries, with practised vigour and marvellous celerity.[1] Three thousand
muskets were sent down from the Tower, and distributed among the shipwrights and mechanics on the
Government establishment, who already were public
servants, and inured to some sort of discipline. There
soon was plenty of cartridges for great guns, and small.
The Lieutenant-General of the Ordnance took good care
that the cannon, which he had himself planted on the
shores of Plymouth Sound, should not be silent for lack
of powder. Horace Walpole, while driving into London
from Strawberry Hill, met thirty-six tumbrils, on a
single morning, carrying ammunition towards Devonshire. No precaution was neglected which could ensure
the Government building-sheds and storehouses against
a risk of incendiarism. Twelve hundred French prisoners
were transferred to Exeter, where an arrangement of
a novel character was made for their custody. "The
gentlemen of that city," wrote a correspondent from
Plymouth, "have come to a resolution to associate
themselves as a guard over them. The gentlemen of
Bristol have done the same ; and both these cities have
sent the whole of their militia hither." The ranks
of every militia battalion were full ; the officers had
been taught their duty ; and the privates had long
ere this been fashioned into excellent soldiers. On
the twenty-first of August there were seven thousand

---

[1] Lord Shuldham, the Port Admiral, who was the life and soul of the
defence, gave it as his opinion that the Mount Edgecumbe woods were so
placed as to favour and conceal the operations of a besieging force. The
citizens were reluctant to part with trees which were the glory of their
native town; but the owner of the domain, who was also a Vice-Admiral of
the Blue, at once pronounced himself in favour of the sacrifice. "If," he
said, "it be absolutely necessary for the preservation of the dockyard
that Mount Edgecumbe be destroyed, you have my ready consent, even
to the last shrub; " and "above one hundred ancient oaks, growing exactly
where they ought," were felled to the ground. *Walpole to the Countess of
Ossory;* August 16, 1780.

trained infantry in Plymouth, "besides many gentle-men-volunteers from London"; and, a few days after-wards, the garrison could turn out on parade with a strength of ten thousand bayonets. The patriotism of West-countrymen had placed their great dock-yard beyond the reach of peril; and it was the heart-felt prayer of all their regimental messes that Admiral d'Orvilliers would re-visit Plymouth, and that on the next occasion he would not forget to bring the French army with him.[1]

Charles Fox, who was still only thirty years of age, had been all on fire with excitement when news reached London that French and Spanish ships of war, in enormous force, had interposed themselves between Plymouth and the British fleet. He at once posted down to Saltram, the seat of John Parker, one of the members for Devonshire, — a country-house, full of noble Sir Joshuas, which was situated near at hand to the threatened town. Here he was in the very centre of the situation; for several vessels of the line, which had been fitted out in hot haste to reinforce Sir Charles Hardy, were waiting for orders in Torbay; and, at the speed which Fox habitually used when he rode or drove, he could reach Torbay from Saltram within the three hours. The officers of the squadron were surprised and delighted when the most genial of companions descended upon them as it were from the clouds; and, like true sailors, they responded cordially to the intense interest with which he listened to all that they had to tell him. He dined each evening with one or another of the captains, among whom was John Jervis of the Foudroyant, the largest two-decked ship in the Royal Navy, — a devoted admirer, and life-long ally, of Charles Fox. Fox extracted from his friend a pledge to take

---

[1] The account in this paragraph is largely derived from the columns of the *London Evening Post*, the *Public Advertiser* and the *Morning Post and Daily Advertiser*, between August the 19th and August the 31st, 1779. Something has been taken from the *Gentleman's Magazine* of the same month and year.

him on board whenever there was a prospect of a battle. He put off all his racing engagements, and let his correspondents at Brooks's, and in Norfolk, know that he must not be hurried to fix a date for his return. To those who reminded him that the first of September was approaching, Fox replied that, in the part of England where he now found himself, there was a probability of more serious sport than partridge-shooting. "If the French," (so he told Richard Fitzpatrick,) "should come again, I cannot think they will go away as they did before, and that there must, either at sea or land, be *quelque chose à voir;* in which case I should be very much vexed indeed to have left the country before the sight begins."[1]

When the storm subsided which had expelled the allies from the Channel they were already within a few leagues of Sir Charles Hardy's fleet ; and they made a half-hearted attempt to bring him to a general action. But he eluded their onset, and out-sailed their pursuit ; and then, picking up Jervis and his consorts on the way, he continued his progress eastward until he reached Spithead, where he was heartily welcomed. The garrison of Portsmouth was strong, and could be strengthened at brief notice. It was the head-quarters of the Royal Marines, who, seldom as they were given their due chance of distinguishing themselves, were a highly disciplined and most formidable infantry. Four regiments of dragoons were encamped in the immediate neighbourhood ; and Cox Heath, the Aldershot of that war, where as many militia battalions as would have made up a modern army-corps were collected under the orders of a very efficient general, lay at a distance of only three forced marches. Portsmouth was impregnable by land ; but the shipping at St. Helen's, and in the Solent, was exposed to the attack of an enemy who

---

[1] Most of the letters in which Fox described his excursion to the West are in *The Memorials and Correspondence.* The first of them, which is addressed to Lord Ossory, is wrongly assigned to the month of April. The correct date, of August 17, is on the original letter.

approached by sea. The arrival of Sir Charles Hardy, and the British fleet, made all safe in that quarter likewise ; and his return to Spithead, without having lost any of his ships, was hailed by the Ministerial newspapers, in that day of small mercies, with almost as much jubilation as if it had been a naval victory.

King George, however, was less easily satisfied. He had set his heart upon having a battle royal at the earliest opportunity. In that respect Charles Fox and his Sovereign, for once in their lives, were both of one mind. The King had not the slightest intention to keep the crews of his Channel fleet splicing ropes, and eating fresh beef, inside Portsmouth harbour; and he wasted no time before making his will and pleasure known. Sir Charles Hardy had cast anchor at Spithead on the third of September ; and, by eleven o'clock on the morning of the fourth, the Earl of Sandwich had already been ordered down to Portsmouth, at an hour's notice, with peremptory injunctions to inform the admiral by word of mouth that His Majesty expected "that the enemy would not be permitted to leave the Channel without feeling the chastisement which so base a conduct deserved." The King showed a fine spirit ; and his view was confirmed by the judgment of the best informed experts, who, with John Jervis at their head, were now all in favour of forcing on an immediate action.[1] Brilliant results were anticipated from the personal qualities of the British officers ; for it was universally agreed that such a set of captains had never before sailed in one and the same fleet. Most of them had been commanders of frigates, or dashing First-lieutenants, in Chatham's war ; and the older men, who

[1] Seven times, in the course of two months, the King had expressed to Lord North his desire that the quarrel with France and Spain should without delay be submitted to the ordeal of battle; and he never had written better letters. " I have not," (he said on the eighteenth July,) " the smallest anxiety if the ships already under the command of Sir Charles Hardy can bring the combined fleet to a close action. I have the fullest confidence in the Divine Providence, and that the officers and men of my fleet will act with the ardour that the times require."

had fought together in line of battle under Hawke and Saunders, had acquired a well-grounded confidence in each other's professional skill, and mutual loyalty. Meanwhile, in the course of the last week, the number of Sir Charles Hardy's vessels had been increased from about one half to something better than two thirds of the hostile force. That proportion, in the last resort, was good enough for a British admiral; as was shown by Jervis himself when, twenty years afterwards, he triumphed at Cape St. Vincent with only fifteen ships to twenty-seven of the Spaniards, and barely one gun to every two of theirs.

There was no battle; but one of the combatants experienced the miseries of war in a sad and dreadful form. When the French set out on their voyage from Brest on the fourth of June 1779 they had small-pox, and putrid fever, on board; and yet some of their vessels sailed unprovided with the regulation medicines, and others did not carry a single doctor. Six weeks afterwards Admiral d'Orvilliers, before leaving the coast of Spain for the British Channel, had put five hundred of the worst cases ashore at Corunna ; but he took at least four times as many sick men with him. A French line-of-battle ship of the eighteenth century was nothing else than a forcing-bed for disease, whenever the germs of disease existed. This generation can form no adequate conception of the sufferings endured by a thousand, or eleven hundred, human beings cooped up with their badly-cured provisions and noisome drinking-water, during the four hottest months of the year, in an ark a hundred and seventy feet by fifty; where all the free spaces were encumbered, and the port-holes blocked, by a hundred great cannon; while a continuous row of hammocks, between any two of which a man could with difficulty insert his head, hung close beneath the planking of the roof along the whole extent of the stifling lower decks. At the end of August the Comte de Guichen, one of 'the Lieutenants-General of the fleet, had five hundred of his crew incapacitated for service ; and sixty of their dead bodies had been committed to the waves. Six hundred had been struck down on board another vessel, of whom seventy had already died; and in a third ship, which had a complement of eight hundred, only three hundred and sixty turned out to keep watch. The bulk of the returns sent in by the commanding officers showed five hundred, four hundred, or three hundred names excused from duty. One captain, who came of a notable family of warriors, reported that those of his men, who still had strength to go aloft, were too few to make sail; and that, if he encountered an enemy, he would be unable to muster sufficient hands to prepare his ship for action, or to serve her lower tier of guns.[1] When September came, d'Orvilliers sent eight of his floating hospitals back to Brest; and those which kept the sea were hardly in better case. He informed his Government that their fleet was incapable of manœuvring in the fairest of weather, and most certainly could not ride out a gale, or survive a battle. That statement was the more important because, in a confidential letter, he had already expressed his conviction that the Spaniards would make a very poor show indeed if the French were not in a condition to take more than their own share of the fighting. "I am persuaded," he wrote, "that our allies are brave and loyal; but what I see of their seamanship confirms me more than ever in the opinion that they have no claim to the title of good naval officers."[2]

The rulers of France were unable to disregard the frank and earnest representations of their trustworthy

[1] *Chef d'Escadre de Rochechouart au Comte d'Orvilliers:* late August, or early September, 1779.

[2] The spread of disease on board the French fleet is narrated in the Fifth Book of Chevalier's *Histoire de la Marine Française, pendant la Guerre de l'Indépendance Américaine.* Full justice is there done to the remarkable story. The principles of naval sanitation were better understood, and more carefully and humanely practised, in England than in France. "Les Anglais," (wrote the Comte de Ségur,) "connaissaient seuls alors ces salutaires précautions qu'enseigne la science de l'hygiène pour conserver la santé des équipages. Nos ministres étaient à cet égard dans la plus fatale incurie."

servant. On the fourteenth of September, by orders
from Versailles, the allied fleet sought an asylum in
Brest harbour. The Spanish ships, after no long while,
made their way home to Cadiz ; the army of invasion
was broken up and dispersed ; and the famous plan,
which Vergennes had elaborated for affecting a descent
upon the coast of England, was consigned to the Limbo
whither so many promising schemes for the achievement
of the same object have preceded or followed it. D'Orvilliers, — whose son, a fine young naval officer, had
died of putrid fever on board the Comte de Guichen's
ship, — came back to France broken-hearted by patriotic
chagrin and private sorrow. The unhappy man resigned
his command, and disappeared from the world so completely that he was believed to have sought seclusion in
a religious house. Louis the Sixteenth's ministers, who
were the real culprits, endeavoured to throw the responsibility of failure upon the admiral ; but they had to do
with a nation which was far too clever to be deluded.
All the coffee-houses, and drawing-rooms, and theatres
were in bitter and sarcastic opposition ; and for some
months to come " it rained pamphlets and epigrams."
The Parisian public, disappointed of their expected *Te
Deum*, were at all events determined to sing something ;
and it was long before the last was heard of a popular
ballad the burden of which was a couplet asserting that
the gold watch worn by a Minister at Versailles was always six months behind time.

CHAPTER VII

BURKE AND THE INDIANS. THE POWER OF THE CROWN.
BURKE AND BRISTOL.

THROUGHOUT the years which elapsed between 1775 and 1782 war raged all the world over, and military reputations were made, and unmade, with startling rapidity. And yet, as far as England was concerned, the most distinguished names which have come down to us from that stirring time are those of civilians, and not of soldiers; for, in the full sense of the phrase, the toga was then more powerful than the sword. In the course of our long parliamentary history the two great parties in the House of Commons have not unfrequently been led by rival statesmen each of whom was an orator of the first order; but, except during the period which coincided with the American Revolution, such a pair of champions as Burke and Fox have seldom indeed fought side by side in the same ranks. They were closely, and, (as it then seemed,) indissolubly united by devotion to a common cause, and by mutual confidence and affection. Fox, devoid of self-conceit, and incapable of envy, regarded Burke with

" That instant reverence,
Dearer to true young hearts than their own praise;"

and the older man took unceasing delight in the company of the younger, and submitted himself willingly and unreservedly to the spell of the extraordinary charm which he, like everybody else, found it impossible to define and analyse.

Very early in the time when they began to work in concert Burke paid Fox the unusual tribute of accepting him as the exponent of his own views on more

than one occasion;[1] and the influence of the two
allies on the proceedings in Parliament was all the more
effective because the one was the precise complement
of the other. " You always," said Wordsworth, " went
from Fox with your feelings excited, and from Burke
with your mind filled."[2] So full and cultured a mind
as Burke's, — so vivid an imagination, and so intense
and catholic an interest in all human affairs, past and
present, — have never been placed at the service of the
state by any one except by Cicero. A famous author,
in the most heartfelt, and therefore perhaps the most
beautiful, passage which he ever wrote, regrets that
Cicero and Burke expended in political controversy
the time, health, and thought which they might have
more profitably bestowed upon literature.[3] But mankind must take thankfully whatever the like of Burke
and Cicero chose to give them ; and it may reasonably
be contended that both of them found the material,
which was best suited to their genius, in the senate
rather than in the library. Unless Cicero had drunk
deep of the ambitions, the passions, — and, in his case,
the sorrows and terrors, — of Roman public life, the
Letters to Atticus would not have been among the
most thrilling and pathetic of extant compositions;
and, if Edmund Burke had stood aside from Parliament, he might have done wonders in history and
philosophy, but he could have created nothing of higher
value than the Speech on Conciliation with America,
or the Thoughts on the Cause of the Present Discontents. It is not for politicians to question the choice
of a career made by the two men who, beyond all

[1] After the discussion on the Address in November 1776 Burke wrote
to his friend Champion to explain his own silence. " I never," (he said,)
"knew Charles Fox better, or indeed any one, on any occasion. His
speech was a noble performance. . . . I did not speak, though up twice.
I was not so much hindered by my cold, which was then but slight. I
waited for the Crown lawyers, expecting some of them would follow
Charles Fox ; but none spoke, and the debate could not lie better than he
left it."

[2] *Haydon's Autobiography;* May 23, 1815.

[3] Macaulay to Ellis; Calcutta, December 30, 1835.

others, have adorned and embellished the vocation of politics.

At this period of his life Burke had a sound instinct for the selection of topics which called into exercise the entire force of his marvellous capacity. He had no time to lose, for he was close upon fifty; a circumstance which went for a great deal in a generation when four men, — the Duke of Grafton, the Marquis of Rocking-ham, Lord North, and the younger Pitt, — became Prime Ministers at an average age of eight-and-twenty. The question of the relations between Great Britain and her American colonies had thrown all other questions into the back-ground; and it was a problem by which Burke, with his vast knowledge and his all-embracing sympathy, was sure to be attracted, and which he was pre-eminently competent to handle. That disastrous controversy would never have reached an acute stage if King George's Cabinet had acted in obedience to those great principles of exalted common sense which were the main articles of Burke's creed. He had been constantly repeating, in a form of words which all readers could understand, and with a force and pregnancy on which no writer who ever lived could improve, that the temper of the people whom he governs should be the first study of a statesman, and that magnanimity in politics is the truest wisdom. Parliament, (so he freely admitted,) had a constitutional right to tax America; but it was a right which, in the condition of feeling that prevailed beyond the Atlantic, no British Minister in his senses would dream of exerting. "Whether," he said, "all this can be reconciled in legal speculation is a matter of no consequence. It is reconciled in policy; and politics ought to be adjusted, not to human reasonings, but to human nature, of which the reason is but a part, and by no means the greatest part." [1] That was the view which Burke earnestly impressed upon the leaders of his own party, who had hitherto been slow to recog-

[1] *Observations on a Late Publication, entitled, "The Present State of the Nation,"* 1769.

nise the full gravity of the American crisis. He rebuked their indolence with a respectful and affectionate
eloquence unsurpassed in the literature of politics; [1]
and before very long, by his precepts and his example,
he succeeded in inspiring them with all his own courage,
and much of his own zeal. They joined in his emphatic
protest against those penal laws which, after a trial
of four calamitous years, were condemned and abandoned by the very Minister who had placed them on
the Statute Book. They argued against the passing
madness of the hour, and they were stigmatised by their
detractors as unpatriotic and un-English; — that taunt
which is, of all others, the most suicidal to the true
interests of England. For a high-minded people, such
as ours, will not consent to learn their national duty
from the criticisms of foreigners; and therefore, if it
be un-English for Englishmen to speak their minds, the
country will never hear the truth at all.

When war had broken out between Great Britain
and her colonies, and when France and Spain had
thrown themselves into the quarrel, Burke directed his
attention to those elements of the situation which lay in
his habitual line of thought, and with regard to which
his advice was especially valuable. He left it for
Charles Fox to animadvert upon the strategical operations in America, and to expose the inadequacy of the
military and naval preparations which had been made
for the defence of our island; and he confined himself,
as his own particular province, to what may fairly be
described as the moral aspects of the war. From the
summer of 1778 onwards the ministers of George the
Third finally and deliberately abandoned their attempt
to re-conquer. the Northern and Central States of the
Union; but they continued to keep the dispute alive
by a series of petty and inconclusive acts of hostility
directed against the civil population, rather than
against the armed forces, of the enemy. It was a

[1] The finest of these memorable compositions was addressed to the
Duke of Richmond on the seventeenth of November, 1772.

species of warfare which served no purpose except to irritate the Americans, and dispose them to persevere in a course of active retaliation at a time when, in their utter weariness, they would otherwise have been inclined to rest quiet, and allow France, Spain, and England to fight until one or other of them was beaten. Burke lost no opportunity of denouncing this resort on the part of the British Government to a system of pin-pricks, where sword-thrusts had failed. He condemned it as futile, and most impolitic ; and he did not shrink from reprobating it as cruel and unrighteous ; for he was one of those who was not afraid to follow where his conscience led him.

When Lord Carlisle and his colleagues, leaving their mission unaccomplished, withdrew themselves from Philadelphia to New York in the wake of Sir Henry Clinton's retreating army, they were in a fit of temper which was not without its excuses. They had been befooled by the Cabinet Ministers who sent them across the ocean ; and their efforts to open a negotiation with Congress had been ignored by that body with an indifference which bordered on contempt. Before taking their passage back to England they exhaled their vexation, and endeavoured to salve their wounded dignity, by the issue of a valedictory Proclamation which they circulated, in an enormous number of copies, throughout the United States. They announced, in dark and ominous terms, that the world must expect a change "in the whole nature, and the future conduct, of the war," and that the British Government would henceforward direct its efforts to desolate the country, and distress the people, of America.

This extraordinary production, which excited anger rather than uneasiness among the Americans whom it was intended to frighten, was read with consternation by all sensible men in Great Britain. The attention of the House of Commons was called to the Manifesto by Coke of Norfolk in the first of those brief and weighty utterances which, for five-and-fifty years to come, were always heard with favour by an assembly to whose taste both speech, and speaker, were in all points precisely suited. He reminded his fellow-members that the plunder and destruction of commercial towns, and defenceless fishing villages, would invite reprisals which the Board of Admiralty had taken no precautions to meet; and the young senator vehemently declared that, apart from considerations of prudence and public safety, such modes of warfare were repugnant to the humanity, and the generous courage, which had in all times distinguished the British nation. A subordinate member of the Government had provided himself with copious extracts from Puffendorf and Grotius to prove that the burning of unfortified towns, "which were the nurseries of soldiers," was perfectly consistent with the accepted rules of war; but all the respect and deference due to those antique pundits was swept away by the flood of indignant rhetoric which poured from the lips of Edmund Burke. "The extremes of war," he said, "and the desolation of a country, were sweet-sounding mutes and liquids; but their meaning was terrible. They meant the killing of man, woman, and child; — burning their houses, and ravaging their lands, and annihilating humanity from the face of the earth, or rendering it so wretched that death was preferable. They exceeded all that the rights of war, as observed between civilised nations, would sanction; and, as no necessity could warrant them, so no argument could excuse them." The impression produced by Burke was so deep that the Prime Minister, and the Attorney-General, rose successively to assure the House that an interpretation had been placed upon the Manifesto which the words would not bear; but they were roughly contradicted by Governor Johnstone, who had been a brother Commissioner of Lord Carlisle, and who therefore spoke with an authority which there was no gain-saying. He had returned to England, breathing fire and fury against the Americans; and in consequence, for the first time in his life, he had been graciously received at Court when he went to pay his respects to His Majesty. Johnstone now told Parliament fiercely and repeatedly that, whatever might be alleged to the contrary, the Proclamation most certainly did mean a war of destruction. " It meant nothing else; it could mean nothing else; and, if he had been on the spot when it was issued, he would himself have signed it. No quarter ought to be shown to the American Congress; and, if the infernals could be let loose on them, he would approve the measure." No Minister of the Crown was able to gainsay a man who knew so accurately what he was talking about, and who, (as North and Wedderburn were both aware,) gave expression to the exact sentiments held by their own strong-willed and masterful Sovereign.

Burke performed a still more notable and durable service to mankind by his protest against the employment of savage auxiliaries in a warfare between civilised Powers. His statesmanlike and impassioned oratory produced an immediate effect upon the opinion, and an ultimate and permanent change in the practice, of our own and other nations. It was said at the time, and it has been repeated since, as an excuse for Lord North's Government, that French and English commanders in former years had often taken the field, or more properly speaking the forest, with a large contingent of Indian warriors in their train. British generals had used red men as scouts for the purpose of exploring the woods, and covering the flank of their columns, during an advance through the wilderness;[1] and the Marquis de Montcalm, in a sad hour for his good fame, led the Iroquois into battle at Fort William Henry as a component part of his fighting force. But the Indians had hitherto been exclusively employed in aid of regular operations directed against an armed and disciplined foe. It was reserved for Lord North and his colleagues to send them forth as executioners to punish a civil

[1] Speech of the Earl of Chatham; *Parliamentary History,* volume XIX, page 411.

population for the crime of rebellion. Cherokees and Senecas, under injunctions sent from Downing Street, were subsidised with public money, and bribed with food and brandy, and then turned loose upon some peaceful country-side in Virginia or Pennsylvania to work their will, and glut their ferocity, amidst a community of English-speaking people who had not a single paid and trained soldier to protect them; and these hordes of savages, on more than one occasion, marched to the scene of slaughter and rapine under the orders of a Loyalist officer who bore His Majesty's commission. Lord Chatham, in the last months of his life, raised his voice in condemnation of this barbarous, — and, as he maintained, this unprecedented, — policy; but he got no satisfaction from a Secretary of State who seemed to have peculiar views of his own about the Third Commandment. "It is allowable," (replied the Earl of Suffolk,) "and perfectly justifiable, to use every means which God has put into our hands." [1]

That statement was made in the House of Lords in November 1777; and, before the year was out, full particulars of the catastrophe of Saratoga arrived in England. The history of Burgoyne's expedition was one long object lesson on the military value, and moral

---

[1] The real character of an Indian raid upon an unarmed and civilised population has been forgotten in our time, for the very sufficient reason that the details and incidents of those raids are indescribable in decent histories. But it is possible, without defiling the printed page, to give a specimen of Indian barbarity. An interesting personal narrative of General Sullivan's punitive march through the Seneca country in the Fall of 1779 has recently been published in Philadelphia; and in the course of that march a small party of Sullivan's people fell into the hands of the Indian warriors. "In this place," writes one of their comrades, " we found the body of the brave, but unfortunate, Lieutenant Boyd, and one Rifleman, massacred in the most cruel and barbarous manner that the human mind can possibly conceive, the savages having first put them to the most excruciating torments by plucking their nails from hands and feet, and then spearing, cutting, and whipping them, and mangling their bodies, and then cutting off the flesh from their shoulders by pieces, tomahawking their heads from their bodies, and leaving them a prey to their dogs. O Britain, behold, and blush!"

That was how the Indians treated their male captives. For the women they too often reserved a yet more horrible fate.

characteristics, of our Indian allies; and Burke chose
an early opportunity for driving that lesson home to
the conscience of Parliament. He spoke for more than
three hours to a crowded and entranced assembly.
Strangers, including of course the newspaper reporters,
had been rigorously excluded from the Gallery; and,
though Burke was urgently entreated to publish his
speech, he could not find the leisure, nor perhaps the
inclination, to rekindle in the solitude of his study that
flame of rhetoric which had blazed up spontaneously
under the genial influence of universal admiration, and
all but universal sympathy. It was generally allowed
that he had surpassed all his earlier performances. He
left no aspect of the question untouched; he stated, in
due sequence, every important argument; and, when he
let his fancy loose, he traversed the whole scale of oratorical emotion, from the depth of pathos to the height
of unrestrained, audacious, and quite irresistible humour.

Burke began by laying the solid foundation for his
case in a series of closely-reasoned passages of which
only the outlines remain on record. These Indian
tribes, (he said,) had in the course of years been so
reduced in number and power that they were now only
formidable from their cruelty; and to use them for
warlike purposes was merely to be cruel ourselves in
their persons. He called attention to the salient distinction between their employment " against armed and
trained soldiers, embodied and encamped, and against
unarmed and defenceless men, women, and children,
dispersed in their several habitations " over the whole
extent of a prosperous and industrious district. He
attributed Burgoyne's defeat to the horror excited in
the American mind by the prospect of an Indian invasion. The manly and resolute determination of the
New England farmers to save their families and their
homesteads from these barbarians led them " without
regard to party, or to political principle, and in despite
of military indisposition, to become soldiers, and to
unite as one man in the common defence. Thus was the

spectacle exhibited of a resistless army springing up in
the woods and deserts." Indians, (said Burke,) were the
most useless, and the most expensive, of all auxiliaries.
Each of their so-called braves cost as much as five of
the best European musketeers; and, after eating double
rations so long as the provisions lasted, they kept out
of sight on a day of battle, and deserted wholesale at
the first appearance of ill-success. They were not less
faithless than inefficacious. When Colonel St. Leger
found himself in difficulties they turned their weapons,
with insolent treachery, against their civilised comrades;
and over a circuit of many miles around Burgoyne's
camp they plundered, and butchered, and scalped
with entire indifference to the sex, the age, and the
political opinions of their victims. Burke told the
story of the poor Scotch girl's murder, on the eve of her
intended marriage to an officer of the King's troops,
with an effect on the nerves of his audience which perhaps was never equalled except by his own description,
during the trial of Warren Hastings, of the treatment
inflicted by the Nabob Vizier on the Oude princesses.
Many of his hearers were moved to tears; — a spectacle
which, in the British Parliament, is seen hardly once
in a generation;[1] and Governor Johnstone congratu-
lated the Ministry that there were no strangers in the
Gallery, because they would have been worked up to
such a pitch of excitement that Lord North, and Lord
George Germaine, must have run a serious risk from
popular violence as soon as they emerged into the street
from the sanctuary of the House of Commons.

And then Burke changed his note, and convulsed
his audience by a parody of Burgoyne's address to the
Indians. It was a passage which Horace Walpole, who

[1] "Mr. Burke never displayed the powers of oratory so strongly as the
other day when the affair of the contracts with the Indians was agitated.
His speech drew tears from the whole House, particularly that part of it
where he described the murder of Miss McReay. I had not the pleasure
of hearing him, as it is at present a standing order that nobody is to be
admitted into the Gallery." Letter from Sir Michael le Fleming; Berkeley
Square, Feb. 9, 1778.

had collected his knowledge of it in detached morsels from many sources, pronounced to be a *chef-d'œuvre* of wit, humour, and just satire. "I wish," (he wrote,) "I could give an idea of that superlative oration. How cold, how inadequate will be my fragment of a sketch from second, third, and thousandth hands!" Burke related how the British general harangued a throng of warriors drawn from seventeen separate Indian nations, who, so far from understanding the Burgoynese dialect, could not even follow the meaning of a speech made in plain English; how he invited them, — by their reverence for the Christian religion, and their well-known, and well-considered, views on the right of taxation inherent in the Parliament at Westminster, — to grasp their tomahawks, and rally round His Majesty's standard; and how he adjured them, "by the same divine and human laws," not to touch a hair on the head of man, woman, or child while living, though he was willing to deal with them for scalps of the dead, inasmuch as he was a nice and distinguished judge between the scalp taken from a dead person, and from the head of a person who had died of being scalped. "Let us illustrate this Christian exhortation, and Christian injunction," said Burke, "by a more familiar picture. Suppose the case of a riot on Tower Hill. What would the keeper of His Majesty's lions do? Would he not leave open the dens of the wild beasts, and address them thus : ' My gentle lions, my humane bears, my tender-hearted hyænas, go forth against the seditious mob on your mission of repression and retribution; but I exhort you as you are Christians, and members of a civilised society, to take care not to hurt man, woman, or child.'" Burke, like Mr. Gladstone after him, was said to be deficient in humour;[1] but a great orator depends for his lighter effects not on a store of prepared jests and epigrams, but on the unforced gaiety by which he himself is swayed at the moment, and which he has the art and the power to

[1] *Boswell's Tour to the Hebrides;* August 15, 1773.

diffuse among his hearers. The walls of the chamber
fairly shook with applause; Lord North himself "was
almost suffocated by laughter"; and Colonel Barré
declared that, if Burke would only print the speech,
he, on his part, would undertake that it should be nailed
to the door of every parish church beneath the notice
proclaiming a day of general fasting and humiliation
on account of the surrender of Saratoga. That speech
would explain, far better than the homily of any
courtly bishop, the real causes of the disaster which
had brought the nation to dust and ashes.

The oration on the employment of Indian auxiliaries,
which by itself would have made the reputation of a
senator, was for Burke nothing more than a splendid
interlude amidst his daily and nightly labours in another
field of politics. It was during the six years of this
parliament that he established his claim to rank in
English history with Sir Robert Walpole, Sir Robert
Peel, and Mr. Gladstone as a financier and economist
of the very highest order. The period of time which he
selected for making his attack upon corrupt and extravagant expenditure may appear at first sight to have
been imprudently chosen. When the nation is engaged
in an arduous war, a jealous and vigilant guardian of
the public resources has for the most part a thankless
office. Laxity of control, favouritism in the allocation
of Government contracts for stores and shipping, and
even connivance in responsible quarters with the
grosser forms of peculation, are too often disguised
under the specious title of a large-minded patriotism
which does not concern itself about trifles when the
safety of the country is in question; and any public
man, who stands forward in defence of thrift and
probity, is sure to be denounced as something little short
of a traitor by all those who are making excessive or
dishonest profits out of the necessities of the state.
But the peers and commoners, who took part with

Edmund Burke in his crusade against jobbery and
prodigality, were silently conscious of the disinterestedness of their own motives, and superbly indifferent
to what was said about them by people whose ill will
was a compliment, and whose good word was the worst
of libels. The Duke of Richmond, and the Marquis of
Rockingham, and the Earl of Shelburne, and Sir George
Savile, and Lord John and Lord Frederic Cavendish,
had each and all of them too unimpeachable a character,
and too large a stake in the welfare of England, to heed
the abuse of mercenary politicians who were paid for
their votes by parcels of scrip which they could sell at a
premium of ten per cent. on the morning after they were
allotted, and of mercantile adventurers who supplied the
Transport Department of the Admiralty with unseaworthy vessels at five shillings in the pound above the
market rate of tonnage. The leaders of the Opposition discriminated carefully between the class of expenditure which it was their duty to provide, and the class
of expenditure which it was equally their duty to
oppose. They never thwarted or obstructed any well-
conceived scheme for strengthening the defences of the
country. In the second year of the French war a Bill
for augmenting the Militia, laid before the House of
Commons on the twenty-first of June, was passed
within the space of four days after long bouts of work
in what was described as " a putrid atmosphere " by
the members who inhaled it ; and in the same week
a Bill for facilitating the enlistment of seamen was
brought forward after midnight, and carried through
all its stages before the House rose on the morrow.[1]
Burke and Fox, as well as all their political allies and
personal followers, opened the national purse-strings
freely to the requirements of military efficiency ; while
they ruthlessly exposed, and fearlessly assailed, a
system of financial practices ruinous to the taxpayer,
and gravely and increasingly dangerous to the liberties
of Britain.

[1] *Parliamentary History;* volume XX, pages 915 to 969.

Those liberties had been in jeopardy from the moment when George the Third, in the full vigour of early manhood, and with a force of will, and determination of purpose, which almost reached the level of genius, set himself deliberately to build up a solid and enduring structure of personal government. To maintain in power ministers of his own choice, irrespective of the estimation in which they were held by their countrymen ; to exercise his veto on legislation, not by announcing through the mouth of the Clerk of the Parliaments that the King would further consider the matter, but by contriving that the measures which he disapproved should be defeated in the Lobby of one or another of the two Houses ; "to secure to the Court the unlimited and uncontrolled use of its vast influence, under the sole direction of its private favour ; "[1] those were the objects which he pursued, and attained, by methods opposed to the spirit, but compatible with the processes, of the Constitution. The King had the wit to see "that the forms of a free, and the ends of an arbitrary, government," might be reconciled by a course of action which avoided the outward show of despotism. Before he had been ten years on the throne he was in a fair way to succeed where Charles the First and James the Second had failed ; and his policy, while less fraught with peril to the safety of the monarch than was the policy of the Stuarts, was infinitely more demoralising to the character of the nation. George the Third had no occasion to march his Guards to Westminster, or commit the leaders of the Opposition to the Tower of London, as long as he could make sure of a parliamentary majority by an unscrupulous abuse of Government patronage, and, (where need was,) by direct and downright bribery. "The power of the Crown," said Burke, "almost dead and rotten as Prerogative, has grown up anew, with much more strength, and far less odium, under the name of Influence." Everything, (so this famous patriot declared,) had been drawn from its holdings in the country to the personal favour of the

[1] *Thoughts on the Cause of the Present Discontents.* 1770.

prince. That favour was the sole introduction to office, and the sole tenure by which it was held; until at last servility had become prevalent, and almost universal, "in spite of the dead letter of any laws and institutions whatsoever." [1]

The machinery of corruption was worked under the habitual and minute supervision of the King; and with good reason. In previous reigns the leaders of both parties, — Harley and Bolingbroke, and Walpole, and Newcastle, — had bribed to keep themselves in office; and now George the Third was bribing, on his own account, in order to retain in his own hands the secure possession of autocratic power. The unsavoury revelations that appear on almost every page of the royal letters to Lord North enable us faintly to conjecture the character of those still less avowable secrets which did not bear to be recorded in black and white, and were reserved for a private conversation between the monarch and the minister. The official correspondence which the King most thoroughly enjoyed was that which he exchanged with Mr. John Robinson, the Patronage Secretary of the Treasury, who was proverbially known for as shrewd and shameless a trafficker in the human conscience as ever priced a rotten borough, or slipped a bank-bill into the palm of a wavering senator. All the departments of electoral and parliamentary management were administered by this adroit and devoted servant beneath the close and constant inspection of the master's eye. When a general election was in prospect the King began to save up a special fund to meet the initial expenses of the contest.[2] He knew the circumstances of all the landed proprietors who had a borough at their disposal; — which of them could afford to keep back one of his two seats for a son or a nephew, and which of them was prepared to part with both; how many of

---

[1] *Thoughts on the Cause of the Present Discontents.*

[2] "As the Dissolution is now fixed for Wednesday, August 30th, I think it right to transmit the money to you which completes up to this month the £1000 per month I have laid by. . . . The amount of the notes is £14000." The King to J. R., Windsor Castle; August 21, 1780.

them would be content to take their money in pounds, and how many would stand out for guineas. He condescended even to those ignoble details which the least fastidious of parliamentary candidates leaves to the sinister industry of a subordinate agent. "Lord North," (he wrote,) "acquainted me with his wish of supporting Mr. Powney for the borough of New Windsor. I shall get my tradesmen encouraged to appear for him. I shall order, in consequence of Mr. Robinson's hint, the houses I rent in Windsor to stand in the parish rate in different names of my servants; so that will create six votes." [1]

When the King had got his nominees duly elected to Parliament he did not abandon them to their own devices, but took excellent care that they should perform his behests within the walls of Westminster. Before he sat down to his early breakfast on the morning after a critical division he already had looked to see whether any of their names were missing on the list of ministerial voters. Tellers of the Exchequer, and Storekeepers of the Ordnance, and Vice-Treasurers of Ireland, and Paymasters of Marines, and Rangers of the Royal Forests, and Registrars of the Chancery of Barbadoes, and Grooms of the Bedchamber, and holders of open pensions for life, and holders of secret pensions during pleasure, and Clerks of the Board of Green Cloth, and the eight Lords of Trade marching to order like the section of an infantry regiment, and the whole crowd of place-holders from the King's Turnspit, who hired a poor wretch at two shillings a week to perform his functions in the Royal Kitchen,[2] up to the Envoy Extraordinary at the Court of Savoy, "who made a sinecure of his post, and left a secretary at Turin, while he enjoyed

---

[1] This letter was addressed to the Secretary of the Treasury in May 1780. The member for Windsor, as His Majesty's own local representative, got his full share of the Secret Service money. "Mr. Powney," wrote Lord North to Mr. Robinson, "stipulated at first for only £1000. He has, I believe, had £1500 or £2000. What does he want now?"

[2] Speech of Earl Talbot, Lord Steward of the Household, April 16, 1777.

his friends and his bottle in London ";[1] — these remarkable senators, one and all, were perfectly aware that, while they were free to neglect their official duties at Dublin, or Portsmouth, or in the West Indies, or on the Continent of Europe, they would have to be inside the House of Commons when the door was shut, and the question put, or their gracious sovereign would know the reason why. When there were not enough well-paid appointments to go round the whole circle of expectants those left out in the cold were conciliated by a round sum in hard cash. " Mr. Robinson," said His Majesty, " shewed his usual propriety in transmitting to me last night the list of speakers in the debate, as well as of the division. I take this opportunity of sending £6000 to be placed to the same account as that sent on the 21st of August."[2] The means which the King employed were sanctified in his own mind by the ideal perfection of the object at which he was aiming. " It is attachment to my country," he wrote, " that alone actuates my purposes; and Lord North shall see that at least there is one person willing to preserve unspoiled the most beautiful combination that ever was."[3] It was a combination which has presented itself under a very different aspect to honest and discerning Englishmen. " Of all ingenious instruments of despotism," said Sydney Smith, " I must commend a popular assembly where the majority are paid and hired, and a few bold and able men, by their brave speeches, make the people believe that they are free."

The enormous, and perpetually growing, cost of this flagitious system was ostensibly provided by the King himself from the resources at his own command. George the Third called the tune, because he paid, or was supposed to pay, for the music. A Civil List of three-quarters of a million pounds a year had been settled on him, once for all, at the commencement of his

[1] *Evening Post* of May 11, 1779.
[2] The King to J. R.   Queen's House;   March 6, 1781.
[3] The King to Lord North.   Queen's House;   April 11, 1780.   15 min. past 8 a.m.

reign, and was exempt thenceforward from the control
of Parliament. He enjoyed, on the same agreeable
conditions, the receipts from the Duchies of Cornwall
and Lancaster; whatever surplus he could draw from
the kingdom of Hanover, and the Bishopric of Osna-
burgh; lucrative Admiralty dues, and Crown rights, and
various odds and ends of taxation then regarded as
perquisites of the monarch; — as well as the hereditary
revenues of Scotland, and the Civil List of Ireland, which
was a veritable gold mine of pensions and salaries for
obsequious English politicians who did as the King
bade them at Westminster. The entire sum exceeded a
million annually, at a time when the average expenditure of the country, in a year of peace, fell considerably
short of five millions.[1] The English Civil List was encumbered with the stipends of the Judges, and with the
outfit and maintenance of British Ministers abroad,
whether they were living at their posts in the capitals
to which they were accredited, or whether they were
tippling, and voting, with the Bedfords in London;
but otherwise the whole of this colossal fund was at the
absolute and unfettered disposal of the monarch. It
was amply sufficient to have maintained the Court in
regal splendour and overflowing comfort, and would
have enabled George the Third to give himself the
satisfaction, (which the greatest rulers of all ages and
countries have regarded as their most valued privilege,)
of sparing something, in times of national emergency,
to relieve the distress, and contribute to the safety, of
the State. The appanage of the throne was generous,
and even magnificent, when estimated by the standard
of private incomes which then prevailed. Lord Shelburne, who did not race or gamble, but who lived nobly
in town and country, gave it as his experience that
"a man of high rank, who looked into his own affairs,

[1] In the year 1767 the total expenditure of Great Britain, exclusive of
charges connected with the National Debt, amounted to £4,618,000 ; in
1768 to £4,235,000 ; and in 1769 to £4,304,000. *Return of Public Income
and Expenditure, Part I ; as ordered to be printed by the House of Commons
in July* 1869.

might have all that he ought to have, all that could be of any use or appear with any advantage, for five thousand pounds a year." But the disbursements of the Royal Establishment were in excess of two hundred thousand pounds annually; and never were the current expenses of any household in more extravagant disproportion to the wants and habits of the master.

George the Third lived very sparingly, — a conscientious ascetic amidst a society which sadly needed examples of temperance. His boiled mutton and turnips, and his jug of barley-water, on a hunting-day, and the tea and bread and butter which sustained him during an afternoon of hard toil following upon a morning of ceremonial duties, excited the mockery of the idle, and the admiring envy of the wise.[1] In other respects his ways were those of a great English country gentleman with the eyes of the world upon him. He liked to feel a fine horse under him when he was galloping after his stag-hounds, and to see the villas and garden-walls, which bordered the Western road, fly past his coach-window as he drove in from Kew to take his seat at the head of a Council-board. He knew good furniture from bad; he loved, with a Platonic affection, the aspect of famous and classical books in tall editions and choice bindings; and there were consummate artists among his subjects competent to gratify his taste in both particulars. He gave his dress no less thought, and no more, than became a monarch. His costumes were suited to the manifold, and very genuine, occupations in which he was engaged; on occasions of State their materials were costly, and their colours perfectly chosen; and, excellent husband that he was, his wife could never be too richly and gaily bedecked to please him.[2] Everything that his private inclinations de-

[1] When Samuel Curwen, the Loyalist exile, was shown over the Queen's House at Buckingham Gate, his special attention was called to a silver-gilt vessel, called the King's Cup, in which the water-gruel was served which constituted George the Third's supper.

[2] "The King's dress, as is customary on his Birth-day, was exceedingly plain. His Majesty wore an unornamented green silk coat, and a diamond-

manded, and all the show of parade, and luxury of
hospitality, which the dignity of the British throne
called upon him to display, might have been provided
for half the money which was squandered year by year
within the precincts of his palaces.

In all that appertained to the management of his
domestic affairs the King was negligently, unfaithfully,
or, at the very best, ignorantly and incapably served.
His Court, (to borrow a phrase from Edmund Burke,)
" had lost all that was stately and venerable in the
antique manners, without retrenching anything of the
cumbrous charge of a Gothic establishment." [1] The
principal officers bore titles which came down from
those feudal ages when peers and prelates were waited
upon by hereditary Stewards, and hereditary Chamber-
lains, and even by hereditary Cooks and Cellarers. The
noblemen at the head of the chief departments knew as
much, and as little, about the conditions of purveying
for the needs of a great modern household as their
ancestors who stood round the table at Runnymede.
Below them, in the official hierarchy, came a multitude
of cadets of noble houses, and gentlemen of old families,
with an admixture of less well-born people who had
been useful to the Ministerial candidate at a contested
election. Whatever might be their social station, they
all had been appointed for political reasons ; and for
the same reasons they were seldom or never removed
from office on the score of idleness, or incompetence, or
even on a grave suspicion of dishonesty. Every branch
of the internal administration of the royal palaces was
absurdly over-manned ; everybody, except the humblest
delegates and understrappers, was very lightly worked ;
and the occupants of the best-paid places for the most
part were not worked at all. The household books were

hilted sword. The Queen was very superbly dressed. Her cloaths were
most richly embroidered with gold, and trimmed with a border of flowers.
On her head she carried nine very large jewels, and a diamond crown
of a beautiful form. Her stomacher was one broad glare of splendour."
London Evening Post. June 5, 1779.
[1] Burke's Speech on Economical Reform; February 11, 1780.

kept by two Treasurers, a Comptroller, a Cofferer, and a whole tribe of subordinate clerks and accountants. The royal clothes were in charge of the Master of the Robes, the Keeper of the Wardrobe, the Keeper of the Removing Wardrobe, the Groom of the Stole, the King's Valet, and the King's Valet's Deputy, who knew a great deal more about the contents of the Dress Closet than all his superiors together. It was the same in every corner of the royal household. The Peers, on a notable occasion, were positively thrilled by a frank outburst of irrepressible emotion from Earl Talbot, who, in his vocation of High Steward, did his best to administer, loyally and zealously, the department which he superintended. It was difficult, (said that nobleman,) to keep in order the menial servants of the royal family, when the profits were enjoyed " by persons of a certain rank, and the services were performed by those of another." He had attempted an economical reform in the early part of His Majesty's reign by diminishing the number of daily dinners, the expense of which it was impossible to regulate, and by granting instead a handsome subsistence allowance to some of the leading officials. But these gentry now came back to the Palace at meal-times, and claimed to be fed at the King's cost without forfeiting a single shilling of their board-wages. They insisted, moreover, on eating at separate tables, no less than twenty-three of which were spread daily in various apartments of the Palace. The picking and stealing was incessant. The most flagrant abuses were rampant in the kitchens, the butteries, the stables, the wardrobe, and more especially in the royal nurseries ; [1] and waste

---

[1] " Eleven tables," said Lord Talbot, " are kept for the nurses; there being so many of that description. It is necessary each should have a separate table; for who could trust two women at the same table, and expect that they should long agree ? " A very small part of this ridiculous expenditure went to feed the little princes and princesses. According to a London newspaper of the year 1780 " the Royal children, by his Majesty's command, get up early, have bread and milk for breakfast, and dine on broth and salads, seldom being allowed any butcher's meat, their solids being chiefly chickens. They drink no liquor other than whey, and milk and water, and are sometimes indulged with a glass of weak negus.

and prodigality, as their inevitable consequence, had brought debt and humiliation in their train. "His Lordship," we are told, "drew a most melancholy picture of the domestic situation of the sovereign, and how far his feelings, as a man and a master, were daily wounded. He appealed to his brother Peers if there was one of them could rest quietly on his pillow while he was conscious that his tradesmen were made miserable on his account, and were threatened with bankruptcy and ruin. The very coal merchant who supplied the royal household had six thousand pounds due to him; and so it was in proportion with all the other tradesmen The poor menial servants, who had six quarters of their wages due to them, how pitiable was their position! Their complaints were sufficient to penetrate the most obdurate heart; and he solemnly protested that his own situation was nearly as much to be pitied, being necessarily obliged to hear these stories of distress and wretchedness without having it in his power to alleviate or remove them." Edmund Burke spoke well within the mark when he asserted that not even a royal revenue could support "the accumulated charge of ancient establishment, modern luxury, and parliamentary political corruption."

Lord Talbot's statement of the profusion and malversation which prevailed in the royal household was in no respect exaggerated; but the true cause of His Majesty's financial difficulties must be sought in another quarter. The deficit on the Civil List was not mainly due to the money, and the money's worth, which was mis-spent or stolen at Windsor Castle, and in the Queen's House at the bottom of the Green Park, but to the far larger sums which had been continuously, deliberately, and only too effectively, devoted to the worst of purposes outside the Palace walls. The fact was that most of the ready cash which ought by rights to have gone in paying the King's butcher, and grocer, and

Supper is the same as breakfast. In this manner, till within two years the two eldest princes lived."

coach-maker, had been consumed in buying Members of Parliament; in corrupting the daily Press; in subsidising needy men of letters on a scale of remuneration much higher than their pens would have commanded in the open market; and in persecuting authors, publishers, printers, compositors, and printers' devils for their respective shares in the production of pamphlets and newspaper articles which displeased the Court. Those ruinously expensive operations had been in full swing ever since the date when the young King first made up his mind to assert the power of the Crown by putting Pitt out, and Bute in. George the Third speedily exhausted the hundred and seventy thousand pounds of savings left him by his wise old grandfather, who found it cheaper, as well as less troublesome, to govern through a Minister possessing the confidence of Parliament and the country; he emptied the Privy Purse; and he incurred in addition heavy obligations which he was totally unable to meet. In February 1769 Parliament was asked for a cool half million to defray the King's debts. The essential nature of the demand was analysed and exposed by George Grenville and Barré in the one House, and by Lord Chatham in the other. They openly affirmed, — what every one of their hearers in his secret conscience knew to be true, — that the money, which the British people had contributed in perfect good faith towards supporting their monarch in ease and dignity, was used to debauch the virtue of their own elected representatives, and to poison the wells of politics. But the voice of warning and remonstrance was drowned with clamour in the Commons, and stifled with chilling silence by the Lords; for that worst of bad Parliaments contained hundreds of borough-members, and scores of peers, who stooped to accept those wages of servility the lavish provision of which had embarrassed, and in the end had beggared, their royal master.

Those were halcyon days for the bribed and the briber; but, by the time that the Civil List was again declared to be insolvent, a change had come over the

face of the waters. When in April 1777 the King requested Parliament to enable him to discharge another
debt of over six hundred thousand pounds "incurred
in the expense of his household, and of his civil government," it was evident that the whole rank and file of
the Opposition, and not their leaders only, had taken
the lesson of the past eight years to heart. The wording
of the Royal Message was insidious ; but it did not
beget belief, and it aroused the resentment natural to
men who are invited to take action injurious to their
own interests, and distasteful to their own feelings, on
transparently false pretences. When it was suggested
that the Master of the Horse, and the Treasurer of the
Royal Chamber, should be called upon to supply
details of expenditure in their several departments
those functionaries returned for answer that they had
"no material suitable for that purpose," and that it
was impossible for them to make up any such accounts
as the economists in the House of Commons demanded.
But on the other hand it came out that within the last
few years a sum of six hundred thousand pounds, — as
nearly as possible the exact amount of the excess on the
Civil List, — had been disbursed under the head of
Secret Service, for objects with which, in the great
majority of instances, no one was acquainted except
the King, the Prime Minister, and the Patronage
Secretary of the Treasury. Furthermore it appeared
that in a single twelvemonth there had been an increase
of seventy thousand pounds in the outgoings of the
officer charged with the payment of annuities, tenable
during the King's pleasure, to certain favoured members
of both Houses, and their relatives and dependants,
whose names were, in the majority of cases, concealed
from public knowledge.[1] The most innocent-minded
of politicians could not blind himself to the conviction
that the Court party, by bribing out of the resources

[1] *Annual Register* of 1777, chapter 5 of *The History of Europe;
Parliamentary History*, volume XIX, pages 103 to 187 ; *Return of Public
Income and Expenditure, July* 1869.

of the Civil List, and then summoning the House of Commons to pay the King's debts and ask no questions, had obtained an unlimited power to draw upon the British people for the means of suborning the British Parliament. There was already a National Debt, to bear the cost of those foreign wars in which the nation had been engaged ; and now there was a Royal Debt as well, incurred to supply the King with the means of carrying on an internal war against those among his own subjects who did not share his personal views on domestic and colonial politics. That war was prosecuted by George the Third with exceptional zest and relish, as is shown in his confidential letters to Lord North, which contain at least ten words about the iniquities of Rockingham, and Chatham, and Fox, and Burke, and Camden, for every three that are bestowed upon the insolence of the Americans, or the treacheries of France and Spain. The members of the Opposition would have been more, or less, than human if they had silently and obediently voted away large sums of money to be expended in destroying their own careers, and enforcing a policy repugnant to their own cherished doctrines and principles. It was incumbent on the real Whigs, who sat opposite Lord North, to defend the independence of Parliament, the most vital article of their time-honoured party creed, against the sham Whigs who sat behind him.

When it became known that the Government intended to pay off the King's debts, and increase the amount of his Civil List by a hundred thousand pounds a year, Lord John Cavendish moved a Resolution preparing the way for a Parliamentary enquiry into the financial aspects of the question. Wilkes took the floor, and addressed the House at a length proportioned to that enormous amount of Secret Service money which the King's ministers had spent over their reiterated attempts to ruin him. He was heard by his brother members eagerly and sympathetically at first, and patiently and respectfully to the end. There was a general feeling that, having been wrongfully kept outside Parliament during so many years, he now had a right to make up for his lost opportunities. When Wilkes had resumed his seat, and handed his manuscript to the reporters, the argument rose to a level worthy of the occasion. Burke was in his very happiest vein; and Charles Fox, — the record of whose masterly performance occupies less than three columns in the Parliamentary History, as against sixteen columns of John Wilkes, — "made a speech that even courtiers allowed to be one of his finest orations."[1] But the advocacy of Fox and Burke was soon overshadowed in importance by an expression of opinion from an unusual, and most unexpected, quarter. The proposals of the Government were adopted after some long debates, and crowded divisions; and on Wednesday the seventh of May "the King, seated on the throne, adorned with his crown and regal ornaments, and attended by his Officers of State, the Lords being in their robes," commanded the attendance of the Commons at the bar of the House of Peers.[2] The Speaker, at the head of his flock, presented to His Majesty the Bill for the better support of the Royal Household, and then proceeded to address the Sovereign in language which recalled the dignified traditions of the great Parliaments in the first forty years of the seventeenth century. "At a time," he said, "of public distress, full of difficulty and danger, their constituents labouring under burdens almost too heavy to be borne, your faithful Commons postponed all other business, and, with as much despatch as the nature of their proceedings would admit, have not only granted to your Majesty a large present supply, but also a very great additional revenue; — great, beyond example; great, beyond your Majesty's highest expense.[3] All this, Sir, they have done in a well-grounded confi-

---

[1] *Walpole's Last Journals;* April 18, 1777.

[2] *Parliamentary History;* volume XIX, page 213.

[3] " Several members, who took notes of this speech, wrote ʻwants' instead of ʻexpense.' " The supposed distinction between the force of those two words became the text for much comment.

dence that you will apply wisely what they have granted liberally."

Sir Fletcher Norton had correctly interpreted the better mind of the assembly over which he presided. When the Commons were once again beneath their own roof, it was moved that his Address to the King should be printed; and the motion was carried *nem. con.* — a phrase which, in the Journals of Parliament, signifies that no sounds of dissent were audible when the question was put from the Chair. One member of the House, however, was not in harmony with the general feeling. Rigby had behaved with unmeasured effrontery throughout the discussions on the Civil List; [1] and now, on Friday the ninth of May, while discoursing on a kindred topic, " he turned with vehemence towards the Chair, and arraigned the conduct of the Speaker with great acrimony." [2]   The Speaker, in few and impressive words, appealed to the Vote which stood on the Journals of the House as a proof that the sentiments which he had expressed were the sentiments of the House, and not his own particular sentiments, as the Paymaster of the Forces had asserted; but Sir Fletcher Norton's protest only served to draw down a fresh, and fiercer, attack from the Right Honourable Gentleman. " Mr. Rigby," according to the official account, " spoke of the Chair in terms very nearly bordering on disrespect, and proceeded to great heat, which seemed to make the Treasury Bench uneasy." Uneasiness deepened into positive panic when Charles Fox started up, and, snatching his chance with the promptitude of a born tactician, moved that " Mr. Speaker, in his speech to His Majesty, did

[1] On an afternoon when Lord North had replied with courtesy to a great many questions from various quarters of the House about the details of the Civil List, Rigby got up, and " attacked the Opposition very violently. No accounts, (he said,) were ever given, or ought to be given. He was astonished how the Noble Lord could waste his time in answering all the trifling questions which had been put to him. For his part, if he were in the Noble Lord's situation, he would make it a rule never to answer a question put by an individual member in his place." *Parliamentary History;* volume XIX, page 156.

[2] *Parliamentary History;* volume XIX, page 224.

express, with just and proper energy, the zeal of this House for the honour and dignity of the Crown." The Ministers tried every expedient to divert Fox from his purpose. Welbore Ellis was put up to cajole and entreat, and Thurlow to bully; but Fox replied that no power on earth should induce him to withdraw his motion. "He was satisfied," (so the report runs,) "that the House would never consent to their own degradation and disgrace in the person of their Speaker, nor would contradict on a Friday what they had approved on the Wednesday immediately preceding. It had been said that the speech was not grammar. If the speech was not grammar, it abounded in good sense, and conveyed the true, unbiassed, sense of the House, and of every man on either side who had not been bought over to a sacrifice of his principles and his conscience." The fire and sincerity of the young orator swept the air clear, and aroused cordial enthusiasm in the virtuous and the honest, and a touch of penitence in some who had dallied with corruption. Rigby himself was cowed, and grumbled out the semblance of an apology; Fox saw his Resolution passed without a division; and then, on the motion of an independent member, the thanks of the House were specifically and unanimously voted to Mr. Speaker for his speech to His Majesty. That was the first defeat inflicted upon the Court in the memorable series of parliamentary campaigns which now was opening. The King had reason on his side when, at fifteen minutes past ten on that same evening, he wrote to the Prime Minister to say that Mr. Rigby would have done well to let the matter rest.

When Edmund Burke consented to stand for Bristol he had told his future constituents that he could not answer for his own abilities, but that of his industry he was sure. That was no vain pledge; for during the six years of his connection with Bristol City he set an example which since his day has been followed by many, but surpassed by none. It may be affirmed, broadly but truly, that Burke's course of action between 1774 and 1780 elevated the conception of senatorial duty to a higher level than it ever reached since the early days of the Long Parliament, and conspicuously higher than it had maintained during the fifteen years which had elapsed since George the Third ascended the Throne. Those years had been wasted in a barren and acrimonious struggle for place and salary. The King's Ministers, and the King's Friends, could spare no attention to the accumulating arrears of current legislation which the needs of the country imperatively demanded ; and the whole period of Personal Government had been sterile of all fruit which did not, sooner or later, turn bitter in the mouth. It was left for Burke to remove that reproach from the fair fame of the House of Commons, and to prove what might be accomplished by a private member, who was likewise a genuine patriot, amidst the din of arms abroad, and the clash and clamour of selfish interests at home. The worthy forerunner of Romilly, and Lord Ashley, and Richard Cobden, he found leisure, in those crowded and noisy Sessions, to initiate many valuable reforms, and to carry some of them to completion. Not the least noteworthy of his undertakings, and his successes, was the extension of religious toleration to a great body of his fellow-countrymen whose conduct had long ago ceased to afford any sort of excuse for the cruel and insulting treatment to which they continued to be subjected.

The Roman Catholics of Great Britain had remained at the mercy of those oppressive laws which dated from the time when their predecessors were unfriendly to the dynasty established by the Great Revolution. They still were forbidden to acquire land by purchase. The entailed estates of heirs, who had been educated in Jesuit schools and colleges on the Continent of Europe, were liable to forfeiture in favour of the Protestant who stood next in the succession ; and a Roman Catholic priest, who officiated in the services of his Church, might be condemned to imprisonment for life at the instance of a common informer. Lord Mansfield and Lord Camden, — fearless and righteous magistrates who were the ornaments of the two great parties in the State, — had done their utmost to protect the liberty and property of these innocent people; and the Crown was not slow to grant a free pardon in cases where the Courts of Justice had no choice except to convict on evidence, and sentence the condemned man to a barbarous punishment. The executive authority had every disposition to mitigate the severities of the Statute Book; but Roman Catholics were tired of living on sufferance; and they knew only too well that dormant laws might at any moment be awakened into baleful operation by a sudden frenzy of popular passion. They had long ere this begun to resent the invidious and unfounded suspicion of disloyalty under which they laboured; and now, when a new French war had broken out, and their country was in dire peril, they had no mind to be accounted among the enemies of England. In May 1779 a humble address was placed in the King's hands by Lord Petre, who in the course of the following autumn entertained his sovereign so royally during his inspection of the Militia Camp upon Warley Common. It was signed by the Duke of Norfolk, the Earls of Surrey and Shrewsbury, Lord Clifford, and Lord Arundell, and a great multitude of peers and commoners, many of whom bore names hardly less historical than those which headed the list. These eminent representatives of their ancient faith united in assuring His Majesty that, "in a time of public danger, when his subjects could have but one interest, and ought to have but one wish and one sentiment," they, and their co-religionists, held no opinions adverse to his government, or repugnant to the duty of good citizens; and they emphatically asserted their attachment to the civil constitution of their country "as perfected by that Revolution which had placed his illustrious house on the throne of these Kingdoms."

In face of such a declaration the penal legislation of King William the Third was a scandal and an anach-

ronism, which no leading man on either side of politics
was able to defend, or willing to perpetuate.   A time
arrived, only too soon, when the great conservative reaction, attendant upon the excesses of the French Revolution, terrified the majority of our statesmen, — including
alas! Edmund Burke himself, — into the paths of religious intolerance ; but the earlier parliaments of George
the Third were notably free from any trace of bigotry.
The House of Commons contained many high-minded
and thoughtful men admirably capable of vindicating,
by speech and action, the freedom of the human conscience ; and the rank and file of their colleagues, who
enjoyed the good things of the present moment, and
who took a superficial, and all too easy, view of moral
problems, had at all events the qualities of their defects,
and were genuine Epicureans in their reluctance to
tyrannise over the beliefs of others.   There was only
one man among them who could have written the Fifteenth and Twenty-first Chapters of the Decline and Fall
of the Roman Empire; but they all were readers of
Gibbon's book, and few of them had any fault to find
with his treatment of ecclesiastical questions.   Roman
Catholics, who petitioned for the relaxation of the penal
laws, had no reason to anticipate difficulties within the
walls of Parliament ; though the perils which threatened
them outside those walls were of a gravity which it was
impossible to exaggerate.   A gay and good-humoured
scepticism was the tone among the upper ranks of society, while the middle and lower classes were still
swayed by intense and uncompromising emotions.   The
prejudices and antipathies kindled by two centuries of
mutual persecutions and proscriptions still smouldered
in many thousand breasts; and the cry of No Popery,
that most potent of all incitements to violence and disorder, only waited for a demagogue unprincipled enough
to raise it.   But Edmund Burke, who was the exact opposite of a demagogue, was diligent in the redress of
grievances even in cases where he was quite sure to suffer for it at the polling-booth.   He undertook to forward

the claims of the Roman Catholics; and he cared so much for the success of their cause that he was willing to obey a sound instinct which taught him to keep his own personality in the back-ground. He began by enlisting the influence of Charles Fox on behalf of his clients, which was no hard matter; for throughout Fox's life any project, which appealed to his sense of justice and humanity, had all the greater fascination for him in proportion as the espousal of it seemed likely to damage his own political interests. A Catholic Relief Bill, — which Burke had suggested, and probably had drafted, — was committed to the charge of Sir George Savile, on the ground that such a proposal, " would come with more weight from an opulent and respected country gentleman." [1] That was by no means an exhaustive description of Savile's qualifications for the task; inasmuch as a long course of self-education in theological research had made him unusually competent to handle such a topic.[2] The introduction of the measure was seconded by Dunning, the ablest of the Opposition lawyers. The Bill, lucidly explained, and forcibly recommended, traversed all its stages in the Lower House without a single hostile vote, and almost without a cavil; and received, as it was, with equal respect by the Peers, it became law within a bare fortnight of the day that it had been laid on the table of Parliament.

Burke's exertions on behalf of the Roman Catholic community in England produced an indirect consequence which was eminently gratifying to his deeply-rooted affection for Ireland. He had an Irish heart; and, Protestant as he was, he never could bring himself

---

[1] *Memoir of the Life and Character of the Right Hon. Edmund Burke*, by James Prior; London, 1826, volume I, chapter 6.

[2] " Though Sir George Savile's reason was sharp, his soul was candid, having none of the acrimony or vengeance of party. He had a head as acutely argumentative as if it had been made by a German logician for a model." *Walpole's Memoires of George the Third*, volume I, chapter 24. The distinguished part which Savile played in the debate of February 1772 on Clerical Subscription in the Church of England is related in the Ninth Chapter of *The Early History of Charles James Fox*.

to believe that the harsh and inequitable treatment inflicted upon the old religion was conducive to the true
interests of his native island. When he crossed the
Channel to seek his political future in London he left
behind him a state-paper, of remarkable merit, insisting upon the hardship of that penal law under which
the children of an Irish Roman Catholic, in case they
thought fit to announce their conversion to Protestant-
ism, could deprive their father of all power over the
ultimate disposition of his own estate, and in the meanwhile could plunder him of half his income. The exposure and condemnation of that unspeakable injustice
had, in the year 1764, been Burke's political legacy to
Ireland; and by the summer of 1778 public opinion had
grown ripe for reform, and the example set at Westminster was copied in Dublin. A measure of Roman
Catholic Relief was introduced by Mr. Luke Gardiner,
one of the very few members of the Irish Parliament
whose principles, (according to the grudging testimony
of Mr. Froude,) were above suspicion.[1] The Bill became
law. The Roman Catholics paid their gratitude in the
quarter where gratitude was due ;[2] and not the Roman
Catholics only, for the satisfaction felt by the best men
of both parties was embodied in a letter to Burke from
the Speaker of the Irish House of Commons. " On
this happy event," (the Right Honourable Gentleman
wrote,) " I sincerely congratulate you, being fully per-

---

[1] Mr. Froude goes on to say that Luke Gardiner, " as Lord Mountjoy,
was to learn the real meaning of Catholic Emancipation when he was
piked and hacked to death at New Ross." It is difficult to understand
that Mr. Froude can have been serious in attributing the Wexford out-
rages of 1798 to the circumstance that the sons of a Roman Catholic landed
proprietor were no longer permitted by law to rob their father. *The
English in Ireland, by James Anthony Froude ;* book VI, chapter 1.

[2] " That Address and Petition, which you left with me in the year 1764,
was found by us here so excellent a performance in every respect, and set
forth our grievances in so affecting a manner, that we happily resolved to
begin our humble suit by laying it before the Viceroy, and requesting he
would transmit it to be laid before His Majesty ; which, we are sure, made
such an impression as was in a great measure productive of what has since
followed, far beyond expectations." *John Curry to Edmund Burke, Esq.
Dublin,* Aug. 18, 1778.

suaded that it is of more real importance to our country than any law that has been passed during my time."

It was not the only, or the most signal, service which Edmund Burke, during those distracting years of internal tumult and foreign war, was enabled to do for Ireland. The commercial welfare of that country had been subordinated, — or rather, to speak more accurately, had been sacrificed, — to the selfish interests of Great Britain. Just a century had elapsed since merchant vessels built in Ireland, and owned and navigated by Irishmen, had been excluded from the privilege of trading with British colonies and plantations beyond the seas. Half a generation later the Parliament at Westminster, without so much as consulting, or even forewarning, the Parliament at Dublin, placed on the Statute Book an Act which intentionally, instantaneously, and irreparably crushed to extinction the woollen industries of the dependent island. The utter prostration of Irish commerce had never been more painfully felt than during the earlier months of this French war. All access to markets on the Continent of Europe was barred by the activity of the American privateers; the monopoly of trade with the East and West Indies was reserved as strictly as ever for Scotch and English shipowners; and Belfast, and Cork, and Londonderry, and Waterford might have been frontier towns on the confines of Bohemia for all the advantage they derived from their proximity to the ocean. "Our trade here," (wrote the Speaker of the Irish House of Commons from Limerick,) " is entirely ruined. There is not a ship in our port, or the least business doing." [1] The prospect had seldom appeared more hopeless for Irish merchants and manufacturers, those helots of English commerce; but the hour of their emancipation was already on the eve of striking. A sincere and growing conviction that Ireland had been shamefully used was noticeable in the British House of Commons, as well as a consciousness that she was fast becoming

[1] *Right Hon. Edmund Sexton Pery to Edmund Burke, Esq.;* August 26, 1778.

too formidable to be trifled with ; and among the leading orators of that assembly was a patriotic Irishman deeply versed in the philosophy, and the practical bearings, of trade and finance in all their branches. "Burke," (said Adam Smith,) "is the only man I ever met who thinks on economic subjects exactly as I do, without any previous communications having passed between us." A sincere and intelligent friend both of England and Ireland, Burke appealed in his speeches not only to the fears, and not only to the consciences, of his parliamentary colleagues. He directed his main efforts to awaken in their minds a rational sense of their true policy as custodians of the common and universal interests of the British empire. After the question was finally decided he reviewed the course of the controversy in a published letter. " The part," (he wrote,) "to which I attached myself most particularly was to fix the principle of a free trade in all the ports of these islands as founded in justice, and beneficial to the whole, but principally to this island of Great Britain, the seat of supreme power." [1]

Burke kept the claims of Ireland before the attention of the House of Commons with an assiduity most unsuited to the Ministerial view of appropriate times and seasons. As late as February 1779 Lord North told Parliament that more than enough had already been done for Ireland, and complained that the only evidence of her gratitude for one boon was that she immediately proceeded to ask for another. Mr. Burke, (we are told,) exploded the Noble Lord's argument with keenness and satire. He exclaimed that such horrid reasoning was too gross to dwell upon. " It was that narrow and illiberal policy which had lost us America, and would in all probability, one day or another, endanger the very existence of the British Empire." [2] That day was not long in coming. Ireland had been made disagreeably aware that King George's Government was powerless

---

[1] *Letter to Thomas Burgh, Esq., from Edmund Burke ; Beaconsfield, New Year's Day,* 1780.

[2] *Parliamentary History;* volume XX, page 137.

to defend her, and that, for the protection of her coasts and cities from insult and invasion, she must rely on her own valour and her own resources.[1] In April 1778 Captain Paul Jones appeared unexpectedly in St. George's Channel; made prize of a Waterford brig, a Dublin merchant vessel, and two smaller Irish traders; and ended by capturing, after a desperate engagement, the only royal man-of-war which the Admiralty at Whitehall could spare to mount guard over the commerce of Ulster. The effect on the North-country Irish was instant and tremendous. That pugnacious race of civilians was stirred into universal and spontaneous action by a passion of shame and resentment, accompanied by just that moderate dose of panic which renders a brave man the most formidable of adversaries. Forty thousand Volunteers, Presbyterians and Episcopalians alike, were speedily enrolled, and equipped for battle, with peers and great commoners, and in one case even a fighting bishop, for their colonels and generals, and squires and squireens for their regimental officers. When Paul Jones, in the course of the autumn, returned with a powerful squadron, manned by two thousand sailors, he was informed by his friends on shore that he would find himself in a hornets' nest if he ventured to land an armed party at any point on the Irish seaboard.

Such an enterprise was beyond the courage of even a Paul Jones, and he sailed away to the North-east coast of England, to reap fresh laurels on an element where he was more at home. Disappointed of any immediate prospect of a brush with a foreign enemy, the Irish Volunteers determined to take advantage of

---

[1] Mr. Thomas Conolly, a great Irish landlord, — who sat in the British Parliament, where he was held in high account, — complained to the House of Commons that "the unfortunate kingdom of Ireland, which had no hand in the American War, and was never to reap any benefit from it, lay exposed everywhere to the descent of the enemy." Dublin itself, (he said,) had been open to invasion till the latter end of the summer of 1778, when two "Newcastle Cats," — or, in other words, two colliers from the Tyne, — were mounted with sixteen guns each, and stationed as guardships at the entrance of the harbour.

so unique an opportunity for extorting the redress of their national grievances from the reluctant hands of a British ministry. On the fourth of November, the anniversary of King William the Third's birthday, many thousand musketeers paraded in front of his statue on College Green, firing volleys, waving flags emblazoned with ominous and significant devices, and trailing cannon placarded with the motto " Free Trade or This." King George and his Cabinet were once more faced by the old difficulty, — much nearer their own doors, and, if possible, in a more alarming shape. Their regular army was on the other side of the Atlantic, engaged in an attempt to enforce the payment of a customs-duty imposed upon America by the Parliament of Great Britain ; their home garrison was composed almost exclusively of militia ; and, if they insisted on maintaining the right of taxing Ireland without her own consent, there would be nothing for it but to leave Portsmouth and Plymouth bare of troops, and transport all our militiamen across St. George's Channel to fight the Irish Volunteers.

That was an extreme of folly too outrageous even for the Cabinet which had invented the Boston Port Bill. Before the end of November Parliament met at Westminster for the winter session; and the King's Speech contained a passage indicating, with even more than the usual circumlocution and obscurity, that his Government was prepared favourably to consider the demands of Ireland.[1] Those hazy and per- functory phrases were not enough to satisfy the House of Commons, and the great majority of Edmund Burke's colleagues desired to have a statement of the situation from a public man who understood the nature of the Irish demands, and who had been con- sistent in his support of them. " Mr. Burke," (according

---

[1] " I have not been inattentive to the state of my loyal and faithful kingdom of Ireland ; . . . and I recommend it to you to consider what further benefits and advantages may be extended to that kingdom by such regulations, and such methods, as may most effectually promote the common strength, wealth, and interests of all my dominions."

to the official account,) "rose to speak; but, finding
a great difficulty in making himself heard on account
of a violent cold and hoarseness, he sat down once or
twice, and would have declined speaking, had he not
been pressed and solicited by the unanimous sense of
the House of Commons." The House was rewarded
by hearing a fine explanation of the intrinsic justice
and expediency of those concessions into which Lord
North and his colleagues had been frightened by a
menace of rebellion. Three weeks afterwards a colder,
and less sympathetic, assembly listened while the Prime
Minister, in an unapplauded speech, introduced Resolutions granting to Ireland the free export of her products
and manufactures, as well as the privilege of trading
with the British colonies under exactly the same conditions and restrictions as were enforced in the case
of Scotch and English vessels. Charles Fox, in his
character of Opposition leader, uttered a few sentences
of cautious and guarded approval; but Burke, — the
mark of all eyes, and the centre of all thoughts, —
remained in his place tranquil and silent, with the
silence of a wise man who has gained his point, and
who leaves well alone.

James Boswell, who watched his contemporaries
intently, and not ungenerously, has put upon record
his impressions of Burke a little before this period of
his public career. "Few men, if any," said Boswell,
"enjoy continual happiness in this life. I have a kind
of belief that Edmund Burke does. He has so much
knowledge, so much animation, and so much fame." [1]
There seldom has been a more striking exemplification
of Bacon's profound saying that great persons have
need to borrow other men's opinions to think themselves
happy. Burke had his private difficulties and troubles,
the full extent of which was known only to himself;
and he bore them as became a man, without impatience,
and with few complaints. During these very years, —
when his action in the House of Commons afforded a

[1] Boswell to Temple; Edinburgh, 12 August, 1775.

model to all time of an industrious, a useful, and an honoured senator, — his relations with his constituents were a never-failing source of trouble and anxiety. The business men of Bristol had for some while past been sore and uneasy on account of the growing importance of Liverpool, which was rapidly displacing their city from the proud position of the second port in the kingdom, after London. But Bristol still retained its hold upon the trade with our West Indian islands, which was a source of exceptional profit to the whole community, and not to the richer merchants only; and the citizens of Bristol now learned with anger and dismay that the gains of what had been virtually a local monopoly must henceforward be shared with the capitalists and ship-owners of Cork, Belfast, and Waterford.[1] It was true that the Act for the Relief of Irish Commerce was a Government measure, introduced and carried by the chief of the Cabinet himself; but, as long as human nature remains what it is, people who dislike a law will always vent their wrath upon an eminent public man who has been an honest and earnest advocate of the unpopular policy, rather than upon the time-serving Minister who, at the eleventh hour, has been forced by the pressure of circumstances to adopt that policy as his own. Burke's sincerity was his crying sin in the view of the Bristol electors. He might, (so he remarked in caustic terms,) have successfully faced his constituents if he had been a rival to Lord North in the glory of having refused some small insignificant concessions, in favour of Ireland, to the arguments and supplications of English members of Parliament; and if then, "in the very next session, on the demand of forty thousand Irish bayonets," he had made a speech two hours long to prove that his former conduct was founded upon no one right principle of policy, justice, and commerce.

[1] Bristol shop-keepers, the very class of voters who had been Edmund Burke's heartiest supporters, had long been accustomed to invest their savings in a larger or smaller venture on board vessels bound to Barbadoes or Jamaica.

"I never," added Burke, "heard a more elaborate, more able, more convincing, and more shameful speech. The debater obtained credit, but the statesman was disgraced for ever."[1]

There was yet another question of prime importance on which Bristol was out of touch with its illustrious representative. The Roman Catholic Relief Bill had been accepted by the governing powers of the country with absolute unanimity. It met the approbation, (to quote Burke's words,) of "the *whole* House of Commons; the *whole* House of Lords, the *whole* Bench of bishops; the King; the Ministry; the Opposition; all the distinguished clergy of the establishment; all the eminent lights, (for they were consulted,) of the dissenting churches. This according voice of national wisdom ought to be listened to with reverence." But the payment of that long out-standing debt to justice and mercy was very differently regarded by a large section of the British people. The newspapers, most of which then reflected public opinion with singular fidelity, were outspoken in condemnation of the Catholic Relief Act; and journalists of either party strove to throw the responsibility for so unpopular a measure upon their political opponents. Whig writers laid the blame upon the Court. What, (they asked,) could induce His Majesty to accept the hospitality of Lord Petre? The company of a Roman Catholic ought to be shunned by the King of England like the plague. How could his throne be established in righteousness unless he paid respect to the established religion of the country? Was the Court of England to become the abode of those Jesuits whom even Roman Catholic monarchs had banished from the countries which they governed? Was history to be read backwards? Was Queen Mary to be accounted as a saint, and the Paris and Irish massacres as a fiction?[2] The Ministe-

[1] *Letter from Edmund Burke to John Merlott, Esq., an eminent merchant of the City of Bristol.*

[2] *London Evening Post* of November 1778. Letter signed by *Aratus* in the same newspaper.

rialist papers followed suit, and fastened the discredit
of the obnoxious policy upon the leaders of the Opposition. The King, (they wrote,) governed the Church, as
well as the State; and Sir George Savile had incurred
the guilt of spiritual High Treason when he moved His
Majesty to show indulgence towards believers in Tran-
substantiation. Roman Catholics were heretics; and no
heretic could be a faithful subject. Let Sir George Savile, and his abettors, prove that heresy and allegiance
were compatible; and English Churchmen might then
be freed from the apprehension of having their throats
cut by Papist assassins.[1]

The most envenomed shafts in the arsenal of party
warfare were directed against Edmund Burke, who was
held up to execration as the author of a deep-laid plot
contrived for the ruin of the Protestant religion. All
the other conspirators, (it was alleged,) were puppets in
his hand, while he himself was an Irish papist, and a
Jesuit in disguise. For many consecutive months he
was branded in the columns of the ministerial journals
by the significant nickname of "The son of St. Omer."
That spiteful story soon made its way down from London to the West of England, and Burke found it incumbent on him to explain the motives of his public conduct
before a crowded meeting assembled in the Guildhall
at Bristol. The oration which he there delivered has
taken rank among the celebrated speeches of the world.
He protested, in lofty and almost contemptuous language, that he and his political associates had done
justice to Roman Catholics, not because they themselves
were Roman Catholics, but from their extreme zeal for
the Protestant religion, which was "utterly disgraced"
by the penal laws enacted in the year 1699; and from
their rooted hatred to every kind of oppression, under
any colour, or upon any pretence whatsoever.[2] On the

[1] *Morning Post;* May 30, 1778.
[2] The same line of thought has since been more pithily expressed by an
English prelate. Dr. Mackarness, the Bishop of Oxford, when denouncing
the Bulgarian atrocities in the autumn of 1876, defended himself from the

same occasion he defined the limits of the obligations which, as a member of Parliament, he owed to his constituents. He was ready, (so he assured them,) to perform their reasonable behests at any sacrifice of health and comfort; but his conscience was his own, and on high questions of public policy he was bound to follow the road towards which, in his judgment, the interests of the nation pointed. If the people of Bristol wanted a member who would obey their orders as blindly and submissively as Lord North, and his colleagues, obeyed the orders of the King, they must look for some one else than Edmund Burke to represent them. "It is the plan of the Court," he said, "to make its servants insignificant. If the people should fall into the same humour, and should choose *their* servants on the same principles of mere obsequiousness and flexibility, and total vacancy and indifference of opinion in all public matters, then no part of the State will be sound, and it will be vain to think of saving it."

A statesman, who is not so entirely absorbed by ambition as to lose sight of everything else that makes life worth having, will always set a high value on the enforced holiday which falls to his lot when his political adversaries are in power. The freedom and the leisure, which may be called the sweets of Opposition, were keenly appreciated by the group of eminent men who did their utmost to counteract the policy of Lord North's government; and none amongst them was endowed with such a capacity for rational enjoyment, such a wealth of intellectual resources, such an ardent and varied interest in all the circumstances of daily life, and such complete and unalloyed satisfaction in his domestic surroundings, as Edmund Burke. In his Buckinghamshire homestead, which was situated within a short walk of the river Thames at the exact point of its rarest beauty, and en-

charge of being actuated by religious prejudice against the Mahomedan faith. "We sympathise," he said, "with the oppressed nationalities in European Turkey not because *they* are Christians, but because *we* are Christians."

compassed by his few hundred acres, every square yard of which was familiar to him, he had no reason to envy the richest of the great landholders who looked up to him as their political mentor. Most of them played at farming ; but Burke's domain was not too large for the inspection of the master's eye, and the minute details of agriculture were at once his business, and his pastime. He knew, as exactly as any nobleman's bailiff, what it cost to produce his wheat, his hay, his barley, and his bacon, and what they would fetch, on any given week, in the local market ; and his voluminous letters on the processes and statistics of rural industry, which occupied much of his time on a wet day, when nothing was doing out of doors, may still be read with pleasure and profit. He never was dull, and never solitary. A morning's drive brought the friends of his choice down from London ; and in the intervals between their visits he found company worthy of himself on the shelves of his library. He was intensely happy with a beloved wife,[1] and a son sufficiently graced by nature to arouse fond and extravagant hopes in the most partial and indulgent of fathers. His strong Irish sense of family clanship was displayed in his relations to a brother and a cousin, whom he treated with fraternal confidence and affection, and an absence of censoriousness carried to a degree of tolerance which unfortunately cannot be accounted among his virtues. The three kinsmen all lived together, keeping a common purse, a well-stocked cellar, and a bountiful table, and driving about the country behind a team of four black horses. A Bristol constituent, who was honoured by an invitation to Beaconsfield, found them still at breakfast at eleven o'clock in the morning. "They had," (so this gentleman wrote,) "no form about them. Everyone was at liberty to do as he pleased, and was as free and easy as if the house was his own."

---

[1] Richard Champion, Burke's favourite and faithful political ally, presented Mrs. Burke with a Bristol tea-service of his own exquisite manufacture. A good many years ago some of the pieces sold "for thrice their weight in solid gold." The largest of them bore a Latin inscription signifying that they were dedicated to Jane Burke, the Best of British Matrons.

Such was Edmund Burke's home, which he had arranged in all respects precisely to his liking; and he desired nothing better than to spend in that secure and peaceful retreat the whole of every month that he was not engaged in debating at Westminster. But, after he became member for Bristol, he no longer remained at his own disposal. His constituents regarded him in the light of a universal providence for the accomplishment of their personal, and sometimes extremely selfish, ends and objects; and there was no business so intricate and onerous that they scrupled to impose it on his overburdened shoulders. He could not have believed, (he said,) how very little interest they felt in the general line of public conduct observed by their representative, and how exclusively they judged him by his merits as their special agent in their private affairs.[1] As soon as each parliamentary session came to a close Burke's real troubles began. He was forced to apologise, almost abjectly, for reserving a very few idle days, and tranquil nights, to recover himself from the immense fatigues of his senatorial labours. "I really," (he pleaded on one such occasion,) "should have gone to town to look after all sorts of business with minuteness and vigour; but, in truth, I want a little fresh air, and repose of mind, and exercise of body. For a long time I have had very little of any of them. I am not yet a week in the country. Forbear with me a little, and I will pay thee all."

The Bristol traders had no mercy on him. They deluged him with commissions; and they were seldom at the pains of collecting beforehand such information as would enable him to perform their errands without undue and excessive drudgery to himself. He devoted an entire fortnight of one hard-earned vacation to getting their tobacco out of bond. He carried through a lengthy negotiation on behalf of a ring of soap-dealers who could not so much as supply him with the name and address of the Master of the Soap-makers Hall.

[1] Edmund Burke to Richard Champion; June 26, 1777.

In order to obtain leave for a merchant-ship to sail for the West Indies he was forced to make himself acquainted with the intricate questions of seamen's wages and of demurrage, with no assistance whatever from the owner of the vessel.[1] The most distasteful, and disquieting, of all his obligations was the necessity for repeated migrations to, and from, the West of England. He descanted to Lord Rockingham on the "horrid expense" of these expeditions of two hundred miles in a post-chaise, and on the dangers which an unprotected traveller was liable to encounter. Burke was robbed by two highwaymen, on Finchley Common, when on his way to Bristol; but no gentleman of the road would have found it worth his while to stop him on his homeward journey, for he always returned with empty pockets. His presence in their city was a reminder to his constituents that they had a claim on his money, as well as on his services. Five guineas for the nurse of a baby for whom he had been asked to stand as sponsor, an offer of fifty guineas reward for the discovery of a miscreant who had set fire to the warehouses on the Avon quay,[2] the presentation to an influential elector of a service of Bristol porcelain "on which was expended all the resources of the art," and the provision of a grand banquet to his political adherents, with fourteen orthodox Whig toasts to follow; — those were some examples of the ceaseless, and heterogeneous calls upon Burke's slender income. A more costly sacrifice still was the futile consumption of his time, his peace of mind, and his energies. The members of both parties in Bristol, while they were agreed upon nothing else, united in demanding his frequent presence in their midst. His friends were sincerely desirous to accost and welcome their member, and his opponents wanted to have him

---

[1] "You did not," (so Burke represented to his correspondent,) "send the number of men or tonnage. I set the tonnage down at a hundred and seventy, and the men at twenty, inclusive of the master and the mate."

[2] Burke was urgently advised by his friends at Bristol to adopt this course because his political adversaries had been putting about that he was in sympathy with the enemies of England.

amongst them in order to humiliate and affront him. They inserted paragraphs in the London newspapers to the effect that Mr. Burke represented Bristol, not on the ground of his property or his social position, but by virtue of his pamphlets and speeches, and that it was therefore high time for him to gratify his constituents with less stingy specimens of his oratorical talent. It was said that he held himself too stiffly, and esteemed his conversation too valuable to be wasted upon people of ordinary cleverness. He was, (so the accusation ran,) the first member for Bristol who had omitted to make a round of calls on the freeholders in the course of every twelvemonth, and to dine, as much richer men than himself had been willing enough to dine, every afternoon, for weeks together, with the Mayor and Corporation of the most hospitable and luxurious municipality in England. Burke defended himself from these imputations in a fine passage of earnest, but calmly worded, remonstrance. " My canvass of you," (so he reminded his constituents,) "was not on the Exchange, nor in the County Meetings, nor in the clubs of this city. It was in the House of Commons ; it was at the Privy Council ; it was at the Treasury ; it was at the Admiralty. I canvassed you through your affairs, and not your person. I was not only your representative as a body. I was the agent, the solicitor, of individuals ; and, in acting for you, I often appeared rather as a shipbroker than as a member of parliament."

Burke led a severe existence, and it told visibly on his physical strength, and his vital powers. He was wasted, (he said,) by fatigue and want of sleep, which in his case was always attendant on heavy labour.[1] He confessed to a very old friend, who had known him well in Ireland, that his present life was nothing better than a warfare. His bodily condition had an injurious effect upon his political action. Over-work and over-worry, as was inevitable with such a temperament, betrayed him into occasional outbreaks of sudden, and very formidable,

---

[1] Edmund Burke to Joseph Harford; April 4, 1780.

anger.[1] When his nervous system was unduly strained, his rhetoric became too emphatic, the vehemence of his language was exaggerated almost to grotesqueness, and metaphors and similes poured from his lips in a turbid and incessant stream ; — for, like smaller men, when weary and out of sorts he seemed unable to bring his speeches to a finish.   Joseph Galloway, the same American Loyalist who bore reluctant witness to the ascendancy which Charles Fox exercised over the House of Commons, thus wrote of Edmund Burke : " He cannot watch the passions, or accommodate himself to the temper, of his audience.   He plays with the most diffi-cult subject.   He leads it through the winding mazes of his fancy.   He places it in a thousand lights.   He gives it an infinity of colours.   We admire for a time the splendour of the dress ; but the eye becomes tired with the glare.   His purpled robes resemble a patched garment.   He often debases the sublimest thought by the coarsest allusion, and mingles vulgarity of idiom with the most delicate graces of expression."   It is impossible to deny that such a criticism was well founded, and that Burke, during the period of the American War, was already not sufficiently careful to keep the quality of his speaking up, and the quantity down.   Nor did he mend of his faults as the years rolled on.   Fox was more acceptable to his hearers ; and, so far as parliamentary success is the test of eloquence, Burke was surpassed in his earlier days by Chatham, and in later life by Chatham's famous son.   But at his best, and at his third and fourth best, he was a noble orator. " What," asked Sheridan, " will they think in after times of the public speaking of this age when they read Mr. Burke's speeches, and are told that, in his day, he was not accounted either the first, or second, speaker ? "

[1] It was admitted by a journalist of his own party that "the amiable-ness of Mr. Burke's disposition, the pleasantness of his nature, and the benevolence and liberality of sentiment which marked his character in private life, made his friends the more regret, and his enemies rejoice at, the want of judgment, and the violence of temper," which were too often observable in his public conduct. *London Evening Post* of June 1779.

CHAPTER VIII

THE Ministers of George the Third, in deeds, though not in words, had confessed their own incapacity to terminate that American War which was strangling England. The region covering the whole space between the St. Lawrence and the Potomac rivers, hardly less in area than France and Spain together, was the core of the American community; the seat of wealth, and commercial industry, and popular education, and political habits and instincts; the district which had been the breeding-ground, and which to the end remained the stronghold, of the rebellion. That vast expanse of ground was never again trodden by the invading columns of a British army. Lord North and his colleagues had abandoned any present intention, (and, if they had been candid enough to admit the whole truth, any future hope,) of recovering the Northern and Central States by force of arms ; but nevertheless they could not bring themselves to treat with Congress on the only terms which Congress would for a moment consider. They were quite as well aware as Burke, or Savile, or Rockingham that the past errors of their American policy were by this time irreparable, and that it was an act of weakness and folly, rather than of heroism, to keep the flower of our army on the other shore of the Atlantic when the real danger was at our own doors. But King George's orders had to be obeyed, and King George's system of government was at stake ; and it seemed to them a matter of pressing importance that the true condition, and the full gravity, of the American question should as far as possible be veiled from the knowledge of the British people.

The Ministerial journalists, calculating upon the remoteness of the seat of war, and the uncertainty of communication by sailing-ship across so many thousand miles of ocean, made a practice of doctoring for public consumption the news which arrived from America. They displayed an almost inconceivable audacity in suppressing British reverses, and magnifying British successes. When the garrison of Fort Mifflin withdrew themselves under cover of the darkness, leaving behind them five or six score of their comrades interred beneath the soil of that shot-ravaged mud-bank, the Government papers in London reported that six thousand rebels had been put to the sword when the work was captured, " scarce one being left to tell the melancholy tale." Washington's army was killed several times over, and died several times over of hunger and disease, in the columns of the Morning Post and the Morning Chronicle. The history of Burgoyne's operations took a fantastic shape in the inspired newspapers. " Yesterday," (so the town was told early in November,) " an express arrived with letters from Quebec which advised that General Burgoyne had brought the Americans to a second engagement in which, after great slaughter on the side of the rebels, Arnold himself was made prisoner, together with seven thousand of his men, and all his artillery, stores, and baggage." On the twenty-ninth of the same month London was assured " on very good authority that Generals Clinton and Vaughan had reinforced Burgoyne, and that in consequence of their assistance he had attacked Arnold, and routed his army " ; for the one element of truth in these amazing bulletins was the prominence attributed to General Arnold, and the absence of all mention of General Gates. Some few days afterwards a report of Burgoyne's surrender was conveyed to England in a Boston newspaper. " A Boston newspaper ! " — such was the comment. " What credit can be given to the representatives of the Press at a place where the liberty of the Press could not possibly exist, and where an editor would be tarred and feathered unless he consented to publish false American victories ? " The hack authors, who were in the pay of the Bedfords, did not miss so apt an opportunity for calumniating a great public servant who had deserved well of England. "The captivity of Burgoyne's army," they wrote, "begins more and more to be doubted; and some go so far as to condemn Sir Guy Carleton for catching so eagerly at the report of his rival's overthrow, and transmitting such an unauthenticated account to Government under the sanction of his name."

As years went on, and the unpopularity of the Ministry deepened with the increasing burden of national dangers and difficulties, the ministerial press-writers laid aside all sense of responsibility in their dealings with their readers. In October 1780, at King's Mountain on the border-line between the Caro-linas, the backwoodsmen of the western forest, shooting as coolly as if they had encircled a herd of deer, de-stroyed or captured the whole of a brave and well-commanded force of Royal infantry and Loyalist partisans. It was an event more ominous for the ultimate success of British arms on the south of the Potomac than even Bunker's Hill had been for the subjugation of New England; but the only prominent notice taken of it by the leading Government print was a contradiction of the report of Major Ferguson's defeat at King's Mountain as "a ridiculous rumour." For many months together the American intelligence sup-plied by the ministerial journalists consisted mainly in generalities about the distress and discontent of the rebels, illustrated by mendacious anecdotes, and supported by preposterous statistics. Long after the capitulation at Saratoga, and the abandonment of Philadelphia by Sir Henry Clinton, these scribblers were still assuring their public that forty thousand Americans, or one man in ten of the whole population, had died by sickness, or in battle; that all their willing soldiers had perished; that Congress was at its last shift; and that the reduction of America was not, nor ever had been, a very difficult matter, to which nothing

was wanting but vigorous and determined conduct on
the part of Britain.   In July 1780 the financial world
of London was treated to what did duty for a money
article.   "It is known as a fact," (so the tale ran,) "to
many merchants in this city that Mr. Washington has
a second time remonstrated to Congress on the folly
of pretending any longer to carry on the war.   He
positively asserts that, if terms of accommodation are
not made to Great Britain, he will resign his command,
and avoid the disgrace of laying down the American
arms at the feet of the British forces.   These are the
truths that have made the Stocks rise."   The Three
per Cent. Consols, as a matter of fact, had lately risen
from sixty-two and an eighth to sixty-two and a quarter,
after a steady and continuous fall of twenty-seven points
below the figure at which they were standing when
Lord North's Cabinet embarked upon the policy of taxing America for the relief of the British Treasury.

Morning after morning the citizens of London were
dosed, and for the most part sickened, with scurrilous
attacks upon American statesmen and warriors for
whom they entertained the respect due to eminent
adversaries.   Doctor Franklin, "though on the brink of
the grave," had young damsels constantly about him.
Paul Jones, the victor in the most murderous frigate
duel which the naval annals of the world record,[1] was
described as a noted coward, who had been thrashed

---

[1] The battle, in all the essential circumstances, has been told by Walt
Whitman in a noble prose poem.

"Did you read in the sea-books of the old-fashioned frigate fight?
    Did you learn who won by the light of the moon and stars?

Our foe was no skulk in his ship, I tell you.
    His was the English pluck, and there is no tougher or truer, and never
        was, and never will be.
    Along the lowered eve he came, horribly raking us.

We closed with him.   The yards entangled.   The cannon touched.
    My captain lashed fast with his own hands. — "

So the piece begins, and so it continues.   Any reader, who loves a fine
ballad, might do worse than get it by heart.

by an Irish lieutenant. It was repeatedly and positively stated that the Comte de Vergennes was scheming for the establishment of a French monarchy in America, and that he had bought over George Washington to assist him in the plot. The Ministers at Versailles, (such was the form which in one case the allegation took,) had secured "that rebellious apostate" to their interest by raising him to the rank of a Marshal of France, with pay and appointments reaching a total of ten thousand francs a month. That charge was framed with the hope of lowering Washington in the estimation of his own countrymen; and another lie, equally circumstantial, and still more invidious in its intention, was set going in order to render him an object of detestation to Englishmen. It was deliberately announced that there was in existence a secret correspondence between John Hancock and General Washington, of a nature indicating that the Commander-in-Chief of the American army had been privy to the conspiracy for burning down London which had so narrowly failed of success at the time of the Gordon riots. Hancock was represented as condoling with Washington about the capture of Charleston by the royal fleet and army. "But the victory of Britain," (so the ex-President of Congress was made to say,) "will be short-lived. We have friends who are working such a mine as will blow up all their triumphal schemes; and, if Providence favours us, the news of the surrender will come to their ears a day too late for their rejoicing in London." Thereupon followed about twenty lines of cipher, "in strange figures, somewhat like Hebrew characters, explanatory, no doubt, of the intended fire in London."

Venal pens, on the other side of the Atlantic, were busily engaged in traducing Washington. James Rivington, the King's printer in the City of New York, owned and edited a newspaper entitled the Royal Gazette, which was conducted with considerable ability, but with an attitude towards the obligations of morality, and the laws of honour, which it is superfluous to characterise by an epithet. In February 1778 there appeared in this periodical a number of letters signed "George Washington," some of which the General had actually written, while others, addressed to his wife, and to various members of his home circle, were fabricated from the first word to the last. They contained passages which implied that the writer disapproved the action of Congress in declaring national independence, and in summoning the colonies to armed rebellion against the Crown. If taken for authentic, they exhibited the Commander-in-Chief of the American army as an adventurer who, in the most important action of his life, had sacrificed conscience to ambition, and had acquired the confidence and attachment of his followers on false pretences. The batch of documents was headed by an editorial preface vouching for their genuineness, and explaining how they were found in a portmanteau entrusted by Washington to a mulatto servant who had been taken by the British at Fort Lee in the summer of 1776. Washington has specifically stated that this servant never was captured at Fort Lee, or elsewhere ; and that no part of his own baggage, and none of his attendants, ever fell into the hands of the enemy ; [1] — and George Washington's word is good for more than that. "It is no easy matter," he wrote, "to decide whether the villainy or artifice of these letters is the greatest. They were written by a person who had some knowledge about the component parts of my family ; and yet they are so deficient in circumstances and facts as to run into egregious misrepresentations of both." [2] The view of the matter taken by the General's friends was curtly expressed by Richard Henry Lee, the celebrated orator. "The design of the forger," said Lee, "is evident ; and no doubt it gained him a good beef-steak from his masters." [3]

[1] Washington to Timothy Pickering, Secretary of State ; Philadelphia, 3 March, 1797.

[2] Washington to Landon Carter ; Valley Forge, 30 May, 1778.

[3] Literary forgeries were then much in fashion. One of the most famous, and perhaps the most obviously fictitious, was a letter which in

Washington's countrymen did not take their estimate of him from the New York Gazette, or the London Morning Post. They were fully conscious that they owed him a great and an increasing debt; and their obligations to him had begun from the first hour when New England rushed to arms. The wounded pride of the British monarch, the harsh and overbearing speeches of Ministers and ministerial supporters in the British Parliament, and the ruthless tone of the ministerial newspapers before, and immediately after, Lexington, were very ominous of the fate which seemed to be in store for the American insurgents. A more serious symptom still was the political hostility, and the social and professional contempt, which at the outbreak of the war very generally coloured the sentiments entertained by royal officers of all ranks towards the army of the Revolution. That army was nothing else than a hasty levy of husbandmen and artisans, with extemporised colonels and captains drawn from the middle classes of society. It was very much such an army, in composition and character, as that which in the year 1685 followed the banners of the unhappy Duke of Monmouth; and, if the revolt had been crushed, the Whigs of Massachusetts and Connecticut, — with due allowance made for the improved humanity of the age, — might expect to be

1777 went the round of the London newspapers, purporting to have been written by Montcalm, and dated just three weeks before the battle of Quebec. The sham Marquis professed to foretell that he himself would be defeated, and killed ; but that he would not fall unavenged, because, within a few years after the French lost Canada, the American colonies were sure to be in hot revolt against Great Britain. "If Mr. Wolfe," he wrote, "understands his trade, he has only to receive our first volley, and then advance at quick-step until he can fire point-blank into our ranks. My Canadians, undisciplined, and unprovided with bayonets, will break and run, leaving me beaten without resource." Montcalm, while he was about it, might as well have given the complete story, and have informed his correspondent that General Wolfe would be shot once through the wrist, and twice through the body. This letter was respectfully quoted by Lord Mansfield in the House of Peers, and was treated by Mr. Carlyle, in his History of Frederic the Great, as a prediction sagacious and statesman-like almost to a miracle.

treated as the Whigs of Devonshire and Somersetshire were treated after the battle of Sedgemoor. But
Congress was called upon to select a general; and, in
a fortunate hour for the relations between the bellige-
rent nations, the choice fell upon George Washington.
That son of Virginia already possessed, not perhaps
what can strictly be called a European reputation,
but at all events a name which had reached Europe.
He had come to the front very creditably, and very
early in life; and for a good many years past intelligent
strangers from England, and other European countries,
had been in the habit of paying a visit to the southern
bank of the Potomac in order to admire the prospect
from Mount Vernon, and seek an interview with its
proprietor as one of the very rare celebrities of colonial
America. Washington was still remembered in British
mess-rooms as a trusty and popular comrade, and an
able and successful soldier; and eminent officers, who
had campaigned with him in Pitt's war, regretted sincerely that the spirit and rules of their service had not
allowed his name to appear on the list of generals in the
royal army.

During the earlier years of the Revolutionary War the
established authority of Washington, his military prestige,
and his recognised social position, were of untold value
to the American cause. He utilised all his own personal advantages in order to maintain the dignity of
Congress, to transact business on equal terms with
British generals in all the official communications which
from time to time passed between the two camps, and
(above all) to protect his humbler comrades in arms
from the terrible fate of being punished as rebels.
He was determined to secure for them the full benefit
of those laws of civilised and chivalrous warfare which
governed the relations of opposing armies on the continent of Europe. With that end in view he at once
applied himself to the task of converting his homely
crowd of minutemen and militiamen into as near a
resemblance to regular troops as the slender resources

at his disposal would permit. In the dearth of martial finery which prevailed in the camp before Boston he gave directions that regimental officers should be distinguished from the rank and file by cockades and ribands, and sergeants and corporals by strips of red and green cloth sewn on to the shoulder of their farming jackets ; and he used diligence to see that his troops were furnished, first with hunting-shirts, and then with sober brown uniforms, — until, in the fifth year of the war, they appeared in all the splendour of blue coats with buff or white facings. At the first breathing space which occurred during that fierce and continuous struggle he handed over his soldiers, most of whom were already veterans, to the tuition of Baron von Steuben, that they might be taught to march in step, and wheel in line, and hold their heads as straight on parade as they held their rifle-barrels in battle. And, as the most pressing of all his duties, he attended vigilantly to the moral side of military discipline. He saw to it that his army should not be a curse and a terror to the civil population. He called marauders and incendiaries to strict account, and visited their crimes upon them with all the more inexorable severity when they endeavoured to conciliate him by pleading that their victims were Loyalists. He condemned gambling, and drunkenness, and profanity, and uncleanliness of person and conduct, in a series of earnest and fatherly General Orders, so that the young fellows under his charge felt themselves almost as closely watched as if they were beneath the eye of the parish Minister and Deacons in their native village.

While George Washington trained his soldiers to respect themselves, he stoutly and persistently refused, on principle, to allow them to be treated with disrespect by the enemy. He neglected no fit opportunity for defending the doctrine that the rank conferred upon a military officer by Congress was of equal validity with a commission which bore the sign manual of the King of England. That, and no paltry vanity, was his motive for declining to receive and open the letter from General

Gage which was addressed to him as a civilian.   When
Charles Lee was captured by Colonel Harcourt there
was talk at Sir William Howe's headquarters of sending
him to a Court-Martial as a deserter ; but Washington
insisted that the prisoner should be regarded, not as a
Lieutenant-colonel in the royal service, but as a General
in the American army.   "I give you warning," (so his
protest ran,) "that Major-General Lee is an officer belonging to, and under the protection of, the United Independent States of America ; and any violence you
may commit on his life, or liberty, will be severely retali-
ated upon the lives and liberties of the British officers,
or those of their foreign allies, at present in our hands."
If an American officer, or private soldier, was threatened
with the gallows for having carried arms against the
Crown, Washington never failed to let it clearly be
known that hanging was a grim game at which two sides
could play.   He was met half-way in his efforts to
humanise the war by several of the English generals
who were   kindly gentlemen, with a statesmanlike
knowledge of the American point of view, and a respect
and liking for the American character.   Washington's
policy was crowned with success over the whole area
where his personal influence could penetrate.   In the
distant regions of Georgia and the Carolinas mutual cruel-
ties, and even atrocities, were practised by the more
violent men of both the contending armies ; but all over
the States of Pennsylvania, and New Jersey, and New
York, and throughout New England, there was neither
shooting, nor hanging, of prisoners taken in battle.[1]   The
Revolutionary War afforded in this respect a marked contrast to the treatment of the Jacobites after Culloden, and
of the Irish insurgents in the rebellion of Ninety-eight.

Washington's firm resolution of permitting no liberties
whatsoever to be taken with the government that he

[1] Towards the close of the war an American officer was hanged near
New York, not by the British authorities, but by a set of fellows who
styled themselves the Board of Loyalists.   Washington on that occasion
took such vigorous and exceptional measures that the outrage never was
repeated.

served, and the army that he commanded, was mainly
responsible for his course of action at a memorable and
tragic conjuncture which for human interest, and for the
light which it throws upon personal character, stands
alone and apart in the history of the American War.
Benedict Arnold, after being shot down in the moment
of victory on the seventh October 1777, had been carried
off the field of battle to the hospital at Albany, where
he lay for the space of several months in cruel suffering;
and many more weeks elapsed before he finally left his
bed, a cripple.   Eager, with the fevered impatience which
swayed all his movements, to find himself once more in
his native Connecticut, he started on his homeward
journey as soon as spring commenced.   But he was reduced to travel by short stages, with long intervals of
repose; at one of his stopping-places " his wound was
in such a condition that a door-post had to be removed
to make room for his litter to enter the house where he
was to pass the night; " [1] and it was not until May 1778
that he arrived at New Haven, where he was welcomed
by his fellow-townsmen with every possible testimony of
sympathy, and of neighbourly pride and delight.[2]   Not
long afterwards he paid a visit to Valley Forge, where
Washington, in view of an impending, and perhaps a
decisive, battle would gladly have given so doughty a

[1] *The Life of Benedict Arnold, by Isaac N. Arnold;* chapter 11.
[2] Arnold's residence at New Haven, according to *The Field-book of the
Revolution*, was " a handsome frame building, embowered in shrubbery,"
with a balustrade enclosing the flat roof, and two pillars in front supporting
a pediment over the centre of the first floor, in old colonial fashion, and
with a sufficiently pleasing effect.   Half a century after Arnold left America a sign-board, which used to hang over his shop in Water Street, was
found in the garret.   " It was black, with white letters, and painted precisely alike on both sides,

B. Arnold, Druggist,
Bookseller, &c.,
From London.
Sibi Totique."

The last words were probably intended to signify " For the benefit of himself and the public."   Arnold was fond of tags of Latin.   While he was
fighting his way to fame he adopted the motto "Gloria Sursum."   After
his fall he had his seal engraved with "Nil Desperandum."

warrior a foremost station in the ranks of his own army. Most assuredly there would have been a more rousing narrative to tell if Benedict Arnold, instead of Charles Lee, had led the American vanguard at Monmouth Court House. But Arnold could not as yet mount the charger with which the gratitude of his countrymen had replaced the horse killed under him at Danbury; and Washington, determined not to leave him unemployed and unrewarded, appointed him to the military command of Philadelphia on the morning after the British evacuated that city.

An eminent surgeon in the American army, drawing upon his immense experience throughout the War of the Secession, used to aver that a soldier, who had once been desperately wounded, was never the same man afterwards except when he was saved from deterioration by high moral qualities; and moral qualities had never been Benedict Arnold's strongest point. It would have tried a cooler head, and a less self-engrossed and domineering temper, to be military governor of a capital city on the morrow of its recovery from the possession of an enemy. Philadelphia, moreover, was at all times noted as a place of varied and infinite temptations; and Arnold had an enjoying nature. For some years past his tendency to ostentation and prodigality had been kept in check by the life of adventure, hardship, and peril which his bodily infirmity for the present closed against him; and he now gave full swing to his less noble tastes, and his poorer ambitions. He resided in the heart of the city, in a fine mansion which had been the head-quarters of Sir William Howe, where he kept house on the same magnificent scale as that royal general who drew the very liberal pay of a British Commander-in-Chief, increased by the exorbitant salary of a Commissioner for Arranging Terms of Peace with the Revolted Colonies. Arnold drove his coach-and-four, and gave splendid entertainments, costly out of all proportion to his means, to a great circle of Members of Congress, military officers, foreign visitors of rank, and unofficial Pennsylvanians belonging to both political parties. In March 1779 he purchased Mount Pleasant, then a delightful country-seat standing in a spacious and well-planted park overlooking the waters of the Schuylkill River; and in the course of the next month he was married to Margaret Shippen, who had been the confidante and playmate of the young and gallant André, and the reigning toast of Philadelphia dining-rooms during the gay and jovial period of the British occupation. It has been lightly, and often, stated and believed that the poor lady ruined Arnold by her extravagance, and sapped his patriotism by inspiring him with her own aversion for republican institutions; but that was a baseless charge. Arnold was the waster; and his wife, during a hard and lifelong struggle with adversity, showed herself a notable saver and manager for the protection of her husband's financial credit, and of her children's future. And the beginning and end of Margaret Arnold's reputed disaffection to the American cause was that as a girl she had danced minuets with royal officers, and that as a married woman she had refused to exclude from her ball-room the wives and daughters of Loyalists and Tories.

Arnold was impelled to his fate by graver and deeper motives than the influence of a beautiful woman upon the uxorious folly of an elderly husband. He bitterly resented the ungrateful treatment inflicted on him by the rulers of the country which he had served and saved. The knot of intriguers, who were the authors of the worst mistakes and misdeeds of Congress, disliked him on his own account, and detested him still more heartily as the friend and client of Washington, at whom they did not dare to aim a direct blow. Every upward step in Arnold's career, and every public recognition of his valour and merit, had been extorted from Congress by the insistence of the Commander-in-Chief, and had even then been doled out with a very sparing hand. For a long while past Arnold had been deluged with slights, and annoyances, and rebuffs; and the time now arrived when he was menaced with a very serious danger. As long as the hero of Valcour Island, the saviour of Fort Stanwix, the real victor of Saratoga, was fighting sword in hand in the front of war, his political enemies were powerless to ruin him; but as military commander in Philadelphia, — a city where tranquillity and order reigned, and which was as secure from hostile invasion as Leeds or Birmingham, — he was in a false position, and thenceforward they had him at their mercy. Arnold's notions of administration had been acquired during the stress and hurry of arduous and distant campaigns, and he chafed under the trammels of routine and formality. The Executive Council of Pennsylvania, sure of a glad and ready hearing in that prejudiced quarter, laid before Congress a budget of complaints against his offhand and imperious methods of transacting public business; and Congress ordered him a Court-Martial. Arnold, with his character and peace of mind at stake, begged to be put out of his anxiety by a speedy trial. " Delay," (so he told Washington,) "was worse than death;" but his accusers, on one pretext or another, kept the matter hanging over him for three-quarters of a year, during which he was nursing his grievances, and gloomily contemplating his prospects. At last, in December 1779, he appeared before his judges, a most striking and pathetic figure. His stern and weather-beaten features gave him a look of ten years older than his age; he walked and stood with difficulty on a leg broken above the knee at Saratoga, and below the knee at Quebec; and, though his sword had been taken from him, he wore his buff and blue uniform, with the sword-knot and the epaulettes which had been adjudged to him by Washington as bravest among the brave in the national army. He was called upon to defend himself from a string of charges of which the most damaging were unsupported by evidence, while the rest were trumpery to the last degree. After a very long and careful investigation he was fully acquitted of everything that touched his honour and probity; but he was found

guilty of having exceeded his powers by giving a pass
to a trading-vessel without the knowledge of the Commander-in-Chief, and by employing without due author-
isation certain public waggons, at a time when they
were lying idle, for the purpose of removing private
property which was in imminent danger from the enemy.
The Court directed that he should receive a reprimand
for his " imprudence." Congress approved the finding,
and peremptorily insisted on the sentence being carried
into effect; and Washington had no choice except to
censure his brother officer in terms as delicate and con-
siderate as pen could frame. But Arnold had confidently expected a triumphant and unconditional acquittal;
and no complimentary phrases could salve his aching
pride, and extenuate his disappointment. The shaft
had gone home, and the wound was incurable.

The twenty-eighth of June 1778, when three-score
unwounded British soldiers were officially returned as
having been killed by the heat at the battle of Monmouth Court House, was the most scorching summer
day ever known in America; and the following January
was the coldest month recorded in a series of observations which has been carefully and continuously noted
down in Pennsylvania over the space of very nearly two
centuries. A regular traffic of loaded sledges was established across ten miles of ice between the town of
Annapolis and the opposite shore of Chesapeake Bay.
Lord Stirling marched his troops dryfoot over a salt-
water channel in New York Bay, and raided the British
cantonments on Staten Island; and ten days afterwards
a detachment of British infantry and dragoons penetrated
by the same road into New Jersey, and warmed their
hands by setting on fire a meeting-house and an academy.
The snow lay from four to six feet deep over the whole
country. Wild animals were almost exterminated, from
deer and turkeys down to squirrels and partridges; and
the soil was frozen so hard, and so far beneath the

surface, that, when spring-time came, ploughing was difficult, and deep spade-work altogether impracticable.[1] The alternations of heat and cold, which assailed the young republic at the crisis of its fortunes, would have been chronicled by an historian of the old Roman republic among his list of prodigies and omens; and it cannot be denied that the events of the war bore a striking analogy to the climatic conditions of the atmosphere. The victory of Saratoga, the recovery of Philadelphia, and the triumphant conclusion of the French alliance, illuminated the cause of America with a blaze of sunshine; but then the weather changed, and the year 1780 was long remembered by the partisans of that cause as a season of chill, and almost uncheered, depression.

Lord George Germaine had empowered Sir Henry Clinton to transfer the war from the Northern to the Southern States ; and the general had the skill to discern, and the energy to seize, a favourable opportunity for carrying into effect the wishes of the minister. Benjamin Lincoln, who commanded the Republican forces beyond the Potomac, had recently made an attack upon the important town of Savannah in conjunction with the French fleet and army. The allies advanced briskly to the assault, and vied with each other in dash and courage. The Stars and Stripes, and the Fleurs-de-lys, were planted side by side on the rampart; but there were as good men, and better, within the wall, and the storming-parties were beaten back with a heavy sacrifice of men and officers. Six or seven hundred of the French were killed and wounded, and the Comte d'Estaing was hit by two bullets. Fairly sickened of the transatlantic war by his experiences at Rhode Island, and before Savannah, he carried his ships home to France ; and Lincoln, with a disheartened army, shorn of the reputation which he had won in the cam-

[1] *Pennsylvania Weather Records between the years* 1664 *and* 1835, *collected and compiled by William M. Darlington, Esq., formerly Vice-President of the Historical Society of Pennsylvania.*

paign of Saratoga, returned to his headquarters in Charleston.

The possession of that city had long been Sir Henry Clinton's prime object. He regarded Charleston as the key to the two Carolinas. Four years previously he had besieged it in vain ; and the idea of succeeding where he had failed exercised over him an attraction which, like an officer of spirit, he found it impossible to resist. It was a case of now or never. The French navy, for an unknown, but not illimitable, period, had vanished from American waters ; and the long stretch of coast between Sandy Hook, and the mouth of the Savannah river, was left clear of a European enemy. With a following wind a British expedition might reach Charleston in ten days ; while a relieving army, if despatched from Washington's camp in the Jerseys, might well take three whole months to accomplish the journey by land.

Clinton embarked at New York on the twenty-sixth of December, 1779. He fell in with heavy gales, which mauled and scattered his fleet. Some of his transports foundered, and others were taken by American privateers ; but the rest of his ships gradually re-assembled at the place of rendezvous on the Georgian coast, and he appeared in front of Charleston before the middle of February. What with the regiments which sailed with him, and the local troops whom he collected on the spot, and a reinforcement of three thousand additional infantry whom Lord Rawdon brought from New York during the progress of the siege, Sir Henry had at his disposal a force of twelve thousand soldiers ; and they were so good that he could have done with less.[1] General Lincoln would have been well advised if he had retreated from the neighbourhood of the coast, and kept the war alive in the interior of the State. His small but

[1] The returns in the British State Papers Office put Clinton's effective force at 12,847 men. A letter in Rivington's *Royal Gazette* of June 1780 stated that "the retinue of the royal army under Sir Henry Clinton amounted to thirteen thousand five hundred and seventy-two men." *The History of South Carolina in the Revolution, by Edward McCrady, LL.D. ; New York and London,* 1902.

well-trained force would have been a rallying-point for the hardy Whig militiamen of the Carolinas, and for the more formidable mountaineers of the frontier settlements. Beyond all question he should have made up his mind to abandon the city of Charleston, as Washington abandoned the city of New York in 1776, and the city of Philadelphia in 1777; but, with the habitual and fatal instinct of a second-rate strategist, he clung to his fortifications, and established himself inside the walls of the beleaguered place with the whole of his infantry. His horsemen, commanded by Colonel William Washington, — who was endowed by nature with the qualities of a military leader, but who still had something to learn, — ranged the open country, and maintained a line of supply between the besieged garrison and the inexhaustible resources of the plantations in the rural districts.

The movements of the Republican cavalry were closely watched and attended by Colonel Banastre Tarleton, who, at this stage in their respective careers, was Colonel Washington's master in the field. Tarleton commanded a mixed force of dragoons, and of light infantry who rode whenever they could find horses. Their title on the roll of the army was the "British Legion," but they were familiarly and widely known by the appellation of "Tarleton's Greens." Recruited at New York from among ardent Loyalists, who had been driven from their homes by the Revolution, they waged war in the vindictive spirit of political partisans. Their unchecked habits of plunder, and their occasional outbursts of merciless ferocity, injured the King's cause even more than it was helped by their undoubted valour. They were splendidly led on the march and in the combat. A little older than Rupert at Edgehill, and a little younger than Kellermann at Marengo, Tarleton was just turning six-and-twenty, which was no bad age for a cavalry officer. He had lost most of his horses at sea, and it was only by dint of unsparing exertions that he was able to provide his people with slow and sorry marsh ponies from the islands along the coast.[1] But that want was soon mended, for on the thirteenth of April he surprised, routed, and utterly dispersed the American cavalry, capturing all their stores and ammunition, a hundred prisoners, and chargers enough to replace those which had gone to the bottom of the ocean. Among the spoils were sixty pedigree horses; and Tarleton and his officers thenceforward were as well mounted as so many Virginian gentlemen.

From that moment onwards Charleston was narrowly blockaded both by land and sea, and its surrender became a question of time. The town was bombarded night and day by the British war-ships and batteries. Dwelling-houses were wrecked and burned. Magazines were exploded. A chance shell from an English mortar carried away an arm from the statue of Mr. Secretary Pitt in front of the City Hall. The steeple of Saint Michael's Church, which was used as a watch-tower by the garrison, was struck more than once; but it survived to be battered eighty years afterwards by American cannon in the War of the Secession. Time, and the turn of events, in both those instances, played strange pranks with History. There were numerous casualties among the soldiers on the ramparts, and some few among the civil inhabitants; but it was famine which did the work. By the end of the first week in May the ration was reduced to six ounces of meal in the twenty-four hours; and on the twelfth of the month, after prolonged parleys, Lincoln delivered up the town, and his army with it. The return of the prisoners, as made out by Major André, the Deputy Adjutant-General of the British forces, showed a total figure of nearly six thousand men. An American regiment, which had been operating outside the town in rear of Clinton's lines, endeavoured to escape across the Santee river; but Tarle-

---

[1] The *Morning Post* of October 1780 described Tarleton's cavalry as "mounted on horses of all colours and sexes; their uniforms light green, waistcoats without skirts, and black cuffs and capes; their arms one sabre and one pistol. Their spare holster holds their bread and cheese."

ton and his dragoons started in pursuit of the fugitives, caught them up after a forced march of a hundred and fifty-four miles in fifty-four hours, refused them quarter, and, in the most literal sense of the word, cut them to pieces. Sir Henry Clinton was justified in reporting to Lord George Germaine that victory was overwhelming and universal. " I may venture to assert," (so he wrote on the fourth of June,) " that there are few men in South Carolina who are not either our prisoners, or in arms with us ; " and next day he weighed anchor for his voyage back to New York, leaving Lord Cornwallis behind him, with a very slender force, to protect and extend his conquests.

Some weeks before Charleston fell Baron de Kalb had marched southwards with the Marylanders and Delawares of the regular Continental army, and he gathered up on his way the militia of those States through which he passed. Washington had advised that the management of the campaign should be entrusted to Nathanael Greene, as the most likely match for Lord Cornwallis ; but Congress obstinately insisted on employing Gates, who on this occasion had no Benedict Arnold to disobey and over-ride the orders of the general in command, and so make him a conqueror in his own despite. Cornwallis advanced to the encounter with the handful of troops whom he could spare from the duty of policing Charleston, and towards the middle of August 1780 the opposing forces met in the vicinity of Camden, on the Catawba river. The odds seemed not unequal. Cornwallis had with him two thousand men, for the most part of the finest quality ; while the Americans were three thousand in number, of whom the full half were good for little at the best, and were absolutely worthless if unskilfully handled. From the moment that Gates took over the charge of the army he had committed every fault that any general could have found time to commit. Two days before the engagement he had sent off some hundreds of his choicest troops on a fool's errand. His dispositions for battle were beneath criticism. He placed his worst troops in the front of danger, and did not go with them to see that they behaved themselves, while Cornwallis forced the fighting in his wonted style. The Twenty-third and Thirty-third of the British Line, the Volunteers of Ireland, and the infantry of Tarleton's Legion, came on volleying and hurrahing; and the American Militia threw away their arms, and fled. Neglecting the runaways, the British turned upon the Continental troops who had been stationed in reserve, with Baron de Kalb for their leader. The dispute was stiff and doubtful, but by the end of three-quarters of an hour all was over. Baron de Kalb had gone down with ten or a dozen bayonet-thrusts in his old body. The Delawares were exterminated, and every other man of the Marylanders lay dead on the ground with his musket beside him. Tarleton's horse followed up the routed army for twenty miles. The Ministerial press in London remarked with justice that, although many battles had been well fought in America, and many victories been gained, the nineteenth of August was the only instance in which the pursuit had been driven home.[1] Cornwallis reported in his despatch that the enemy lost all their cannon, all their ammunition, all their waggons, and almost all their firelocks, and that two-thirds of them had been killed or taken.

Baron de Kalb lingered for a few hours, perishing for a cause that was not his national cause, like the exiled Count Pulaski, who some months previously had been shot dead in the assault of Savannah. There was one prominent American at Camden who, unlike these gallant foreigners, had no intention whatever of giving his life for American freedom. General Gates retired from the field betimes, — swept away, (it was alleged,) by the torrent of fugitives. Mounted on a racehorse of some note, he soon shook himself clear of the crowd, leaving it to the sabres of Tarleton's cavalry. He rode night and day, and on the fourth evening he got out of

---

[1] *Morning Post;* Oct. 22, 1780.

the saddle at Hillsborough in North Carolina, with two
hundred miles of highway behind him.   A writer, who
did not love him, has acknowledged that he might have
pleaded the example of Frederic the Great at Mollwitz
for leaving the field in an undignified hurry.[1]   But
Mollwitz was Frederic's first battle ; and on all future
occasions, whenever fortune went against that King, his
attendants found the greatest difficulty in getting him
away from the scene of peril and slaughter.   Horatio
Gates, on the other hand, was never under fire subsequently to his defeat at Camden ; and his detractors
went so far as to assert that in his earlier campaigns
he had so contrived matters as never to have been under fire before.   His last exploit was too much for the
fidelity and affection of his admirers in Congress, and
the safety and honour of an American army were not
again committed to his charge.

These successive budgets of evil news from South
Carolina reached the cities and townships of the North
at a time when the popular mind was disposed to take a
very gloomy view of the situation.   The ship of state,
if a simile may be permitted, was in a plight very familiar to any Yankee skipper who had ever sailed to a port
in the Spanish colonies on the south of the Equator.
" For a space of time," said one who had gone through
that disagreeable experience, " we were condemned to
the sufferings of purgatory.   We had entered the Dol-
drums, — that strip of baffling weather which lies between the Trade Winds."   Week after week, (so the
writer proceeds,) the ship drifted aimlessly about, with
stores wasting, and water rotting in the tanks ; and then
of a sudden the change came, and all was well.   The
ropes sang, the canvas bellied, and the vessel shot forward on her course, — " for we had picked up the North
East Trades."

In the spring and summer of 1780 the citizens of
America were traversing a most anxious period of sus-

[1] Fiske's *American Revolution;* chapter 13.

pense and dejection. During the opening years of the
Revolution they had exerted themselves with passionate
energy to repel the invasion of their political rights, to
ward off the worst penalties of rebellion, and to achieve
the liberation of their country. Their personal life and
liberty, and their national independence, were now secured; but they still were floundering deep in a morass
of trouble which seemed to have neither shore nor bottom. Enthusiasm had subsided, the hope of a prosperous issue was dim and distant, and weariness and
dissatisfaction ruled the hour.[1] The war, though more
expensive than ever, was languid, inglorious, and unut-
terably stupid and uninteresting. The British no
longer entertained the thought of attacking Boston or
Philadelphia; and, so far as any hostile intention on the
part of the American army went, the fortifications of
New York were as safe as the Tower of London. The
generals on both sides had valid reasons for their inaction. Sir Henry Clinton, after so many failures, knew
better than to attempt another invasion of a region inhabited by a population of sturdy farmers, "bred to the
gun,"—averse indeed to the restraints of a professional
military career, but always ready, at the call of danger,
to turn out and do battle for hearth and home. On the
other hand the anticipations which Congress had founded
on the French Alliance had resulted in flat disappointment, and mutual recriminations. D'Estaing was al-

[1] "In Committee of Congress,
Camp Tappan,
19 August, 1780.
"Sir,—When America stood alone against one of the most powerful
nations of the earth the spirit of liberty seemed to animate her sons to
the noblest exertions, and each man contributed his aid in support of her
dearest rights. When the hand of tyranny seemed to bear its greatest
weight on this devoted country their virtue and perseverance appeared
most conspicuous, and rose superior to every difficulty. If then such
patriotism manifested itself throughout all ranks and orders of men among
us, shall it be said at this day, this early day of our enfranchisement and
independence, that America has grown tired of being free?"
Those are the opening sentences of a singularly manly and judicious
letter addressed to Governor Trumbull by John Mathews, one of the
Congressmen for South Carolina.

ready on his way back to Brest and Cherbourg, and there was not a white uniform nearer the American coast than the Island of Martinique. Washington had no help except in himself, and in the native army which he commanded; and his power to undertake offensive operations on his own account had by this time sunk to a very low point indeed.

The underlying cause which had brought about a stagnation in American military operations was the deplorable condition of American finance. By the end of 1779 Congress, and the State Governments, had issued between them four hundred and fifty millions of dollars in paper money. The value of their notes had gone down thirty-three per cent. by January 1777, seventy-five per cent. by January 1778, and ninety per cent. by January 1779; and then it began to fall like a collapsed balloon.[1] In the June of that year fifty dollars were paid in Philadelphia for two pairs of shoes, and sixty dollars for two silk handkerchiefs. Fish-hooks, in that piscatorial city, cost half a dollar apiece.[2] In October 1780 beef sold in Boston for ten dollars a pound, and butter for twelve dollars. Indian corn cost a hundred and fifty dollars a bushel, and a barrel of wheat-flour fifteen hundred. Samuel Adams, who was not a dressy man, paid two thousand dollars for a hat and a suit of clothes. The rise in the price of coffee had long ere this disturbed the tranquillity of the city. Bostonians had listened to more than one orator of the soft-money party in their State Assembly as he inveighed against merchants and shop-keepers who refused to take Government notes, at face value, in payment for goods. They had heard such people vigorously denounced as engrossers, and forestallers, and regraters, and, — a word the meaning of which they understood much better, — as Tories; and the housewives of Boston saw no reason why, in the case of over-priced coffee, they

[1] *The Monetary History of the United States, by Charles J. Bullock, Ph.D., Assistant Professor of Economics in Williams College;* chapter 5.
[2] *Philadelphia Society One Hundred Years Ago, by Frederick D. Stone.*

should not follow the immortal example set by their own husbands in their dealing with imported tea. " A number of women, mostly from the North part of the town, assembled under the direction of one Mrs. Colter. They were not your Maggies, but reputable clean-dressed women, some of them with silk gowns. On they went to Boylston's warehouse, where they insisted on having his coffee at their price. He refused; and they without ceremony put him into a cart, and drove him some way up the wharf. He found it impossible to withstand, and gave them his keys. They took one cask, and carried it off, intending to pay him for it. Poor Boylston was never so sweated since he was born. He was very roughly handled." [1] Scenes of that character, marked by greater violence and cruelty, were often repeated during the next five years in ruder and less cultured neighbourhoods than the residential quarter of Boston.

In the later years of the war, — if any accurate, or even approximate, reckoning could be taken of such shadowy values, — the Government paper was at a discount of three hundred, seven hundred, and at last of a thousand, to one. A blight settled down upon all the transactions and the relations of human society. Honest commerce withered and shrank; but it was a rare harvest-time for unscrupulous money-jobbers, and pettifogging attorneys, and downright knaves and rascals. Bad men speedily discerned an opportunity for a form of rapine against which the Courts of Justice afforded very dubious protection; for litigation had become nothing else than a lottery under a state of things altogether novel to the law. Ancient mortgages, and long outstanding debts, were in many cases discharged by the proffer of a sackful of worthless paper; and there were trustees who sought to acquit themselves of their most sacred obligations by paying off the claims of widows and orphans with a fiftieth, or a seventieth, part of their due. " Instead of the creditor pursuing

[1] John Scollay to Samuel P. Savage ; Boston, July 25, 1777. *Proceedings of the Massachusetts Historical Society for June 1911.*

the debtor, the debtor pursued the creditor with an offer of Continental money, and forced the bond out of his hand." [1] Pelatiah Webster, — an old-fashioned patriot who so lived and acted as to justify his right to the Biblical name which, after the New England custom, his god-parents had given him,[2] — had courageously and persistently endeavoured to shame his countrymen into defraying the expenses of the war out of the proceeds of taxation. His advice was rejected in favour of a less sound and self-denying financial policy; and he soon had reason to express it as his sad and settled conviction that the scandals and iniquities of the currency had polluted the law, had corrupted the public administration, and had gone far to destroy the morality of the people. The nation, (said Webster,) had suffered more from this cause than from the arms of the enemy.

" A bankrupt, faithless, republic would be a novelty in the political world, and would appear among respectable nations like a common prostitute among chaste matrons." So Congress proclaimed to the world in a public address of September 1779, and none the less in March 1780 it calmly passed a law enacting that forty dollars in paper were thenceforward to be the equivalent of one dollar in specie. In other words the American Government declared itself bankrupt to the extent of nineteen shillings and sixpence in the pound. That announcement killed the public credit, swept the market bare of cash, and demolished every vestige of commercial utility that still attached itself to the Government paper. The evil consequences fell with intense severity upon the comfort, the discipline, and

---

[1] *The Financial History of the United States, by Alfred Bolles, formerly Professor of Finance and Economy in the University of Philadelphia;* chapter 9.

[2] " It came to pass," wrote the prophet Ezekiel, "that Pelatiah the son of Benaiah, died. Then fell I down upon my face, and cried with a loud voice, and said, ' Ah, Lord God ! Wilt Thou make a full end of the remnant of Israel ? ' " The name of another Pelatiah was on Nehemiah's list of the Jewish notables who sealed the covenant after the return from the captivity.

the efficiency of the army. Congress found it all but impossible to enlist fresh troops, and very difficult to feed and clothe those whom it had already. The soldiers in the Continental camps, except that they spent more nights in bed, were hardly better off than at Valley Forge. During the summer of 1780 they sometimes had no meat, and sometimes no bread ; and they were placed on a half, and a quarter, and even on one eighth, of the regulation allowance of food for several days together. The pittance of money due to them was often in arrear, and the value of it had fallen so low that it did not greatly matter whether it was in arrear or not. The officers of the Jersey Line complained to their State Legislature that four months' pay of a private would not procure for his family a single bushel of wheat, that the pay of a colonel would not keep his horse in oats, and that a common labourer received four times as much wages as an American officer. It was evident that nothing short of exceptional induce-ments, or the most ardent and self-sacrificing public spirit, could any longer attract men into such a service. Voluntary recruiting on the old conditions had be-come a thing of the past. Lavish bounties in money, outfit, and titles to a goodly acreage of vacant land, were offered by Congress ; and those bounties were supplemented by the State Governments until the combined amount was raised to a preposterous figure. Already, nearly a year before this time, a portion of the recruits from Massachusetts were said to be mere children, " hired at about fifteen hundred dollars each, for nine months' service." [1]

The favours heaped upon these new-comers aroused a natural and pardonable jealousy in veterans who had given to the country their all but gratuitous ser-vices, and in many cases not a little of their blood, during those five years which had elapsed since the commencement of the war. Several of the old regiments

[1] Washington to President Reed ; West Point, July 27, 1779.

were constantly on the brink, and sometimes over the
verge, of mutiny. In August 1780, before the news of
Camden had reached his head-quarters at Orangetown,
Washington addressed a letter to the President of
Congress, reminding him that the term of engagement
of half the troops then in arms would expire on the
first of January following. "The shadow of an army
that will remain," (so the Commander-in-Chief solemnly
warned his correspondent,) "will have every motive,
except mere patriotism, to abandon the service, without
the hope, which has hitherto supported them, of a change
for the better. This is almost extinguished now, and
certainly will not outlive the campaign unless it finds
something more substantial to rest upon. This is a
truth of which every spectator of the distresses of the
army cannot help being convinced. Those at a distance may speculate differently ; but, on the spot, an
opinion to the contrary, judging human nature on the
usual scale, would be chimerical. . . .   To me it will
appear miraculous if our affairs can maintain themselves much longer in their present strain." So felt
the chief and leader who carried the burden of responsibility, and upon whom the very existence of the
nation, as a nation, depended. Men of less resolute
heart than George Washington began to fear that the
sun of American freedom had sunk for ever ; and yet,
if they had only known it, the period of gloom through
which they then were passing was but the dark hour
that precedes the dawn.

CHAPTER IX

MAJOR ANDRÉ. BENEDICT ARNOLD.

THE clouded aspect of public affairs had thrown a
deeper shadow than ever upon the dark and stormy
soul of Benedict Arnold.   He despaired of the republic;
and he was not in the mood to bind up his fortunes indissolubly with a cause which he regarded as on the eve
of ruin.   A paper in his hand-writing, prepared in the
autumn of 1780, contains a detailed statement of the
enfeebled plight to which the troops under Washington's
command had been reduced.   Congress, (Arnold said,)
had appealed to the nation for thirty-five thousand
men; but their entire force now consisted of less than
twelve thousand, "illy clad, badly fed, and worse paid,
having in general two or three years' pay due to them;"
and he declared it to be his opinion that the rebellion, if
taken boldly and firmly by the throat, would soon be at
its last gasp.

Arnold was thoroughly acquainted with the numbers
and the condition of the American army; but he
cherished a fatal self-deception with regard to the
sentiments of the American people.   As military governor of Philadelphia he was beset and courted by influential townsmen who were out of sympathy with the
Revolution, and who plied him with talk to which, as
they gradually began to perceive, he lent a pleased and
credulous ear.   He allowed himself to be persuaded
that America, like England in the spring of 1660, was
ripe for a monarchical Restoration.   History has its
fashions which recur at intervals over a certain number
of years, and then fade, and pass away for ever; and
in the latter part of the eighteenth century the example
of General Monk had still a singular and powerful
attraction for ambitious men of the sword.   In France,
under the Directorate, when the reaction against the

Jacobin rule had set in with irresistible force, the admirers of more than one Republican general fondly expected that their hero would consent to play a part
analogous to that of the cool-headed and stout-hearted
soldier who took the tide at the turn, and landed Charles
the Second safely on the throne. There then were
Royalists, and many Royalists, who carried infatuation
to such a height, and ignorance of personal character to
such a depth, as to entertain a hope that Napoleon Bon-
aparte had possibly made the Eighteenth Brumaire in
the interest of his legitimate sovereign. And so, by a
diseased and perverted mental process, Benedict Arnold
contrived to delude himself into the notion that the great
majority of his fellow-countrymen were impatient to
undo the work of the Revolution, and forswear the
Declaration of Independence ; and that any prominent
American general who had the will, and the power, to
revive the policy of Monk would earn the same public
gratitude, and win for himself the same splendid and
unstinted rewards.

Arnold justified his action, as far as Congress was
concerned, by the abominable usage which he had
experienced at the hands of his political enemies ; but
nothing could excuse, or explain away, his meditated
disloyalty to George Washington, in whom he had
always found a staunch friend, and a zealous champion.
It was in Feburary 1779 that Arnold's assailants in
Philadelphia opened their attack upon his career and
reputation ; and in the course of that month he wrote
from the camp in New Jersey, where he was on a visit
to his companions in arms, a letter assuring the lady
whom he was soon to marry that she need have no uneasiness about his future. " I am treated," he said,
" with the greatest politeness by General Washington,
and the officers of the army, who bitterly execrate Mr.
Reed and the Council for their villainous attempt to
injure me." And in July 1780, soon after the Court-
Martial was over, and the sentence had been pronounced,
Washington showed his disapprobation of the action

taken by Congress, and his unabated trust in Arnold's good faith and military talents, by inviting him to join the fighting army, and " command the left wing, the post of honour." But the unhappy man had already other views in prospect.

Access to the town of Albany, and to the interior parts of the State of New York, was effectually barred against the British by the fortress of West Point, which was the Vicksburg, or the Ehrenbreitstein, of the Hudson River. American engineers had long ago been busy in that quarter under the direction of Count Kosciusko ; and redoubt had since then been added to redoubt, and battery to battery, until the line of bluffs which over- looked the stream was covered to the extent of several leagues by works of great strength, and admirable con- trivance. The citadel itself was reckoned to be impreg- nable by land ; and, in order to block the passage against a hostile fleet, an enormous chain, containing a hundred and eighty tons of iron, had been stretched across the current from shore to shore. By the end of 1779 West Point was the principal military post in the United States. There the Revolutionary government had stored its precious reserve of gunpowder, together with an immense supply of munitions of war which had been purchased with French gold, or had been issued from French arsenals. West Point had gained in importance now that General Washington's field army was too weak for aggressive warfare; and he had spared from his scanty numbers a garrison of more than three thousand men to protect a stronghold which was the key of his defence, and the pivot of his strategy. The place, and its surroundings, were remarkable for their extraordi- nary beauty, of a nature to which justice would more fitly be done by a scene-painter than by the artist of an easel picture ; and in the Fall of the year 1780 it became the theatre for a drama of crime and passion, of intrigue and adventure, with a complicated plot, a swift succes- sion of thrilling incidents, and a tragic ending.[1]

[1] West Point is described in a private letter from a President of the

As far back as February 1779 Arnold was in secret
communication with the Commander-in-Chief of the
British army at New York. His letters, in a disguised
hand, and under a false signature, were deceptively
framed in the cant terms of a commercial correspondence ; and the replies were written by young André,
Sir Henry Clinton's favourite aide-de-camp, who subscribed himself " John Anderson," a name which was
soon to acquire a melancholy celebrity. But, with every
desire in the world to imitate Monk, Arnold was at a
disadvantage when compared to the famous general of
the Restoration. Monk, as the military administrator
of Scotland, had at his command the devotion of a well-
appointed army, and the resources of a large province,
which not very long before had been a separate kingdom ; whereas Benedict Arnold, the governor of a
peaceful city, bare of troops, possessed nothing to offer,
and nothing wherewith to bargain, in his negotiations
with the British authorities. He accordingly determined
to mend his hand with a high trump-card before sitting
down to a final deal in the game of treachery ; and, in
a spirit of sinister forethought and almost inconceivable
audacity, he set his friends at work to obtain for him
the command of West Point. His claims to that employment were warmly urged by Philip Schuyler and
Robert Livingston, both of them honourable men, completely unsuspicious of the purpose for which their influence was sought and used ; and in the first week of
August 1780 Washington, who could refuse Arnold
nothing, put him in charge of the fortress, and of all its
dependencies, from Fishkill in the Northern highlands

Alpine Club, familiar with noble and picturesque, and in some cases all
but inaccessible, scenery in many quarters of the world. "We have,"
(wrote Mr. Bryce to the author,) "just been up to the part of the Hudson
River whence Arnold fled, and have been wishing you could have been
here to see these romantic stretches of water under splendidly bold and
richly wooded hills. It is something like what the Rhine used to be
between Bingen and Coblenz; only the hills are higher, and the wood far
more beautiful, and the stream, — it is really a long, winding fiord, with a
tide running up and down it, — much wider."

to King's Ferry which lay fifteen miles down the river.[1]

Arnold transferred his head-quarters to a pleasant country-house situated within the limits of his new command: and he was followed thither by his young wife, with a baby son whose advent into the world had been welcomed with hearty congratulations by her husband's old comrades, from George Washington downwards. But the poor lady's domestic tranquillity was not of long duration. The house began to be frequented by an equivocal, and most disagreeable, personage, — a certain Joshua Smith, who resided on the West bank of the Hudson river, some little distance below King's Ferry. His sneering remarks about the American cause, and the American paper money, were intolerable to the officers of Arnold's staff, who one and all were ardent patriots. They agreed among themselves that, whenever occasion offered, they would put an affront on the stranger in the presence of their chief. Arnold took up the cudgels in defence of his guest, and the table was soon in an uproar; for the warriors of the Revolution were capable of using strong language elsewhere than on the field of battle. Colonel Varick, the senior officer on the staff, "cursed Smith as a rascal, a scoundrel, and a spy;" and the general told him in return that, if he asked the Devil to dine with him, he should expect the gentlemen of his family to treat him with civility. The fact was that Arnold had already placed himself in Joshua Smith's power. No sooner was he in command at West Point than he began, with his irrepressible instinct for decisive action, to hurry forward the arrange-

[1] The latest letter written by Arnold to Major André under the disguise of a pretended mercantile transaction is dated August 30, 1780. "A speculation," (so it runs,) "might at this time be easily made to some advantage with *ready money;* but there is not the quantity of goods *at market* which your partner seems to suppose; and the number of speculators below, I think, will be against your making an immediate purchase." The "partner" was, of course, Sir Henry Clinton. The "goods at market" were the regiments under Arnold's own command, and the "speculators below" those American forces which lay further down the river between West Point and New York.

ments for the prosecution of his enterprise. He requested Sir Henry Clinton to send him a responsible agent, with whom he might treat in full confidence, and on an equality ; a man, as he quaintly phrased it, " of his own mensuration."[1] He expressed a strong prefer- ence for Major André, who had come back from the siege of Charleston with an increased reputation for valour and ability, and who now was Adjutant-General of the British army. Sir Henry acceded to the suggestion with some misgivings ; for he loved André, like everyone else who knew him ; and he did not let the young man de- part until he had warned him never to carry compromis- ing documents about his person, and had exacted from him a promise always to wear his uniform.[2]

André was conveyed up the Hudson by the Vulture, a British sloop of war. On the evening of Thursday the twenty-first September he met Arnold by appoint- ment, and conferred with him for the space of many hours, first in a grove of fir-trees near the landing-place, and then beneath Joshua Smith's roof. Like practical men they fell to the business at once, and brought it to a finish before they separated. André gave Arnold a positive assurance that a conjoint expedition should be despatched to the attack of West Point, starting on a concerted day, and arriving at a concerted hour. The flotilla was to be commanded by no less competent a sailor than Sir George Rodney, who had brought his fleet on a visit to New York in the very nick of time ; while the land army was to be conducted by General Knyphausen, who had distinguished himself at Fort Washington, and who, — now that Von Donop had been killed, and Von Riedesel had been taken prisoner, —was

[1] Sir Henry Clinton to Lord George Germaine ; New York, October 11, 1780.
[2] Sir Henry Clinton informed the Secretary of State that he had de- sired André " to wear his uniform, and on no account to take papers." " Major André," wrote Arnold, " went on shore without changing his dress ; and he declared to Colonel Robinson and Captain Sutherland that he dared not do it, as he had received the Commander-in-Chief's positive orders to the contrary." B. Arnold to Colonel Robinson ; September 21, 1780.

the best German officer available for such a service. Arnold, on his part, promised to facilitate the passage of the British war-vessels by removing, on pretext of repairs, a link of a great chain two feet in length, and a hundred and forty pounds in weight. What was still more to the purpose, he engaged to paralyse the defence by issuing confused and dilatory orders, and to disperse his own troops in such a manner that they could be attacked and defeated in driblets. A code of signals was arranged by which Arnold would be informed of the approach of Rodney's ships, and the Royal commanders would in return be assured that all had been made smooth for their reception within the fortress. And then Arnold handed over to André six documents which he had been preparing carefully for a fortnight past. Five were in his own handwriting; and, when read together, they gave a comprehensive account of the numbers and composition of the garrison, and minutely specified where every battalion, and every battery of cannon, was to be posted in order that General Knyphausen might have them at his mercy. André stowed the documents away, some within, and some beneath, the soles of his stockings; and the wrinkles in the paper made by the pressure of his feet may be seen to this hour. They talked through the night, and all the next morning; and at noon on the Friday Benedict Arnold returned to West Point after obtaining an understanding from Joshua Smith to put André on board the Vulture as soon as darkness fell, — or, (in case it was thought better to travel on horseback,) to accompany him in person until he was safely deposited within the British lines. In order to avoid any difficulty with the American sentries Arnold wrote out a permission for John Anderson, and Joshua Smith, to pass the guards in the neighbourhood of White Plains, "they being," (so the paper was worded,) "on public business by my direction."

The scheme of the great betrayal, a dire menace to the cause of America, had been planned with rare skill and judgment, sharpened on the part of Sir Henry Clinton, and Major André, by professional zeal, and in the case of Benedict Arnold by motives into which it is painful closely to enquire.[1] Nothing had been neglected which could ensure success ; but from this point onwards foresight and caution were baffled by the accident of events, and blind chance made cruel sport with human destiny. Early on Friday morning, just as Arnold and André were snatching a hasty breakfast, they had heard the alarming sound of heavy guns at no very remote distance. A smart American officer, acting on his own responsibility, with ultimate results of which he little dreamed, was cannonading His Majesty's ship the Vulture with such effect that she hoisted her anchors, and found a safer berth some miles down the stream. Joshua Smith was not a hero ; and his nerves were so shaken by the firing that, when the hour of departure arrived, he refused to trust himself upon the water. He insisted upon going by road ; and André, unmindful of Sir Henry Clinton's fatherly injunctions, started upon his journey muffled in a civilian's great-coat, and with the heels of his boots stuffed full of incriminating documents. At sunrise on the following morning Smith deserted his companion, and returned home ; and André, left to his own guidance, was already within a few miles of the British lines when he approached a thicket where three Whig militiamen were lying in ambush, on the look-out for cattle stealers. If Joshua Smith, whose face was familiar to them, had been of the party the pair would have been allowed to ride by unquestioned ; but André, as a stranger, was stopped by a musket presented at his breast, and was summoned to give an account of himself.

It so happened that one of these three young men,

---

[1] " Mr. M——e flatters himself that in the course of ten days he will have the pleasure of seeing you. He requests me to advise you that he has ordered a draft on you in favour of our mutual friend S——y for £300, which you will charge on account of the *tobacco*." Letter of August 30, 1780, from " Gustavus " to " John Anderson."

On the thirtieth of September Governor Trumbull was informed by a member of Congress, who afterwards was Chief Justice of Connecticut, that " General Arnold was to have £30,000 for delivering up the fort."

John Paulding by name, who had been a prisoner of war in New York, had escaped from that city only three days previously in the clothes of a Hessian Chasseur; and he still had them on when he emerged from his hiding place, and confronted André. Deceived by the well-known green uniform, and glad to be done with pretence, and to appear before friends in his true character, André disclosed that he was a British officer, "out in the country on particular business." As soon as he learned his fatal error he changed his story, and hastened to show Arnold's pass, and announce himself as plain John Anderson; but it was now too late, and he had aroused the suspicions of three specimen members of a quick-witted people.[1] They took him aside into the bushes, undressed him from head to foot, and discovered the hidden papers. "By God, he is a spy!" said the man in the Hessian coat, as soon as he had mastered the nature of their contents. André offered a large sum of money for his freedom, and a discussion arose about the amount of a ransom. The unfortunate Englishman was in deadly earnest, although his captors apparently spoke in irony, for they ended by declaring that they would not take ten thousand guineas to let him go. They conducted André to the nearest military post, and delivered him over to Colonel Jameson of the Continental Army, a puzzle-headed man, who reported to General Arnold that he was keeping under arrest a certain John Anderson. "He had a passport," wrote Jameson, "signed in your name, and a parcel of concealed papers taken in his stockings, which I think of a very dangerous tendency;" and then he went on to say that, as his duty seemed to require, he had forwarded the papers to His Excellency, General Washington. It is difficult to understand the precise theory which the Colonel had formed in his own mind as to what had taken place between André and Arnold.[2]

[1] "Had he pulled out General Arnold's pass first," (said Paulding,) "I should have let him go."

[2] "But for the egregious folly, or the bewildered conception, of Lieu-

Jameson sent off his messengers on the afternoon of Saturday the twenty-third of September. Washington was expected to arrive at West Point on the Monday, attended by the Marquis de Lafayette and Alexander Hamilton; — for even the minor actors in this strange episode were men of historic fame. The indignation against Arnold, which was soon to be all but universal throughout America, was heightened by a very reasonable belief that he had so timed his treachery as to surrender his own Commander-in-Chief into the power of the enemy. In view of the relation which had always subsisted between the two men, that would have been a crime little short of parricide; and Washington himself more than doubted whether any such notion had crossed Arnold's mind.[1] When Monday morning came Washington, accompanied by General Knox, turned out of the direct road to examine some of the outlying redoubts; but he bade the younger men of the party ride on to West Point, because, (he said,) they stood in need of their breakfasts, and moreover he well knew they were all of them in love with Mrs. Arnold. They alighted at the door of her house, hungry and in high spirits, and sat down "in its cheerful wainscotted dining-room"[2] to a merry repast. They were still at table, and in flowing talk, when Colonel Jameson's letter was placed in Arnold's hand. He read it without changing countenance and finished up the subject of his discourse from the point where he had been interrupted; and then he told the company that he had been called away across the river, and, in the hearing of everybody, he gave orders for his barge to be manned.

tenant-Colonel Jameson, who seemed lost in astonishment, and not to know what he was doing, I should undoubtedly have got Arnold." Washington to Lieutenant-Colonel Laurens; 13 October, 1780.

[1] "How far," (wrote Washington,) "he meant to involve me in the catastrophe of this place does not appear by any indubitable evidence; and I am rather inclined to think that he did not wish to hazard the more important object of his treachery by attempting to combine two events, the less of which might have marred the greater." Washington to Lieutenant-Colonel Laurens; 13 October, 1780.

[2] Fiske's *American Revolution*, chapter 14.

His wife, who had observed him more closely than the
rest, followed him out of the apartment as if to see
him off. He led her into their chamber, and revealed to
her the awful truth. She screamed, and fainted in his
arms ; and, leaving her senseless on the bed, he limped
down stairs, hoisted himself on to his horse, and galloped,
by a break-neck track which still bears the appellation
of "Arnold's path," to the spot on the shore below
where his barge awaited him. Eighteen miles of water
lay between Arnold and the British ship of war; but
he was an old merchant-captain, and he knew how to
make oarsmen drive their boat along. He wrote to
Washington from the cabin of the Vulture, protesting
that Mrs. Arnold had no knowledge of her husband's
schemes, and begging that she might be allowed to
rejoin him at New York, unless she preferred to take
shelter with her own family in Philadelphia. Then
the vessel proceeded on her course ; and, before
twelve hours had elapsed, Benedict Arnold was with
Sir Henry Clinton in the middle of the cantonments
of the British army.

Washington imparted the ill-omened news to Knox
and Lafayette in a broken voice, and with tears rolling
down his cheeks. "Arnold," he said, "is a traitor,
and has fled to the British. Whom can we trust?"
The peril was urgent, and of unknown and unexplored
magnitude. But now that Charles Lee and Horatio
Gates had been laid aside and discredited, and Arnold
had gone over to the enemy, Washington had no longer
anybody about him who was unworthy of trust; and,
above all, he could trust himself. Having despatched
two of his aides-de-camp in vain pursuit of the fugitive
he rode over the whole circuit of the works, detecting
with a practised eye, and correcting with rapid skill and
decision, those arrangements which had been artfully
and treacherously made to ensure the loss of the
fortress, and the success of the enemy. Before nightfall
he had re-distributed the garrison, and had summoned
reinforcements from all the country round in a series of

brief, precise, and passionless letters which remain as a
model of how pen and paper should be used by a great
captain in the throes of a transcendent crisis.[1] General
Greene was at Tappan camp with that left wing of the
field-army the command of which had been offered to
Benedict Arnold. A long day had been spent in an
inspection and a review of the troops by old Baron
Von Steuben, who expressed his entire satisfaction with
their performance. Greene had retired to his tent to
calm his mind for slumber, after his lifelong habit, by
the quiet perusal of a favourite volume; but towards
eleven o'clock at night he was startled by receiving
directions from Washington to put his division in
motion for King's Ferry, in light marching order, with
their heavy baggage to follow. "Transactions," so
the message continued, "of a most interesting nature,
and such as will astonish you, have just been discovered." Greene gave his tired soldiers a few hours'
sleep; and then he had them all aroused at three in
the morning. The bulk of the division was kept in
readiness to start at a moment's notice, and two regiments of the Pennsylvania line were sent off then and
there to West Point. The more immediate danger was
soon over. With Henry Knox to place his cannon,
and Nathanael Greene's musketeers to line his ramparts,
Washington could hold the redoubts at West Point
against three times his number of any soldiers in the
world. In that hour of strain and anxiety he had a
thought for one who was even more distressed and
anxious than himself. "Go to Mrs. Arnold," he said
to an officer; "and tell her that, though my duty requires that no means should be neglected to arrest
General Arnold, I have great pleasure in acquainting
her that he is safe on board a British vessel." Lafayette

---

[1] Letters from General Washington to Colonel Wade, to Lieutenant-
Colonel Gray, to Major Low of the Massachusetts levies, and to Colonel
James Livingston, then in charge of the Fort at Stony Point, — all of
them written, and sent away to their destination, by half past 6 o'clock
on the Monday evening.

and Alexander Hamilton were untiring in their sympathy, and in the delicacy and the efficiency of their good offices, towards a lady whom they described as "the most unhappy of women;" and between them they did her memory the inestimable service of establishing her innocence of all complicity with her husband's guilt. The conduct of the two young men was in complete accordance with that spirit of true gallantry which always reigned in George Washington's military household.[1]

Major André's fate was determined by a Board of Generals assembled in the old Dutch Church at Sleepy Hollow, within the precincts of Tappan Camp. Greene acted as President of the tribunal, which consisted of Baron Von Steuben, the Marquis de Lafayette, and twelve American generals and brigadiers. No Court-Martial on record has been composed of more respectable elements; and none, however constituted, could honestly have returned a different verdict. Lord Stanhope, writing, a generation ago, in a tone which has long been obsolete, spoke slightingly of General Greene as a blacksmith by trade, who had probably not so much as heard the names of Puffendorf and Vattel.[2] Greene had swung a hammer in his father's anchor-yard, just as, in other capacities, he had done a great deal of work that was useful and honourable.

[1] "We are certain that she knew nothing of the plot." So runs a sentence in the letter writen by Lafayette to the Chevalier Luzerne; and still more conclusive is the eloquent, and most graphic, account of the affair which Hamilton sent to Elizabeth Schuyler, his own lady-love and future wife. The calumnies against Mrs. Arnold had their origin in the guile, and were promulgated by the malice, of Aaron Burr, — one of the darkest figures in American history. He, like the others, had formerly been on the staff of General Washington, who got rid of him on account of his "immoralities;" and his character was such that his ill word possessed no weight or value, more especially in the case of a beautiful and virtuous woman. Four-and-twenty years afterwards Aaron Burr killed Alexander Hamilton in a duel in which the chivalry was all on the part of the illustrious victim, and the fell intention on that of the vindictive and implacable slayer.

[2] Lord Stanhope's *History of England from the Peace of Utrecht to the Peace of Versailles;* chapter 62.

But he was as fond of good books as Lord Stanhope himself; he was an early admirer, and a sturdy reader, of Blackstone's Commentaries; and, ever since he had adopted the military profession, he had paid especial attention to military jurisprudence, and had carefully studied and annotated his copy of Vattel.[1] There was nothing in Vattel's pages which could help poor André; for the author of the Law of Nations had expressly pronounced that the enterprise in which that officer had involved himself was the most immoral and reprehensible among all the devices of warfare.[2] The members of the Court, delivering their opinions severally and in turn, unanimously declared that the prisoner must be considered as a spy, and ought to suffer death according to the laws and usages of nations. Mr. Lecky, who has commented on the case of Major André at great length, and in a spirit of responsibility and impartiality that would have befitted a Judge Advocate-General, arrived at the conclusion that "the Americans at this very trying moment showed themselves singularly free from sanguinary passion." No document, (he wrote,) could be more temperate, or better reasoned, than the sentence of the Board of Generals which condemned André.[3]

Sir Henry Clinton, in an agony of regret and remorse, insisted that André had gone up the river under the protection of a flag of truce, and that Major-General Arnold's passport had been granted for his safe return to the British camp. But André, who behaved with rare dignity and composure during the terrible ordeal of his trial, felt himself bound, as a man of honour, to

[1] Fiske's *American Revolution ;* chapter 14. *Life of Nathanael Greene;* volume II, chapter 8.

[2] " Seducing a subject to betray his country, suborning a traitor to set fire to a magazine, practising on the fidelity of a governor, enticing him, persuading him, to deliver up a place, — is prompting such persons to commit detestable crimes. . . . If such practices are at all excusable, it can only be in a very just war, and for saving our country when threatened with ruin by a lawless conqueror." Vattel's *Law of Nations, Translated from the French ;* book III, chapter 10.

[3] Lecky's *History of England;* chapter 14.

repudiate the theory that he was sheltered by a flag of truce on an occasion when he was engaged in transactions of a sort which no flag of truce was ever intended to cover.[1] Nor could the Court, without stultifying and humiliating itself, recognise a safe conduct given by an American general to that very British officer with whom, for a year and a half back, he had been conducting under feigned names a clandestine, and, (so far as Arnold himself was concerned,) a criminal and infamous correspondence. On the thirtieth September Washington approved the finding of the Board of Generals, and two days afterwards André died upon the gallows. He wore the full uniform of a British officer, as one who was not ashamed of having faced the extreme of peril in order to serve his King. He told the commander of the escort that he was reconciled to death, but that he detested the mode. " It will," he said, " be but a momentary pang ; " and he never spoke again except to ask the bystanders to bear witness that he met his fate like a brave man. His youth and grace, his sedate and dauntless bearing, and his evident nobleness of character, evoked the admiration and compassion of all true soldiers throughout the American army.[2]

[1] "'Did you consider yourself under the protection of a flag ?' was one of the questions. 'Certainly not. If I had, I might have returned under it ; ' was the unhesitating answer." *Life of Nathanael Greene;* volume II, chapter 8.

[2] " In my boyhood many of the old soldiers of the Revolution were still living, and from their lips I heard of the events in which they were actors. Both my grandfathers, and great-uncles, were soldiers in the Army; and two were with Stark at Bennington. Our village pastor was a Harvard freshman at Cambridge when the war broke out; and, with an elder brother, he joined the army as a fifer, and stood at attention when Washington took command, and reviewed his army of farmers on Cambridge Common. I sat on his knee while he described to me the scene. 'Washington,' said he, 'was a grand looking man ; and, when he walked by with his staff, I was so impressed that I forgot to remove my hat.' A village neighbour was an old soldier who stood in the ranks at the execution of Major André. 'We all fret badly,' (said he,) 'for the handsome young officer ; and, if we could have captured Arnold, André would not have died as he did.' " These sentences are taken from a letter recently addressed to the author by Mr. Samuel P. Hadley, of Lowell, Massachusetts.

Washington had always yielded a sad and reluctant, but unquestioning, obedience to the stern code of war which prevailed in the eighteenth century. In September 1776, when he was in camp in the northern corner of Manhattan Island, he applied to the Colonel of a Connecticut regiment for the services of a volunteer who would procure him information about the strength of the British army on Long Island, and in New York City. A response came from Nathan Hale, a young officer who, like André, was a gentleman and a scholar; greatly beloved, burning with ardour and devotion, and assured of a brilliant future in the estimation of all his comrades. Like André, " he had assumed a character which he could not sustain, and he was too little accustomed to duplicity to succeed; " [1] and, like André, he was arrested within the hostile lines in the guise of a civilian. When brought up for examination before Sir William Howe he made no effort at self-defence, but frankly confessed the object which had taken him to New York; and he was hanged on the following morning. Washington accepted the blow in silence. Neither then, nor thereafter, did he impugn the justice of the sentence; and Mr. Bancroft, — the most intensely, and sometimes the most obtrusively, partiotic of all historians, — has testified to the fact that Nathan Hale's fellow countrymen " never pretended that the beauty of his character should have exempted him from the penalty which the laws of war impose." André had committed himself more deeply than Nathan Hale; for he had penetrated into the enemy's lines for the purpose not only of gleaning information, but of encouraging an American general to desert his flag, and deliver up the stronghold which had been made over to his safe-keeping. If an Adjutant-General of the American army had stealthily visited Sir William Howe's camp in order to seduce so much as a corporal's guard to be false to their duty, he would have been

[1] Appendix 7 in volume VII of *The Writings of George Washington*, *with a life of the author by Jared Sparks.*

hanged without mercy ; and the remission of André's sentence would have been tantamount to a confession on the part of Washington that what was punishable by death when committed against England might be attempted with impunity as against the United States. The tidings of André's fate aroused pity and emotion in London, and some hard things were said about Washington. But our military men, from the very first, and with few exceptions, admitted that under the circumstances he could not have acted otherwise ; and military opinion, in that warlike century, had a powerful influence upon the judgment of society. The personal respect, with which George Washington had always been regarded by the majority of the English people, was not permanently or substantially affected by his conduct in the matter of Major André.[1]

Miss Anna Seward, the Lichfield poetess, had been the friend of André's early days, and his confidante in the ill-starred love affair which drove him from civil life into the profession of arms.[2] Vain and foolish woman as she was, she had a kindly heart, and she felt it incumbent on her to mourn his death in an elegy nearly three times the length of Milton's Lycidas.

> " Oh Washington! I thought thee great and good,
> Nor knew thy Nero-thirst of guiltless blood.
> Severe to use the power that fortune gave ;
> Thou cool, determined, murderer of the brave !
> .   .   .   .
> Remorseless Washington ! the day shall come
> Of deep repentance for this barbarous doom ;

[1] On the third of December 1780 Samuel Curwen read the story of Arnold " over a dish of tea " at the Coffeehouse in Spring Gardens, and acknowledged to himself that Major André must be ranked in the class of spies, and that his punishment was " justified by the universal practice of all nations, civilised and uncivilised, on persons of that character." If such was the first impression made upon an American loyalist it was pretty sure, in the long run, to become the view of the English people.

[2] André's early story is shortly told in the account of the Meschianza at Philadelphia as given in the thirty-fourth chapter of the author's *History of the American Revolution.*

> When injured André's memory shall inspire
> A kindling army with resistless fire,
> And when thy heart appalled, and vanquished pride,
> Shall vainly ask the mercy they denied.
> With sorrow shalt thou meet the fate you gave,
> Nor pity gild the darkness of thy grave."

That was the quality of verses which did duty for poetry among our great-great-grandfathers during the interval when they had lost Gray and Goldsmith, and had not yet discovered Burns and Cowper. The Monody on Major André soon reached America, where a small English literary reputation still went for a great deal more than its intrinsic worth; and Washington was seriously perturbed at finding himself portrayed in such very lurid colours. After the war was over he commissioned one of his aides-de-camp, who was visiting England, to wait upon Miss Seward; to show her André's letters to himself, and his own answers; and to assure her that no circumstance in his life had ever given him so much pain as the necessary sacrifice of André, "and, (next to that deplorable event,) the censure passed upon himself in a poem which he admired, and for which he loved the author." [1] Miss Seward was touched by the compliment, and quite ready to be convinced by the evidence. "From the hour," (she wrote,) "that I conversed with General Washington's officer, and perused the papers, I have regretted the injustice of which I had been guilty." Although not an event of the first order in the annals of literature, it was a transaction which did honour both to the general and to the lady.

The defection of Arnold, and the arrest of André, came like the shock of an earthquake upon the American people. They awoke to the consciousness of an obscure and incalculable peril which had been brought into the light of day by an accidental stroke of national good luck. The three militiamen at once sprang into heroes,

[1] Anna Seward to Mr. Simmons; Lichfield, Jan. 20, 1802.

and occupied an easily earned niche in the Pantheon of Revolutionary history. Congress voted them handsome pensions for life, and silver medals with patriotic inscriptions in Latin and English, which must have gone some way to exhaust the very scanty stock of that metal in the Treasury of the United States.[1] The nature of the service which they had rendered was acknowledged by Washington in a public letter to the President of Congress. " They have prevented," he wrote, " in all probability our suffering one of the severest strokes that could have been meditated against us."

The revelation of Arnold's treachery created a powerful and lasting reaction in American opinion. Thousands, and tens of thousands, of people who had been grumbling, and croaking, and abusing their Government, and exclaiming against the burdens of the war, discerned as in a flash of lightning the depths of the abyss towards which discontent and disaffection might lead them. The horror excited by this act of treason brought home to these citizens of a four-year old nationality the sense that they had a country which they loved as Frenchmen loved France, and Englishmen England. Arnold's effigy was carried through the streets of Philadelphia in a pageant, disfigured by ghastly and degrading accessories which might well have been spared, and burned amidst the taunts and acclamations of a vast assemblage. The indignation which his conduct aroused was nowhere stronger than among those comrades who had shared his dangers, had gloried in his triumphs, and had loyally and affectionately resented the shabby treatment which he had received at the hands of Congress. General Otho Williams, who was in the front of almost every battle during the latter half of the war, and Colonel Daniel Morgan of the Virginia Rangers, exchanged

---

[1] The widow of one of the three was still drawing her two hundred dollars per annum seventy years after the capture of Major André, and ten years after her husband had been interred " with military honours in the presence of a large concourse of spectators." Note to chapter 32 of Lossing's *Field Book of the Revolution.*

their sentiments about him in the most ferocious epithets that the English language could supply. "Curse on his folly and perfidy!" said Nathanael Greene. "How mortifying to think that he is a New Englander!" And Washington, the most generous and constant of Arnold's admirers, — who had borne with his dark humours, and had watched and fostered his career, — could not mention him without a shudder, and never made a pretence of forgiving him. To bring him to condign punishment was henceforward a prime object with the Commander-in-Chief of the American armies. When Lafayette was campaigning against Arnold in Virginia he was strictly enjoined to hold no communication with the traitor; to refuse him recognition as a Royal officer; and to allow him no mercy, and the shortest of shrifts, if by any chance he was captured in battle. Arnold, on his part, was firmly resolved never to fall alive into the power of his countrymen, and night and day he always kept a brace of loaded pistols ready to his grasp. Colonel Laurens was not far wrong when he told Washington that Arnold was undergoing a more severe punishment than André " in the permanent, increasing torment of a mental hell."[1]

Arnold was made a Brigadier in the British army, and received a gratuity of something over six thousand pounds "to compensate his losses;" but the value of the affection and confidence, which he had flung away for ever, could not have been replaced to him by the entire contents of the British Treasury. Immediately after his arrival in New York he prepared and issued " an Address to the Inhabitants of America," and "a Proclamation to the Officers and Soldiers of the Continental Army who had the real interest of their country at Heart, and who were determined to be no longer the Dupes of Congress or of France." When copies of these publications reached London the adherents of the Ministry confidently asserted that the Rebellion would

[1] Lieutenant-Colonel John Laurens to General Washington; October 4, 1780.

dissolve itself into "a mere rope of sand." [1] But that expectation was doomed to disappointment. The friends of national independence in the United States were more resolute, and more averse to compromise, than ever; and the American Tories, whether few or many, were cowed and silent. After the discovery of Arnold's plot the whole country seemed to be of one way of thinking, like England in the year 1696 after the plot against King William the Third, and like France in the year 1800 after the plot against the First Consul. So it was with the great mass of the inhabitants; and Republican sentiment, then as always, was at the very least as widely spread, and as deeply rooted, in the American army as among the civil population. There was penury and destitution, and much physical suffering, in the Continental camps, — together with a keen and angry sense of the neglect and ingratitude displayed by Congress. Misery had driven a certain number of individuals to desert the colours, especially among those recruits who had been drafted into the ranks under a system of compulsory enlistment; but the veterans of Trenton and Germantown were as little likely to renounce their country, and go over to the enemy, as the English Footguards. General James Robertson, then Governor of New York City, was a foolish officer who, in June 1779, had endeavoured to persuade an incredulous Committee of the House of Commons that two thirds of the American people were faithful and devoted partisans of the Crown. And now, in June 1780, he professed to have obtained authentic, and very important, intelligence about the spirit of unrest and dissatisfaction which prevailed among the American soldiers. The sequel to the story is related by a Hessian captain who had sailed with Sir Henry Clinton on the expedition to South Carolina. "Upon our return to New York," (this gentleman wrote,) " we found General Knyphausen in the Jerseys. He had yielded to the representations of old Robertson, who assured him that, as soon as our

[1] *Morning Post* for November 1780.

troops should appear there, half of the enemy's army would come over to our side. But they came with powder and ball. Our Jäger Corps lost an officer. Seven officers were wounded. Of subalterns and privates there were about one hundred dead and wounded. That fun cost us dearer than the heavy siege of Charleston." [1]

The fighting men of the American Republic did not respond to Arnold's seductions, and saw nothing attractive in his example. The officers of his own staff were the first to repudiate the disloyal action of their chief with unconcealed disgust, and eager volubility. Arnold appealed in vain to the instinctive fidelity, and the implicit obedience, which a naval officer of renown inspires in the common sailors who are in daily attendance about his person. When, after his flight down the Hudson river, he found himself alongside of the Vulture, he told the coxswain of his barge that, if only he would consent to unite his fortunes with those of his old commander, he should have a commission in the Royal service ; to which the man replied that he would be damned if he fought on both sides. [2] That blunt answer expressed the feelings alike of the seamen who had worked the guns on board Arnold's flag-ship at Valcour Island, and of the soldiers who charged behind him through the sally-port of the German redoubt on the evening which decided the campaign at Saratoga. He passed into the British camp unaccompanied and unfollowed, taking nothing with him except his redoubtable sword. It was a weapon which his new employers did not long permit to remain idle.

The British Ministry throughout the later period of the war, while abstaining from all attempts to recapture the Northern and Central States of the Union by dint of arms, continued to harass those districts with sudden and isolated raids and incursions. The officers in

---

[1] *Extracts from the Letter-book of Captain Johann Heinrichs, of the Hessian Jäger Corps ;* 1778-1780.
[2] *The Memoirs of Major-General Heath;* 30th September, 1780.

charge of these expeditions did not confine themselves
to sacking and destroying the military storehouses and
arsenals of the Republican Government. They set fire
to open towns and villages; they swept the neighbourhood bare of such private property as could be carried
away in carts and knapsacks; and they ruined the
factories, the salt-pans, the bleaching yards, and all
the fixed and permanent apparatus of daily industry.
Anything less resembling the course of conduct pursued
by our own Duke of Wellington, when campaigning in
the South of France in the year 1814, it would be impossible to imagine. It was more of a piece with the
conduct of certain generals in the ancient Greek wars
who shocked the opinion of their own time by cutting
down the olive-trees in an invaded country. No state
in the Union suffered so cruelly as Connecticut. As far
back as April 1777 Governor Tryon had landed near
Danbury, and had given over the town to plunder. He
then applied the torch to the local place of worship,
and to all dwelling-houses and granaries which were not
owned or occupied by avowed friends of the British
connection; but, before he could do any further mischief, he was driven back to his ships in disgraceful
rout by the fiery valour of Benedict Arnold, fighting in
defence of the State which was his home and birthplace.
Two years afterwards Tryon once more visited Connecticut, and burned down several streets of warehouses
in New Haven, as well as the smiling and prosperous
hamlets of Fairfield and Norwalk. On this occasion
he got safe off, because Arnold, with his hands full of
business, and his wound still unhealed, was settled down
a hundred and fifty miles away in the Government
House at Philadelphia.

It was a species of warfare which Englishmen learned
to disrelish as soon as they had a taste of it themselves.
In the year 1781 a French naval officer destroyed two
plantations in the British island of Tobago. "Here,"
(wrote a London journalist,) "is barbarian war with a
vengeance! It is a thousand pities that Admiral Rod-

ney had not come up in time, taken the villain in the fact, and either hung him on the spot, or thrown him in to mend the fire of his own making. He would have been justified by all laws of war, justice, or humanity." [1] Connecticut, inhabited by a politically minded and pugnacious race of men, and firmly and sympathetically administered by Jonathan Trumbull, had from the first hour been almost unanimous in favour of the Revolution; and its citizens, so far from being terrified, were angered and alienated, beyond all possibility of reconciliation with the mother country, by these futile and desultory hostilities. The Ministers of Louis the Sixteenth might as well have hoped to intimidate the three Ridings of Yorkshire by bombarding the lodging-houses on the sea-front of Scarborough, or to break the spirit of Devonshire by laying Lynton and Ilfracombe in ashes. But Sir Henry Clinton, undeterred by past experience, re-commenced these ill-judged operations on a larger scale as soon as he had Benedict Arnold's services at his disposal; and Arnold, who did nothing incompletely, carried out his orders with such vigour and thoroughness as to confirm the disapprobation, and inflame the hatred, with which he was already regarded by the enormous majority of his own fellow-countrymen.

Arnold was ready, and able, to give King George full value for the rank and money which had been bestowed upon him; for he was a soldier by the gift of nature. As Pozzo di Borgo said of Wellington, he was born for war as a hound is born for the chase. He transmitted to Downing Street two alternative plans for an aggressive campaign directed against the heart and centre of the American Confederacy; neither of which plans, in his view, demanded a larger force than Sir Henry Clinton had at his disposal. " But an army of fifty thousand men," he added, "will do nothing without energy and enterprise." [2] The British Ministry

---

[1] *Whitehall Evening Post* for September 1781.
[2] Arnold's letter is quoted by Mr. John Fortescue in Book XI, chapter 17, of his *History of the British Army.* " Other soldiers besides Arnold,'

could not rise to the elevation of Arnold's conceptions, and they sent him into Virginia at the head of a small detachment of infantry, with a roving commission to do as much damage as he could contrive to effect. They very soon learned what the words "energy and enterprise" meant in the mouth of Benedict Arnold. He landed in the James River on the third of January. His ships had been overtaken by a violent gale, and a part of his small force had not as yet succeeded in rejoining him; but, without waiting for the laggards, he pushed on for Richmond, the capital of the State; marshalled his handful of men so as to produce an appearance of double their actual numbers; and fairly frightened the garrison out of the town. Before attending to any other business he despatched Colonel Simcoe to get possession of West Ham, the cannon foundry and arsenal of Virginia, which was situated on the James River some miles above Richmond. John Simcoe, a warrior after Arnold's heart, was a young British officer who had come to America just too late for Bunker's Hill, but in plenty of time to be wounded at Brandywine. Full of honourable ambition, and military spirit, he had resigned his adjutancy in a regiment of the Line, and had taken command of the Queen's Rangers, a splendid body of Light Infantry and Hussars, raised in and about New York, but recruited indiscriminately from the Loyalists of every colony. Colonel Simcoe reached his destination as fast as his storm-tossed and road-weary horses could travel, and at once commenced the work of demolition. He broke up a great quantity of muskets, drowned the ammunition in the river, knocked the trunnions off the cannons, blew up the powder-mills and the gun-factories, and made a complete wreck of the whole establishment. Then he brought his troops back to Richmond in time to have their share in a store of rum which would have sufficed the needs of an army corps, and proved to be a great deal more than enough for

writes Mr Fortescue, "had long striven to din the principle of concentration into the deaf ears of Germaine."

Arnold's slender following. Arnold, meanwhile, had made the citizens of Richmond feel the weight of his hand. The town was delivered over to plunder; and many public and private buildings, including a range of warehouses replete with the staple commodity of Virginia, perished in the flames. "There never," it is written, "was such a smell of tobacco in Richmond, before or since, down to the time of the burning of the city in 1865 on its evacuation by Jefferson Davis."[1]

By this time the alarm had been sounded throughout the whole region which lay between the Pamunkey and the Appomattox rivers. Baron von Steuben, and General Nelson, — a Virginian of considerable authority in politics, and some reputation in arms, — had assembled the militia, and were converging upon Richmond from two opposite quarters, in the belief that they had caught the English in a trap. Arnold, as wary and prompt in retreat as he was audacious in attack, gave instant orders to evacuate the town. Colonel Simcoe begged for a respite on behalf of his exhausted men and horses; but Arnold convinced him by an apt illustration drawn from the inexhaustible store of his personal military experiences. If Governor Tryon, (he said,) had set off two hours sooner from Danbury on a certain famous occasion, he would have got back to his ships unmolested: and, if he had delayed his departure for a few more hours, he would never have reached the seacoast at all.[2] Arnold collected all his people, whether drunk or sober: set them on the road with their faces towards the south-east; and, with the countryside buzzing around him, marched them till they were safely ensconced in an intrenched camp at Portsmouth, in touch with the British fleet, on the shores of an estuary a hundred miles down the James River.

The people of Virginia had not yet got quit of Benedict Arnold. He remained amongst them for the space of several months, harrying them and despoiling them

[1] *Life of Benedict Arnold;* chapter 19.
[2] *Simcoe's Military Journal; New York, 1844;* page 164.

on land, and making havoc of the shipping in the interior waterways of their State; for he was skilled beyond any other living man in all the arts and practices of amphibious warfare. In the course of a single expedition he captured, or sank, seven armed brigs and sloops carrying from sixteen to six-and-twenty guns apiece, a score of heavily laden merchantmen, and a large number of smaller vessels, without a man of his own being killed or wounded. He destroyed some important corn-mills, and an abundant magazine of flour; a great tannery full of hides and bark; a government rope-walk, and a building-yard with three ships on the stocks. He carted off, or burned, nearly seven thousand hogsheads of tobacco; and he carried away with him as prisoners an aide-de-camp of Baron von Steuben, and nine other American officers, who had allowed themselves to be surprised while they were waiting for a ferry boat. All that, and more besides, was accomplished by the troops under Arnold's immediate supervision during one fortnight in the early summer of 1781.[1] It was too much for the equanimity of Virginia. The Old Dominion was in a frenzy of rage and consternation; and Thomas Jefferson, the Governor of the State, who had shown in the Declaration of Independence that he knew how to give expression in writing to the more violent passions of his fellow-countrymen, published a proclamation offering a reward of five thousand guineas to anyone who could capture Arnold alive.

Arnold returned to New York before the end of June 1781; and, after a short rest from his labours, he was sent on a raiding excursion against his native state of Connecticut. It was a piece of cruel irony to impose such a task upon the victor of Danbury; but it apparently was accepted without remonstrance, and most cer-

[1] *Benedict Arnold to Sir Henry Clinton; Petersburg, May* 16, 1781. Arnold was just then second in command to General Phillips of the British army, the hero of Minden and Ticonderoga, who had come south from New York with reinforcements. But that noble veteran had been struck down by fever, and died at Petersburg not many days after the date of Arnold's despatch. The story of General Phillips is told in the thirtieth chapter of *The American Revolution.*

tainly was executed without compunction. At daybreak on the sixth September a fleet of twenty-four sail anchored in front of New London, a thriving little seaport on the Thames river, half-way along the coast between New Haven and Narragansett Bay. Arnold came on shore with a brigade of British infantry, a detachment of the dreaded Hessians, and, (which in the eyes of the civil population was a still more formidable apparition,) a strong force of Loyalist partisans. The town was sacked; and the church, the court-house, and more than a hundred shops and private dwellings were consumed by fire. The damage inflicted upon the inhabitants was estimated at very nearly a hundred thousand pounds sterling, but they suffered a more poignant loss which could not be valued in money. The local militia, who were mostly lads, and very ill provided with muskets, had been hastily mustered under the command of Colonel William Ledyard, and posted behind the ramparts of a well-constructed work, called Fort Griswold, on the left bank of the river. They defended themselves gallantly against two battalions of regular infantry, using their pikes with no little effect; but the assailants at last pushed their way through the embrasures, and the defenders of the fort laid down their arms, and asked for quarter. A scene ensued which took many minutes to enact, and does not bear telling in detail. The result was stated by General Arnold himself, without comment or explanation, in his official report to Sir Henry Clinton. "Eighty-five men," (he wrote,) "were found dead in Fort Griswold, and sixty wounded, — most of them mortally." The garrison numbered only a hundred and fifty-seven to begin with, of whom not more than ten or a dozen, at the very outside, had fallen in fight before the place was surrendered. At dawn next morning Colonel Ledyard's niece, — whose uncle had been slain, or, (more properly speaking,) murdered, — entered the enclosure "with a provision of wine, water, and chocolate," and discovered a heart-rending spectacle of horror and anguish.[1]

[1] After Fort Griswold had been taken Major Bromfield, a New Jersey

It was an event stained with a redder dye than any previous incident in a war which, everywhere to the north of the Carolinas, had been conducted with becoming, and sometimes exemplary, respect for the sacredness of human life whenever the necessities of combat did not imperatively require that human life should be taken. In July 1779 Anthony Wayne had carried by assault the fort of Stony Point, on the Hudson river, after a desperate conflict in which both parties lost heavily. Wayne was struck by a musket-ball on the head, and for a time was supposed to be mortally wounded. Between five and six hundred British soldiers laid down their arms. American tradition relates, and Englishmen are not unwilling to believe, that " one old captain refused to surrender, and fell where he stood, fighting to the last; " but, with this exception, no one was killed after the flag was struck, and the garrison pleaded for quarter. A month afterwards Major Henry Lee, father of the Commander-in-Chief of the Confederate armies during the war of the Secession, surprised the stronghold of Paulus Hook, which was situated where Jersey City now stands. Major Lee, when the fighting was over, spared the lives of all the defenders, although he had the greatest difficulty in carrying off his prisoners; and the same honourable forbearance, in the course of the last four years, had been shown on similar occasions by several of King George's generals.

Others, but not Arnold himself, have pleaded in his excuse that he did not lead the storming-party at Fort Griswold, and remained throughout the affair on the opposite bank of the river; but that circumstance was not a matter of common knowledge when the terrible story was first revealed to the world. He, and no one else, was the general in command; and the people of the United States, and more especially the wives and

---

Loyalist, entered by the gateway, and called out to ask who commanded the garrison. Colonel Ledyard mildly replied : "I did, sir ; but you do now," and handed over his sword to the Major, who thereupon ran him through the body with his own weapon.

mothers of Connecticut, held him responsible for the massacre.   The destruction of new London, and the capture of Fort Griswold, were the closing exploits in that chequered and portentous military career.   On the nineteenth of the next month Lord Cornwallis capitulated at Yorktown; the war of the Rebellion, for all practical purposes, came to an end; and Benedict Arnold's occupation was gone.   The time was evidently fast approaching when the United States, and most of all the State of Connecticut, would not be a safe or pleasant home for him and his family; and in December 1781 he sailed for England, pursued by a blast of execration almost strong enough to propel him across the Atlantic.

During the first few days of his life in England everything seemed to promise well for Benedict Arnold. He entered upon his new career under high auspices, and in the best of company.   Lord Cornwallis had been his fellow-passenger on board the man-of-war which brought him from America; he carried a letter from Sir Henry Clinton earnestly commending him to Lord George Germaine's "countenance and protection"; and, when he went to Court, he was ushered into the royal presence leaning on the arm of Sir Guy Carleton. George the Third received him most graciously in public, and conferred with him frequently in private; and he was noticed walking in the London parks and gardens "with the Prince of Wales, and with the King's brother."

Mrs. Arnold excited some compassion, and much curiosity; for her praises had been sung far and wide by the Guardsmen who had known the lovely Miss Peggy Shippen in Philadelphia during Sir William Howe's occupation of that city.   Queen Charlotte desired that marked attention should be paid her by the ladies of the Court; and she was granted a pension of five hundred a year for herself, and one hundred a year for each of her children.   She spent the money well and wisely; and, with Lord Cornwallis for a helpful friend, and King George for a kindly and watchful

patron, she brought up her sons to be good men, useful public servants, and exceedingly gallant soldiers.
Her eldest born became an eminent Indian civilian.
One of her sons was killed, and another very badly
wounded, while fighting for England in the great French
war ; and a grandson met his death in battle in front of
the advanced trenches before Sebastopol.

The favour of the Court, in the case of General
Arnold, did not carry with it the favour of the public.
London society set its face sternly and inexorably against
him. In war, and in politics, men have often welcomed a deserter ; but they invariably despise a traitor.
The Royal officers in Clinton's army, — never very ready
to serve under the orders of a native-born American,
however high his character and blameless his history, —
had evinced the strongest reluctance to be commanded
by such a colonist as Benedict Arnold ; and their feeling about him was shared by English gentlemen who
did not wear the red coat. In political and fashionable
circles he was shunned by most of the Whigs, and by
many Tories. Middle-class citizens had all of them
read the tragic story with which his name was indissolubly connected ; and he walked the streets attended,
in the imagination of spectators, by the ghost of André.[1]
Arnold felt his unpopularity keenly. He led, whenever
he was in England, the retired and solitary life of
a proud and disappointed man ; and he disappeared
from that country often, and sometimes for years
together, while he was prosecuting his multifarious, and
for the most part disastrous, mercantile operations
in Canada and the West Indies.[2] The man himself

[1] Some years after the war was over Mr. Peter Van Schaack, a banished
Loyalist from New York, saw General Arnold, "and a lady who doubtless
was his wife," conversing together in face of the beautiful and touching
little bas-relief on Major André's monument in Westminster Abbey.

[2] Arnold had planted the head-quarters of his commercial business at
St. John in New Brunswick, where he had an establishment for ship-
building, and a storage for goods. In July 1788, while he himself was in
Europe, his warehouse was burned with all the contents, and such was
the prejudice against him that he had to go to law for the insurance money.
The people of the United States, as the least that could be expected of

gradually dropped out of the sight and knowledge of
the London world; but his story was not forgotten.
In May 1792 the Earl of Lauderdale, — a fiery, and not
ineffective, speaker in the House of Lords, — attacked
Mr. Pitt's government for having conferred a military
appointment on the Duke of Richmond, who had
recently changed sides in politics. If apostasy, (he
said,) could justify promotion, the noble duke "was
the most fit person for that command, General Arnold
alone excepted." It so happened that Arnold was in
London; and, as soon as he read the report of the
debate, he sent a peremptory demand for satisfaction.
Lord Lauderdale was surprised, and somewhat taken
aback, by the message; for he had made his speech
with the sole object of insulting his brother peer, and
had only referred to Arnold incidentally as the classic
and historical example of a renegade. In any case,
however, he had been called out; and out he came. The
meeting took place near Kilburn Wells, on the Edgware
road, at seven o'clock on a Sunday morning. Arnold was
attended by Lord Hawke, son of the famous admiral;
while Charles Fox acted for Lord Lauderdale, with the
cheerful serenity which, whether as principal or second,
he never failed to display upon what was then called
the field of honour. Arnold fired, and missed. Lord
Lauderdale, who had not discharged his pistol, invited
his opponent to take another shot; but Arnold refused
to fire again until he had been fired at. The duel
came to a standstill; the seconds had no choice except
to intervene; and Fox, exerting all his powers of persuasion, succeeded in inducing Lauderdale to make, not
indeed an effusive, but a presentable apology. That
was the last gunpowder which Benedict Arnold ever
burned in anger.[1]

them, insisted on believing that Benedict Arnold had set fire to his own
premises in order to defraud the underwriters.
[1] Lord Lauderdale survived to a great age, as befitted one who had come
away alive and unhurt from standing in front of Benedict Arnold's pistol.
As late as the year 1834 he told Lord Broughton that Charles Fox " was
not only the most extraordinary man he had ever seen, but also the best

Margaret Arnold did her best to sustain the respectability of her unhappy and restless husband. It was a dreary and uphill task. She made pitiful complaints to her relatives in Pennsylvania about the high prices of housekeeping in England; but the fact was that Benedict Arnold would have been embarrassed financially if he had had as large an income as Governor Pitt, or Alderman Harley. He was a born spendthrift, and a rash and most unlucky speculator. When the war of the French Revolution broke out Arnold, with an eagerness which had a touch of pathos about it, hastened to place his military and colonial experience at the service of the British government. He submitted to Mr. Pitt a scheme for conquering and annexing the Spanish possessions in the West Indies; he entreated Lord Spencer to employ him on naval duty; and he besought the Duke of York for permission to lead the most desperate expedition, or to run the chances of the most deadly climate. But his applications for an opportunity to prove his mettle, and re-gild his tarnished fame, were encountered by cold neglect in every quarter. Then, as a last resource in his utmost need, he fell back upon a form of enterprise which formerly had been very familiar to him. Great Britain was now again involved in a naval war; and the plunder of mercantile property on the high seas had once more become an authorised and lawful profession. Between 1777 and 1779, when Benedict Arnold was a general in the Continental Army, he had purchased shares in no less than six of the privateers which preyed upon British commerce; and now, in the closing years of the eighteenth century, he obtained letters of marque against France and Spain for armed vessels which he bought and equipped with borrowed money. If he could have sailed and fought his ships himself he might have done something considerable to mend his ruined fortunes; but

man." Fox had rare and noble qualities; and yet there is something almost droll in this unqualified testimonial to his moral excellence from a man whom he had aided and abetted in fighting a duel on Sunday.

his captains did not possess the talent of their trade. They set at nought his specific instructions, which were in a high degree provident and judicious; and he had no effectual means for checking their extravagance, or their dishonesty.[1] The expense of the venture was enormous; and the prizes which these bungling sea-rovers brought safe into a British harbour were few, and for the most part worthless.

Arnold's courage at last gave way; and he fell into melancholy, and deep dejection, which certain sentimental writers have pleased themselves by attributing to repentance and remorse, but which arose from the chagrin of pecuniary distress, and the consciousness of a hopelessly mismanaged life. He was attacked by nervous disease; sleep fled from him; and in June 1801 he died a broken man, leaving his family a heritage of debts and law-suits. It would have been well for him if the memory of his existence upon earth could have perished with him. The time arrived when the mind of America was once again stirred from its depths by the secession of the Southern States. Her historians then had something fresh to write about; but during the whole of the intermediate period between 1782 and 1861 their industry was almost entirely concentrated upon the events and personages of the War

[1] In February 1801 the whole Arnold connection was rejoicing over the capture of some Spanish merchantmen. "They proved," said Mrs. Arnold soon afterwards, "to be worth more than was at first supposed; — at least twenty-five thousand pounds. But they were sacrificed by Captain Neilis's breach of orders, which were to *see* anything which was valuable *himself* into port. Expecting to capture more of the same fleet he sent them off unprotected, and the day following they were re-taken, and he was disappointed in getting more."

"I have lately," (she wrote, after her husband's death,) "had several demands made upon me by the *vile privateers* which I do not know how I can resist, or even if they are just. The claim of the Swede for the detention of the vessel, and total loss of his cargo, is in the Court of Admiralty." There is an account of the whole matter in an article in the *Pennsylvania Gazette* for July 1899, by Edward Shippen, Medical Director of the United States Navy. Doctor Shippen says that the different captains seem to have "humbugged and cheated" the Arnolds out of about fifty thousand pounds.

LORD MACAULAY'S WORKS AND LIFE

THE COMPLETE WORKS OF LORD MACAULAY.
"Albany" Edition. 12 vols., with 12 portraits. Large cr. 8vo.
$12.00.

CRITICAL AND HISTORICAL ESSAYS, WITH LAYS OF ANCIENT ROME. Complete in one volume.
Popular Edition. Cr. 8vo. $1.00.
"Silver Library" Edition. With Portrait and Illustrations to the "Lays" by J. R. WEGUELIN. Cr. 8vo. $1.25.

CRITICAL AND HISTORICAL ESSAYS.
Trevelyan Edition. 2 vols., cr. 8vo. $3.00.

HISTORY OF ENGLAND FROM THE ACCESSION OF JAMES THE SECOND.
Popular Edition. 2 vols., cr. 8vo. $2.00.
Cabinet Edition. 8 vols., post 8vo. $14.00.

LAYS OF ANCIENT ROME.
Illustrated by G. Scharf. Fcp. 4to. $3.75.
Popular Edition. Fcp. 4to. Sewed, 20 cts.; cloth, 40 cts.
Illustrated by J. R. Weguelin. Cr. 8vo, cloth extra, gilt edges.
$1.25.

MISCELLANEOUS WRITINGS AND SPEECHES.
Popular Edition. Cr. 8vo. $1.00.

LONGMANS, GREEN, & CO.,
New York, London, Bombay, Calcutta, and Madras.

SELECTIONS FROM THE WRITINGS OF LORD MACAULAY.
Edited, with Occasional Notes by the Right Hon. Sir G. O. TREVELYAN, Bart. 8vo.

THE LIFE AND LETTERS OF LORD MACAULAY.
By the Right Hon. Sir G. O. TREVELYAN, Bart.
Library Edition. 2 vols., 8vo.
Popular Edition. 1 vol., 12mo.